The Last of the Red Hot Lovers

Adult Reading

Ethel Ann Shaffer
(writing as Eva Sandor)

Printed in the United States of America

ISBN 979-8-89114-209-1 (sc)
ISBN 979-8-89114-211-4 (e)

Library of Congress Preassigned Control Number: 2025914120

2025.09.25

MainSpring Books
5901 W. Century Blvd
Suite 750
Los Angeles, CA, US, 90045

www.mainspringbooks.com

Chapter One

Kurt and I have known one another as children. He spent every summer with his aunt and uncle who live three doors from me. Walking to church every Sunday, I'd see the curtains flutter, and I'd giggle thinking that Kurt might be interested in me. He was the first boy to kiss me, at a friend's tenth birthday party, when we played spin-the-bottle and it landed in front of me. I remember kissing him back.

In our junior year of high school, Kurt moved in permanently with his aunt and uncle; and we graduated high school together in 1947. Then we went our separate ways, married, and had children.

Sixty-two years later, we reconnected, fell in love, and got married. Although this sounds like the usual love story, there's a hitch. We're seniors, and while our peers have tucked away their sexual adventures as memories, we can't keep our hands off each other.

The last time I saw Kurt was at a high school class reunion ten years ago. But a lot can happen in ten years. Pam, Kurt's beloved wife, had passed, and my twenty-year-relationship with Wesley had ended. Kurt emailed me and other friends to tell us about Pam, and I emailed him back my condolences. He responded, and that started an email chain that led to our love affair.

Kurt was one funny guy and had me in stitches. The guy I had remembered from high school was engaging, but no comedian. I guess our life experiences not only matured us, but it graced us with a self-confidence that teenagers only pretend to have.

Both Kurt and I had been popular in high school and still keep in touch with a slew of friends. It's great fun poking into our past and sharing stories about our teenage tribulations and those of our classmates. But there was so much more I wanted to know about Kurt—the guy who had me beguiled by his emails. He must have felt the same way about me because we're having our first date in Las Vegas.

Kurt felt we should meet soon because of our ages. I'm eighty, and he's eighty-one. I suggested we meet half-way between our residences and on neutral ground. After agreeing to the meet-up location, Kurt realized that Las Vegas is about a three-hour flight from his home and an hour's flight from my home. Rather than complain, he laughed at my resourcefulness.

On the hour flight to Vegas, I remembered Kurt from high school. He was good-looking with wide shoulders and light brown wavy hair that fell irresistibly across his forehead. He had a deep, sensual voice, and I imagined him making an appealing newscaster. I found him attractive, but at the time, I was in a relationship with Ned Kanecky, who had graduated two years earlier.

The plane landed while I was still reminiscing. After grabbing my suitcase from the overhead bin, I debarked and boarded the shuttle bus for Bally's. Instead of thinking about how Kurt looked in high school, I started thinking about how he looked at the last reunion. He was just under six feet tall with broad shoulders and tight abs. He walked with a swagger that said he knew who he was and enjoyed being that person. His eyes were blue-green. Although I could picture him at the reunion, that was ten years ago when we were in our seventies. What if I didn't recognize him today? What if he didn't recognize me?

Although I was nervous about meeting Kurt after ten years, I looked forward to it. He readily agreed to separate rooms, and I had the feeling he saw our relationship, through correspondence and phone calls, the same as I did: light-hearted and fun. I had no expectations of romance— just a fun date with an old friend. Who am I kidding? Romance saturated the air.

When the shuttle bus pulled into Bally's, I spied Kurt sitting on a bench near the entrance. He still had a full head of hair, now white, and his shoulders were still broad. No beer belly in sight. I called his name, and a wide smile crossed his face as he eyed my blond hair and slim body in tight jeans. We hugged, and he stepped back. "You're still petite and beautiful."

He towered over me. "I used to be five feet two," I offered, "but I've shrunk two inches."

* * * * *

While entering the lobby, I placed my hand in his, and sparks flew. Kurt told me later he thought that was a very good sign. I saw him sneaking glances at me while I snuck glances back at him. We talked non-stop as he got me settled in my room, four doors down from his.

Promptly at seven, Kurt knocked on my door to take me to dinner. When I opened it, we stared at one another. As his blue-green eyes caressed me, I felt like a sex goddess. An eighty-year-old sex goddess. I remember thinking how preppy he looked. He said my dark brown eyes made a lump gather in his throat. "They are perfect with your blond hair." I didn't tell him that most grey-haired ladies turn into blondes later in life.

Over dinner, we chuckled over how much we had in common. Although seemingly shy in high school, Kurt wasn't shy any longer. He told me he'd attended college at Ohio University in Athens on the ROTC program and had been a pilot flying reconnaissance in the Vietnam War. He retired as a Major. He said he also accepted a job with the State of Ohio and retired from that second job.

I was impressed with what he'd done with his life and with his command of the English language. A good many people from Ohio use *youns* and *ain't*. He used neither. I'll never forget how perturbed I'd get when my first husband commonly used those slang offenders as part of his normal vocabulary.

Kurt interrupted my thoughts by saying he and Pam had both thought I was happily married and living in Beverly Hills.

"On the contrary," I said. "I struggled to raise my two daughters while working as a legal secretary." I told him the law firm where I worked paid for paralegal classes that I attended on Saturdays and evenings at the University of Southern California. "Things got better for us after I became a paralegal." It was fun getting to know the persons Kurt and I had become.

Kurt was saddened to learn of the physical and verbal abuse I'd suffered at the hands of my first husband. "I stuck out that marriage for thirteen years," I said, "worried that I couldn't financially support my daughters. But I left when I saw Ned getting annoyed with Lexie and Susan, and I fretted that his rage would soon be directed at them." I sighed deeply. "After my divorce, I bought a new 1965 black Impala convertible, and I drove to California with my daughters. We stayed at nice motels while crossing country that I really couldn't afford, but I wanted Lexie and Susan to enjoy our move and to look forward instead of backwards."

Kurt intertwined his fingers with mine, and a thrill raced up my spine. "I wondered why you moved to California," he said. "And I can't imagine any guy laying a hand on you."

I told him about the new life that opened up for me that I never would have experienced if I stayed in Ohio. "It's hard to believe I've lived in California for over forty years, arriving in 1965." I told him how well my daughters had adjusted to California. "Lexie was a majorette and played a saxophone and clarinet in the high school band, and Susan was a cheerleader. Their school graduated three hundred in a class, not sixty-two like in our graduating class."

Kurt stroked his chin stubble. "You always came back for our class reunions," he mused. "That impressed Pam and me."

"I guess you could call me a reunion junkie."

"I am, also," he chuckled. "I really enjoy staying connected with our classmates."

Kurt said his service stint had him living all over the country: Mississippi, Texas, Long Island, N.Y., Massachusetts, Alabama, and Vietnam. He told me about some of his war experiences and landing his plane in dangerous situations. What a guy!

I told him my favorite movie was *The Bridges of Toko-Ri*, about a fighter pilot who was forced to come to grips with his ambivalence about the war and a fear of having to bomb a set of highly-defended bridges. "Did you see that movie with William Holden and Grace Kelly?"

Kurt said he remembers that movie well and feels the same atmosphere existed during his service in the Vietnam War.

* * * * *

After a scrumptious shrimp scampi dinner and Sangria at an outdoor cafe, we walked hand in hand around the outside courtyard of Bally's. I'd forgotten how romantic it can be holding hands with a handsome beau. However, I'm getting ahead of myself. Back to the emails that had gotten us together after sixty-two years. My best friend Julie had passed away, and her brother Mo and his wife flew to California for the funeral. Julie and I had been friends since we were seven and five. Kurt knew Julie and Mo, as we were in many of the same high school classes.

"After graduation," I said, "Julie married and moved to California. After my divorce from Ned, she and her husband urged me to move there, also, which I did. Julie cared for my daughters when I needed help, and I moved into her home and stayed with her four children when she and her husband went on vacations. We couldn't have been closer if we were sisters."

"If you will remember, it was after Julie's funeral that you ran into Mo and his wife at the St. Clairsville Mall, and Mo told you about their attending the funeral and seeing me."

"Yeah, and I remember Mo saying that you're single and still look good, and he was right." Kurt laughed. "Mo gave me your address, and I took it, although we'd already been emailing one another." He stroked his stubble again. "I fleetingly wondered whether I should tell him about our emails, but I decided against it."

I thought of how Kurt would email me in the evenings, and I'd respond in the mornings. We'd scan in pictures of ourselves and email them to each other. Kurt said he'd know me in a crowd because of my lips and dark chocolate eyes. Yes, we were getting flirty. Kurt often wrote about his days as a pilot when he flew a Lockheed Constellation. He said there were only four left, and one was at the Camarillo Airport, which he found by surfing the net. I lived in Camarillo at the time and wondered whether this was a sign of some kind.

Kurt came across as an in-control person, although not controlling. I don't know whether one would describe me as controlling, but I'd certainly gotten assertive raising two daughters alone from the time they were seven and eleven, receiving little child support, and worrying about meeting financial obligations. And if anyone got demanding or treated me with disrespect, I turned into a pit bull. Those thirteen years as an abused wife while married to Ned had left scars, and nobody would ever get away with treating me with disrespect again, I vowed.

I have a long list of email friends who send me jokes, and I, in turn, forward them to other friends. Evidently Kurt has the same thing going on because I receive a lot of jokes from him. As jokes flew back and forth, some started to get racy. Kurt said he thought for quite a while before emailing me a video of a dancer who used a red scarf to hide her assets while performing a sizzling dance. I thought it was hilarious and emailed him back that I was planning to buy myself a red scarf. Within days, I received a long, red scarf in the mail from Kurt. I replied by sending Kurt a picture of me wrapped in it, wearing a black bra.

We both got a little bolder after that. I told him about rushing to the nursing home to see Julie the night she died. Something told me I just had to get there, and fast. When I arrived, her oldest daughter Carol was in the room with her. Looking up with tears streaming down her face, Carol said, "Mom died about five minutes ago." Hugging and crying, we sat and waited for the undertaker to come for her body.

I asked whether Julie would be donating any of her organs, and Carol said she wouldn't.

I told her I planned to donate my organs.

"Who would want eighty-year-old organs?" she asked, her eyes half-crossed.

"I've been told my corneas can be used, as well as my skin for fire victims. I don't know what other parts can be utilized, but I have a barely-used vagina."

Carol cracked up, and we both started laughing— exactly what we needed at this sad time.

Later, at Julie's wake, which Mo and his wife attended in California, Carol asked if she could relate the incident of my organ donations. I nodded. I thought Mo was going to pass out from laughter. For a split second, I considered not relating this story to Kurt, but then I typed it up and emailed it to him. Not hearing back about it, I naturally thought he'd gotten offended. When we spoke by phone a couple of days later, Kurt told me he thought it was hilarious but had forgotten to mention it.

In his emails, Kurt often included quotes from famous people. "Men as a rule love with their eyes, but women with their ears." Oscar Wilde. "A woman never falls in love with a man unless she has a better opinion of him than he deserves." Ed Howe. And this one from Kurt: "I was never in the least inclined to take a mistress. Now it is too late."

As for our trip to Vegas, I would be staying three days, and Kurt would stay over an extra day in order to accommodate my arrival and departure. In one of his last emails before our meet-up, he had written: "Gosh, I've never had a romantic tryst. What do they taste like? Warning. I may not let you go. I will have your cat flown into Vegas to attend the wedding ceremony, and we will spend our honeymoon in Tiltonsville." That's a town of approximately eighteen hundred people, one grocery store, a post office, and the high school we graduated from.

What a great sense of humor, I mused, and I emailed him a thought for the day that I'd just received: "GOOD looks catch the eye, but a GOOD personality catches the heart. You're blessed with both." Although someone else had written those words, they fit Kurt perfectly.

Humor is very important to me. In fact, writing humor for local and national magazines and newspapers is how I supplement my income.

After getting the email about honeymooning in Tiltonsville, I wrote back that I planned to give Kurt a big hickey on his neck when I saw him. He responded by saying he'd go four days without eating to get one of those, and he'd sport his hickey all over town.

I now understood how people can fall in love by the written word because I found myself getting amorous about the person that had been making me laugh through daily emails for the past couple of months.

Kurt confessed he'd been doing a considerable amount of day-dreaming about our trip. He said yesterday he wound up at his old venue, ran a number of red lights, and mowed half of his neighbor's lawn. I don't think so, but that email let me know I was on his mind a lot. On the other side of the country, I'd also been doing some day-dreaming. I'd been broken up with my boyfriend, Wes, for ten years. He and I had seen one another exclusively for over twenty years, and it had been a fulfilling relationship. I always fretted about our age difference, though, thinking that in later years my looks would fade, and fearing people would think I was his mother. I recall how quickly my ex had aged, and when he took his mother shopping, on one occasion a salesclerk had referred to her as his wife. I had heard Ned became livid.

No one measured up to Wes, however, so I spent the next ten years volunteering my services and trying to find out who I was before getting involved in another relationship. I served as a commissioner for the Area Housing Authority of Ventura County, as a hospice volunteer for Kaiser Permanente, as a certified ombudsman for the Long-Term Care Services of Ventura County, and I'd also served on the board of directors of the homeowner's association where I lived, consisting of approximately 3,500 residents. I would complete one volunteer assignment before taking on another one, and before I knew it, ten years had passed. While those volunteer jobs were very humbling and rewarding, I began to miss the intimacy of a loving relationship. And I had mixed emotions about never having sex again.

Kurt wrote that his wife had been in ill health for four years and he was her sole caregiver. He related that for a short time Pam was in a local nursing home receiving physical therapy, and that was not a good experience. Seeing that she wasn't being helped by the physical therapy, he took her home, knowing he could do a better job of caring for her needs, and he did just that until she died. He confessed he'd been celibate for six of those caregiver years.

OMG. I'd been celibate for ten years. As I wondered what happens when two celibates meet, an unexpected smile tugged at my lips.

Previously, Kurt sent me photographs of himself, but he recently sent me a picture in his Major's uniform. I set it on my desk where I'd look at it while typing at my computer. It stirred up tingly feelings. Kurt wanted a photo of me, so I emailed him one that had been taken when my romance novel, *Secret Torment*, had been published five years earlier. He said the picture was beautiful and that he'd emailed it to several of his retired air force buddies who want my phone number. (Funny.)

When Kurt found out I'd written a novel, he ordered one from Barnes and Noble and later gave me a flowery critique. I knew he wouldn't want to sabotage a budding relationship with an eighty-year-old near virgin, so I didn't put much weight on his critique.

Kurt's emails started off as: Dear Ms. California, Dear Ms. Tiltonsville, Dear Ms. Hungarian Gypsy, etc., and he would sign off with a bunch of alphabetical letters, such as LFTSU. That was easy—looking forward to seeing you. One day I couldn't figure out what ATSY was, and I asked him to decipher those letters for me. He couldn't, so that made me suspicious whether he just hung some letters together at the end of his emails to keep me busy trying to puzzle them out. Kurt's excuse was that it was so long ago he'd simply forgotten.

In another email, Kurt said he'd sold his home that he and Pam shared. He said it had too much lawn to take care of, and it was in an unincorporated area. His new home is in the city, next door to his sister-in-law Deena. Although she is two years older, we'd been friends in high school. Pam and I had also been friends, hanging out mostly in the seventh and eighth grades.

Kurt sent me a picture of his new home, which is a lovely split level. I told him I lived in a retirement community of active seniors called Leisure Village. I'm not sure how active they are, as I found out later the average age is seventy-two. But the brochures say "active." After moving there, I discovered the residents jokingly call the place Seizure Village because paramedics race through the Village on a regular basis.

Although the Village has an Olympic-sized swimming pool, a 16-hole golf course, two tennis courts, a racquet ball court, pool room, art room where painting classes are offered, plus many clubs, over half of the residents don't use them. A friend learned Chinese brush painting while living there and is now quite renowned for her paintings. She is the exception, however.

Kurt said he loves to swim and would take advantage of the pool. I told him I don't go there any longer because Depends (women's feminine pads) were caught in the drain system twice. I'd been on the board of directors for two years and discovered many of the disadvantages of living in a retirement community. The most distasteful was the increase in association fees to maintain and upgrade the grounds and amenities. Once increased, they are never decreased.

In an email to Kurt, I said that my eldest daughter was urging me to move to Georgia to live closer to her and her husband. Her arguments made sense: property is cheaper; if you're over sixty-five, you don't pay school taxes. In addition, food and gasoline are cheaper. "The key point is that you're getting older, and we'll look in on you," my daughter said.

"You should give it a lot of thought," Kurt said, "because you've said how much you love California."

Chapter Two

On our second day in Vegas, Kurt and I spent a lot of time strolling hand-in-hand from casino to casino. It was October and the air was warm, yet brisk. We were stopped several times as we walked along. One gentleman asked if we were newly-weds. A camera crew asked if we'd mind answering a few questions for a segment of a new television show. We couldn't even answer one. But who would know the tune that was used to advertise Lucky Charms cereal? The 20th president of the United States? What actor played the first Superman role in the movies? Our friendship was headed for romance, and it was evident to people observing us.

We walked to the Riviera to pick up tickets for the comedy show that night, then to the MGM Grand to buy tickets for tomorrow night's Bette Midler Show. Next, we stopped for a latte, and I made a phone call to my cat, Moxie. Kurt laughed, saying he wondered if anyone else called their cat. "I'm sure they do," I said. I left a message on the answering machine that I loved him and missed him. I also sent a lot of noisy kisses. Moxie usually perched on his cat motel, and the answering machine sat nearby, so I knew he'd be excited to hear my voice.

Later that evening, Kurt and I were the first couple in line at the comedy show, still holding hands. The ticket taker, an elderly gentleman with a grey pompadour, joked with us while the line got longer. He then led us into the auditorium and seated us at a front table, near the raised stage. A good spot for hecklers, I thought, or targets for the comedian.

Just as the show was to begin, a couple was ushered to our table. After introducing themselves, the woman whispered, "I'm sorry we're late, but my husband had to phone our cat."

Kurt chuckled as he told them I'd called my cat earlier.

"See, it's not that uncommon," I gloated. During the performance, Kurt and I discovered that we were seated at this particular table to be heckled by the comedian Marko. He asked my name, and I said "Eva." He then asked a lady sitting in the section to our right what her name was, and as she took a moment to respond, Marko said, "Eva knew her name immediately." And that's how the routine went— always coming back to me—usually with insults.

Marko asked the audience to raise their hands if they served in the war, and Kurt raised his hand. Marko asked if Kurt served with Custer. The audience roared. Next, he asked Kurt how long we were together, and Kurt said we'd been married for sixty-two years. That got a loud round of applause. Kurt meant to say that after sixty-two years, we got together. Marko said although I was old, he'd like to bang me. Tapes of the show were for sale, but we didn't buy one. I would have been embarrassed to have my friends listen to my being the target of such bawdy jokes. I'm sorry now, however, that we didn't buy the tape for memory's sake.

As we were leaving, we picked up our photograph that the house photographer had taken. Kurt's arm was around me, holding me close. We looked very cozy and affectionate. I noticed Kurt had his wedding band on. He'd said earlier that he told Pam that as long as she wore hers, he'd wear his. That didn't bother me because they'd been married for over fifty years. I secretly hoped, however, that he'd stop wearing the ring if our relationship heated up.

When we got back to my room, Kurt opened the door and proceeded to pick me up to carry me across the threshold; but we both fell to the floor. I guess he thought I was a featherweight, when I actually topped the scales at 115 pounds. What else he didn't know was that he'd rammed my head into the door jamb. In spite of the pain, the scene seemed very funny—the two of us sprawled out on the hall carpet, laughing so hard that it hurt. Kurt said he hadn't expected me to be so heavy; I said I hadn't expected him to be such a weakling.

The next night when Kurt arrived to take me to dinner, I noticed an edginess about him. After complimenting each other on how nice we looked, Kurt sat on the side of the bed and asked me to sit on his knee. I did, and he put his arms around me. As his fingers caressed my arms, my heart hammered. I felt certain Kurt could hear it. He pulled me closer and brushed his lips ever so lightly against mine; he then pulled away, looking deeply into my eyes. "Is it too soon to say 'I love you?'" I couldn't speak for a minute, shaken by his unexpected ardor. With a slow sigh, I melted against him, and we kissed again. This time a very passionate intensity took over, and as we pulled apart, I mumbled, "It's too soon." He didn't seem daunted by my response; and we struggled to stifle our passion as we left for a night on the town.

Our dinner was very romantic, and we prodded each other with questions trying to find out everything we could about one another. Although we graduated from high school together, in actuality, Kurt only spent the last two years with our class, having moved in with his Aunt Thelma and Uncle Pete who lived around the corner from where I lived. Since Kurt spent most summers with them as a small child, he'd made many pals that remain friends with him to this day. I'd run into him when we were kids, and we hung around at the same places and attended the same parties. In fact, Kurt says he may have been the first boy who kissed me, and I kissed him back. The kiss took place at a friend's tenth birthday party when we played Spin-the-Bottle. It must have been special for the both of us to have remembered it sixty-two years later.

Before moving to Tiltonsville, Kurt said he lived in Brookfield, PA with his mother. But after his mother divorced, she felt the right thing to do would be to keep her younger son with her and have Kurt, who was three years old at the time, go live with his paternal grandmother temporarily until his mother could get her life together. She'd been divorced and remarried several times. But it wasn't until Kurt was thirteen that his mother came back for him. Kurt said it broke his grandmother's heart to have him taken from her. He said he felt a deep sense of loss to have to leave her, but he also felt a sense of excitement for the opportunity to renew his relationship with his mother and to bond with his brother. They lived together for three years—until Kurt moved to Tiltonsville with his aunt and uncle on a permanent basis. His Uncle Pete got him jobs during the summers and encouraged him to live with him and his wife and to attend his last two years of school at Tiltonsville.

Not long after Kurt moved to Tiltonsville, his beloved grandmother moved in with his aunt and uncle, and she and Kurt were together again. Kurt's new family were a guiding influence in his life, teaching him good work ethics and encouraging him to attend college.

Kurt's brother was killed in an auto accident by a drunk driver when he was twenty-three. The drunk driver got off with no jail time because laws weren't as stringent against drunk drivers when that accident occurred, almost ten years ago.

Kurt's mother couldn't get over the loss of her youngest son and committed suicide in her early seventies. Kurt confided, "My mother borrowed a gun from a neighbor, telling the neighbor she needed protection from prowlers." Kurt was devastated. Not only was his brother gone, but now his mother was, as well.

Through emails, Kurt confided that since he was a small child, his dream was to be an airline pilot. He said he stayed fixed on that goal and attended Ohio University after graduating from high school. He worked as a short order cook and took various other jobs while putting himself through college. After two years, he said he dropped out and took a full-time job to build up his college funding, and he then returned to college to fulfill his goal.

Kurt said his relationship with his father was good, although he didn't see him often due to his moving around to find work. That was during the depression years and jobs were scarce. Kurt's father later remarried, and two children were born of that union: Richard and Frieda. Kurt and his half-siblings keep in touch to this day. Kurt said his father got his act together during his second marriage, but that his mother never did. "It's very sad because my mother was beautiful, and everyone who met her liked her. She suffered depression for years and took whatever pills she could get her hands on to make herself feel better. But after my brother died, no amount of pills seemed to help her."

I told Kurt about my childhood and my relationship with my parents, my brother Joey, who was four years older, and my paternal grandpap who lived with us from the time I was born until the day he died. Grandpap and I had a special relationship, similar to what Kurt had with his grandmother. When my parents played cards with friends at their homes, Grandpap would be my sitter. As soon as my parents left, I'd invite friends over, and we'd have taffy-pulling contests and play board games in the basement. Grandpap regularly walked down the stairs to make sure things were under control. The kitchen would be a mess when my parents got home, but under Mother's grilling, Grandpap always said the same thing, "Only Eva and Julie were here."

Upon reflection, I think that because of my close relationship with my grandpap, and of the love lavished upon me by my dad, I thought all men were nice. I found out differently right after marrying Ned at the age of nineteen.

The waiter kept filling our iced tea glasses as Kurt and I shared our lives.

I told Kurt that it had always been a dream of mine to attend college, but my mother wouldn't hear of it. "You'll just get married anyway, and that money will have been wasted."

"Although I attended business school while still in high school, I dreamed of going to college; but no amount of begging would change my mother's mind.

"Why do you think she didn't want you going to college?"

"We didn't have any colleges nearby at that time, and I believe she wanted me to get married and have kids and stay in the same town as her and Daddy, and that's what I did."

"You should have gone to college," Kurt said. "Placing third in our graduating class was an accomplishment."

There were only sixty-two in our class," I laughed.

"High school grades are what matter in getting you into college," Kurt said.

"I finally did go to college," I told Kurt. "When I was in my fifties and after my daughters were raised, I enrolled at Van Nuys Community College and earned an associates degree in Journalism. I later attended the California State University at Northridge, graduating magna cum laude with a batchelors degree in English Literature. I managed to fulfill my college dream, but neither of my parents knew because they had passed away by then."

"What made you pursue college since you were a paralegal?"

"I got tired of writing what someone else wanted me to write. Funny thing, though. I sold more short stories and essays before I got my college degree."

"That's interesting," Kurt replied.

Just then the waiter appeared with more iced tea and our conversation continued.

I asked Kurt if he knew my brother. "I saw him several times, but we never spoke."

"He was four years older than I and volunteered for the army in World War II right after graduating from high school. Then he attended college on the G.I. Bill, earning a degree in Accounting from Ohio State University. When growing up, he didn't want a younger sister shadowing him. But when he was discharged from the service, we shared a close relationship. After having seven children, my brother also got divorced."

"Your brother had seven kids?" Kurt asked, amazement in his voice.

"He sure did. His wife converted to Catholicism and was a registered nurse. They just grew apart."

"Usually I'd fly into Columbus when visiting in Ohio, and I'd stay at my brother's home. We'd have a great time reminiscing. We'd take trips to visit relatives. On one visit my brother confided to me that while we were growing up, he felt Mom was rather distant. I couldn't believe my ears. 'You were always her favorite,' I interrupted. 'Whenever you wanted anything, you got it immediately. I was fourteen before I got a bicycle.'"

"In that way, I guess you're right. But the hugs and kisses were missing."

I confessed to Kurt that this blew my mind…that my brother, Mom's favorite, also felt she didn't love him. And I knew he didn't have the spontaneous love lavished upon him by our dad and grandpap like I had. What an awakening! My brother and I both felt that our mother was a good, Christian woman who just couldn't show affection, and that she was the one who missed out by this flaw in her makeup more than we did. After pausing a moment, reflecting on our relationship, I said, "My brother died eight years ago."

Kurt and I came from the same backgrounds and shared many similar experiences. I told him that Pam and I hung around together when we were in junior high. "In fact, Pam wrote in my autograph book, and so did Deena."

"What did they write?"

"Pam wrote that we'd be friends until the Ohio River wore rubber pants. Then she added, 'But whatever you do, don't get married.'"

"That's very weird," Kurt said. "Did she know about your relationship with Ned?"

"No, she wrote that in the seventh grade, and I didn't start dating Ned until my junior year in high school."

"Wow! Then you marry me." He was silent a moment and then asked, "What did Deena write in your autograph book?"

"She wrote that she hoped my future would be bright."

"You know, it's a comfort to know you and Pam had been friends," Kurt said.

We had a great time processing the information we'd learned about one another, and the time slipped by. We talked for so long and drank so much iced tea that we had to hurry to get to the Bette Midler show on time; and we were both big fans of hers.

* * * * *

After the show, that night in my room, our kisses were bittersweet. We were very aware that this would be our last night together. I was now sorry I'd be leaving after only three days. But when we decided to meet, I was afraid to commit to a longer stay. What if we didn't click? I should have known better because our emails revealed our compatibility.

The next day—my last day in Vegas—Kurt and I enjoyed breakfast together, and then I packed my suitcase. Since Kurt would be spending another night at Bally's, we put my suitcase in his room and did some gambling. We yearned to be alone, yet we were afraid to be alone. Things were moving very fast. About an hour before I was to catch the shuttle to the airport, we went to Kurt's room to get my suitcase and to say our goodbyes. Kurt closed the door and pulled me down on the bed. We just stared at one another while goose bumps gathered on our arms. Leaning over, Kurt placed his mouth on mine. His lips were soft and sweet and very warm. Then he kissed me harder, deeper, and I kissed him back. This kiss wasn't just a kiss. It was a promise. It was a temptation. It was the beginning of something special. This time when Kurt said he loved me, I said those words back to him.

In-between kisses, we talked about our next date. He would fly to Los Angeles to spend time with me. We were completely caught up in one another and very sexually aroused. OMG—did we ever discover what it feels like for two celibates to meet! We struggled to keep our hands off one another as we lay on the bed—blue-green eyes burning into brown eyes. His eyes seemed to melt into mine; and I could feel the heat from his body entering mine. If we'd been in a sauna, we couldn't have been hotter. We just lay there enjoying the wonder of new love.

A few minutes before I was to leave, I pulled up my sweater and bra and flashed Kurt. Kurt, being a boob man, said he thought he died and went to heaven.

As we walked out of his room, Kurt murmured. "Wow! Are you built for a little gal."

"Thirty-eight C," I proudly announced.

A very deep, sensual feeling swept over us as we two celibates got caught up in our passion for one another. I'm sure the process was hurried along by knowing each other as children, although it felt like love at first sight. Whatever it was, it hit hard. We found out that love can happen at any age, and it can be just as intense when you're in your golden years.

After straightening our clothes and taking a couple of deep breaths, we headed for the elevator. Kurt said, a little hesitantly, that he'd like a little souvenir from me. He set down my suitcase and stood in front of me. "I don't know how to ask you this because I've never done anything like this before."

"Just ask me."

He spoke haltingly. "How about giving me a pair of your panties?"

Not missing a beat, I asked. "Before or after I've worn them?"

"After, of course." Kurt grinned sheepishly.

We had a very difficult time leaving each other when the shuttle pulled up. Kurt told me later that he walked the same streets as we had walked earlier, and he experienced a very lonely feeling. He missed me something dreadful, while I, on the shuttle, could think of nothing but Kurt and his sweet, sweet kisses.

Chapter Three

When I got back home from the Vegas trip, I could hardly wait to get Kurt's email. He said how much he enjoyed our time together. He also said he spent some time with his sister-in-law Deena and passed my regards to her. "I told her about the great time we had and about the shows we saw. Now she wants to fly to Las Vegas. She said she would not go alone, so I might find myself in Vegas again soon."

I read that part of the email over and over again, and my stomach twisted into knots. I like Deena a lot, and Kurt said their relationship was platonic. But a trip to Vegas with her? I immediately sent off an email to Kurt saying I was not interested in a three-way relationship. I said I got the impression he thought it was okay to take trips with Deena, but I'm not okay with his taking trips with anyone but me. I let him know that being in a committed relationship meant we didn't take overnight trips with people of the opposite sex.

I was beginning to wonder whether Deena really wanted Kurt to be happy or wanted him for herself. I was mixed up and questioned Kurt's love for me.

I said in my email for Kurt to count me out of this scenario and that I wished him the best but said this was not the best for me. After pushing the send button, I felt sad. I'm Hungarian and often do things impulsively. Was I being impulsive, or was there a jealous streak in me? Probably, but I felt this was deeper than what I could handle; and since our relationship was new, I'd rather break it off sooner than later. Tears gathered on my cheeks. It was late in the evening, so even if Kurt read the message immediately, I knew he wouldn't call me late at night.

About nine the next morning the phone rang, and it was Kurt. His voice sounded shaky as he tried to explain that Deena didn't have any friends interested in going to Vegas, and she wouldn't go alone. He said he thought nothing was wrong in accompanying her.

I asked him if he'd mind my going to Vegas with my son-in-law. It didn't take him long to say he wouldn't like it. He then apologized and said he understood my feelings. "I love you and don't want to lose you," he said. "I guess I just wasn't thinking. Are we okay now?"

I said we were. I could tell Kurt wasn't very savvy about women. Pam was the first gal he'd gotten serious with, and he married her. I'm sure he was still grieving when he and I met up. I remember when my brother had gotten divorced; he joined several singles clubs and dated much younger women. I think it was to show he was still macho. Kurt didn't need to do that because his wife had assured him he was macho. I came to realize that losing a spouse and getting a divorce can cause men to act weird.

Later in the afternoon when I checked my email, there was one from Kurt with the subject matter identified as *Tragedy Averted*. I felt bad. He said that as he read my letter about breaking up, his hands started to tremble and he had trouble picking up the phone.

"All of those wonderful days we had in Vegas passed through my mind, and now I am about to lose only the second woman I ever loved? Yes,

I had second thoughts about what I said in my letter but after I hit the send button there was no going back. Your letter cut me to the bone and that is why I called. As I type this letter I am still a bit shaken. Toward the end of our conversation your voice sounded much more receptive and you have assured me that all is well again. Please confirm this with a short email.

"Last evening I could not sleep because you were on my mind. I think about you all day and try to transcend those many miles between us. I want you in my life until the day I die. You must believe me. This morning you made me feel wonderful when you said I was a good man. That, coming from a devout Catholic woman, reassured me.

"I will speak with Deena. There is no problem here. Sorry to have made you feel so low since my last letter. I am yours. I just made a bad tactical error and it will not be repeated. Do believe that, my love. Seems you have taught me a valuable lesson. The affairs of the heart can set many traps for those who fail their lover's sensitivity. *Love is the emotion that a woman always feels for a poodle, and sometimes for a man.* George Jean Nathan. *Love has the power of making you believe what you would normally treat with the deepest suspicion.* Mirabeau." Sorry I hurt you, Kurt."

We agreed to talk things out in the future rather than jumping to conclusions that could damage our relationship. Yeah, we had a relationship.

A few days later, Kurt sent me a letter by email that he'd received from one of his squadron buddies in response to his confiding about starting a relationship with me. His friend Ken said he and Anne will be together for fifty years, and he can't survive without her. He said the doctor says he's in good shape, and he takes enough vitamins and plenty of Viagra. He said he and Anne think it's wonderful that Kurt is re-establishing a past friendship. "Pam would want you to continue to enjoy life." He ended by saying, "Our hearts are with you. Keep us informed."

That made me happy to know that Kurt was telling his friends about me and that they approve. Kurt still keeps in touch with a lot of his buddies from the Vietnam war, in addition to high school classmates. And here I thought I was the only one still attached to the past.

The next time Kurt called, he wanted to know what I did during the days, and I told him about my Himalayan cat who is twelve, my hundred-year-old Aunt Wilma for whom I hold the power of attorney, and my ninety-six-year-old neighbor, Wanda, who is in a nursing home due to a fractured femur, and for whom I also hold the power of attorney. "I'm busy visiting them and handling their affairs, and I'm also painting my kitchen and bathrooms in case I move to Georgia and need to sell my condo."."

"You're doing what?" he asked.

"I've been single a long time, so I'm accustomed to painting and doing repair work."

"I'll keep that in mind. I didn't realize you were that serious about moving to Georgia. But Georgia is closer to Ohio than California is, so we'll be able to see each other more often."

We were both very eager to see one another again, and our emails had been getting progressively hotter. When I'd email Kurt, I'd often call him "Mr. Yum Yum," "Dearest Love," "Super Kurt." I spent hours choosing cards that expressed how I felt about him. Kurt said he did the same thing. One card Kurt sent me was a picture of a girl and boy (about five years-old) in adult clothing. They strikingly resembled Kurt and me. Then we got on the kick of how many children we'd have had if we'd have married young. "Since you're Catholic, we probably would have had seven or eight," Kurt said. "That would be about five too many for me."

"I have two kids," I replied, "and my brother has seven."

"Maybe it was a good idea not to have pursued our relationship earlier," Kurt joked.

I asked Kurt about his daily routine, and he said he gets up early and goes out for breakfast, comes home and reads the paper, takes a nap, and then goes back out for lunch. "I get antsy when shut up in the house for very long," he said.

In every email, we express our love for one another. One email from Kurt read:

"Dear Ms. Ohio,

"Vegas was a hoot, but not long enough. We couldn't get enough of each other. I'm elated that you want to move up the date when we will meet again. Keep in mind that I can absorb any expense involved. I can fly to your city and drive to your home. It has been less than a week since we were together, but it seems like a year. It will be a thrill to be with you again. The most powerful thing in this universe is…the kiss!

"I lead such an easy life these days. The divorcee across the street sees me leaving the house a number of times every day and probably wonders, 'Now where the hell is he going?' She, too, is divorced from a lawyer and has two daughters.

"Tomorrow I will join the boys at the airport and play first liar doesn't have a chance.

"Gotta go now and resume my retirement. AML – Kurt."

Kurt uses correct English and writes beautifully, but his emails are in reporter style. I wonder whether it's because of his military training.

In one of our phone conversations, Kurt told me he has a hangar at a small airport about ten miles from his home. He and a group of plane aficionados have planes there and meet regularly to fly and shoot the bull. Kurt said he used to have a plane but sold it. He said the gang flew to Oshkosh several times for the air show where he'd run into some of his Vietnam war buddies; and he and some of the gang would fly to another city just for lunch.

In my email to Kurt in response to a card he'd mailed to me:

"I love the card you sent me—I've read it several times. Funny how it expresses exactly the way I feel about you. Isn't it wonderful that the best things in life just happen? I still can't believe how you've stolen my heart, and in such a short time.

"I took *the picture* the photographer had taken in Vegas for my daughter and family to see. My daughter loves it and said we look good together. My grandson said we both look very happy and that makes him happy. My granddaughter said she doesn't doubt that it's love. My son-in-law says to go slow as he doesn't want me hurt. So, it's all out on the table, and my family approves."

Kurt said he's glad my family approves of our relationship and said he's sure his two sons and their wives will like me and approve as well.

The next day's email from Kurt:

"Dear Miss Excitement,

"I really love to open your mail when its subject is **us**. Thank you for taking the time to email me in spite of your workload. I'm glad that the card satisfied your fancy. I was looking around the card section when I happened on this one. It seemed right for what we're both thinking. For me, the words come from the heart. *I really love you.* I think about you all day. You're in my prayers every night. Tell me, what do you see in me?

"I'm assembling a package to send you. Some of the stuff you might want to discard. A few of the items may spike your interest.

"Funny you should comment about envying Pam's time with me. I have often thought the same about you. But not since my sunshine years with Pam have I ever met a woman so desirable as you. I really mean that Eva, my dear.

"I have shown our picture only to Deena so far, but you can bet many more folks will see it. I look at that picture many times a day. I'm going to contact a few other classmates to let them know we've found love. So happy your family approves of our union.

"Have to go now, sweetheart. Be well. Just an average guy. Kurt."

"You're no average guy, or I wouldn't be so crazy about you," I said. I wondered what he sent me. "What did I like about him?" I said I love his looks and gentle style, and his wonderful, deep voice. "Plus, you make me smile inside. Lastly, you were hand-tailored for little Eva."

In another email I told him that about a week after I'd moved Aunt Wilma into a nursing home closer to where I live, I noticed a large hand-printed note on her nightstand. "If I have any complaints about the home or the nurses not treating me well, I should call the ombudsman's number and report them." She'd also printed the phone number and underlined it. I asked where she got this information, and she said it was posted on the wall by the front door, and she wrote it down in case she ever needed it.

I couldn't stop laughing, wondering what the staff thought when they read the note.

My aunt is one hundred and very sharp. She whizzes around the nursing home in a wheelchair with big wheels that she moves with her arms. She also likes men and has made good friends with the staff doctor's brother, who has the beginnings of Dementia.

Kurt replied that he looks forward to meeting Miss Wilma. "One hundred? I hope you inherited her genes." He attached a scanned-in picture of him tinkering with an engine of some kind. My reply was: "Good heavens, do you work on engines of planes a well as fly them? You are out of my league. I'm more familiar with the items on your bathroom vanity."

The next email from Kurt said:

"That was a posed picture. I don't know poop from a spittoon about this type of engine. I use this picture to send to people I do not like (you're the exception, of course). It forces them to change their minds about how stupid they think I am."

I emailed Kurt to ask him if he'd be interested in receiving my writer's club newsletter because I had two articles in it. I said this was the second time I'm president, having been president ten years ago. I told him it's fun but cuts into my writing time. I said I'm also a pro-member of Romance Writers of America but I'm not actively involved in that club. "I'm hooked on writing romance novels, and I'm through with grout, ceramic glue, and paint brushes.

From now on, I'm going to write; and I'm starting another novel titled *Vengeful Heart*, and I'm tired of having to rely on my memory for the love scenes. I need your help. ILU – Eva."

He called me that night and said we should set a date and place for our next meet-up and added that I was in his thoughts constantly. We decided he should come visit me the early part of December, 2009. "I may be able to help you with your love scenes." He laughed wickedly.

That afternoon, the doorbell rang, and the postman handed me a package that contained pictures of Kurt at different stages of his life and a fuchsia sweatshirt hoodie with Ohio University written across the front—the college Kurt had attended. The hoodie was a size small and fit me perfectly. I left it on because it felt so soft and warm. I sent an email to Kurt telling him I loved the hooded sweatshirt and since Novembers are sometimes a little cool in California, this was a most welcome gift, as were the pictures of him that also warmed me up.

Kurt's response was that he was glad I liked the sweatshirt, he'd love to read the newsletters, and he'd like some pictures of me. He then asked me about the men in my life. "Not that it matters," he added.

This wasn't the first time Kurt asked about the men in my life. When we were in Vegas I told him about my abusive first husband who destroyed my self-esteem. "Ned made me believe I was used merchandise and no man would ever want me." I told Kurt that Ned cheated on me with my girlfriend's sister. "I'd lost a lot of weight and was down to ninety-nine pounds. Since my clothes didn't fit, I packed them up and gave them to a girlfriend, who gave them to her sister Etta. My friend told me later that Etta wore those clothes when she cheated with my husband; and one night Ned said to Etta: 'My wife has that same dress,' not knowing it was **the** same dress. Isn't that bizarre? Anyway, I was glad my friend told me about Ned and her sister. Although I suspected Ned cheated, I never knew for sure until my friend confirmed it. She also said I'd probably end up not speaking to her, but she had to take that chance. I threw my arms around her and said I appreciated her telling me about Ned and that we'll always be friends. She's the one who picks me up at the airport when I fly in for class reunions. You may not have known her because she dropped out of school her senior year. Her dad said she needed to get a job to help with family expenses. Later she found out her earnings went towards a prom gown for her older sister her father favored. My friend was heartbroken."

As for Ned, I wrote,

"I filed for divorce from him on the grounds of *Extreme Cruelty*, which was granted. I was also awarded sole custody of our daughters with the stipulation that Ned could address the court in the future, if circumstances should change. However, Ned never did that, which made me believe he wanted a single life again with no one inhibiting him. P.S. Remind me to tell you about my rotten honeymoon one day.

"Will, who later became my second husband, was a lawyer, and we worked together at the law firm. He had a larger-than-life presence, and he made me feel good about myself, and he made me feel loved. He only charged clients what they could afford, and that's one of the things that endeared him to me. He was very thoughtful of other people; but he and I were both carrying curses. Me, with my lowered self-esteem; and he, with his drinking problem. When we dated, he drank a lot; but he convinced me it was only a social thing. But evidently it was more than that, because after we married, Will polished off a quart of Vodka every other night; and it seemed I always had a glass of liquor in my hand. I didn't like how Will's problem was quickly becoming my problem, so I gave Will an ultimatum. 'It's either me or the Vodka;' and the Vodka won out. We still loved one another and dated after we divorced. I'm attaching the poem I wrote about our relationship at the end of this email. Will never saw the poem; but I want you to read it because I know you like poetry. Please remember that this poem was written before you came into my life."

"It was Wesley, however, another lawyer, who made me bloom and soar. He's a very good man and is in many pictures with my family. Since he's eleven years younger than I, his two children were youngsters when we met, while mine were married. We never discussed our age difference, I think, because it didn't matter. I'd always looked ten years younger, and I always attracted younger men. Since Wes was a lawyer, and I was a paralegal, we always had lots of things to talk about. We'd take his kids and my grandkids to various amusement parks and restaurants. He took care of me when I had a blood clot and was hospitalized; and he was always there for me.

"I loved his family, who became my family. His mother and I developed a close relationship and she told me that she felt I was good for her son. His dad enjoyed writing poetry, which he shared with me. I shared my newspaper articles with him. Wes' dad started calling me on Sunday evenings and we'd talk for an hour about the projects we were working on and the books we were reading. Several times Wes was visiting when his dad called. Although Wes acted irritated, I knew he was pleased to see how his family accepted me. And my family loved and accepted Wes.

"Wes and I talked through everything. He wouldn't let me say, 'Never mind, it's not important.' He listened and loved me for who I was. He was non-judgmental and fun to be with. We were together for over twenty years, and he's still very special to me. It was after I moved to Leisure Village that we started drifting apart. I had retired and became involved in community politics and activities, and Wes made new friends through his law practice, and we stopped working on our relationship. Now I'm only in

love with you, Kurt, and it gets stronger the
more I know you."

A LOVE TRIANGLE

Bastard! Liar! Cheater!
I loved you! I hated you!
Nobody knew.
You made my heart do tricks.
It jumped through hoops for you, rolled over, did flips.
You were my boss, my mentor, my lover.
Business only at the office.
Yet everyone knew.
Your body language spoke of love.
My eyes replied with fervor.

You made me promises you never meant to keep.
I know that now.
Liar!
Because of you, I'll never trust
again. I'll never love again.
Letting go of memories is the toughest part of all:
The morning you came to my home, awaking me at five,
a thermos of coffee under your arm,
driving to the beach, watching the sun rise...
Our kisses were sweet, pure.

I remember your first gift to me,'
a small marble urn with delicate gold legs, very pretty,
I didn't know what it was.
"A soap dish," you said. "Every time
you bathe, you'll think of me."

And I did.
When the treasured dish fell and broke,
My heart felt like it, too, had broken.
I spent days gluing it back together.
I was whole again.

I became your wife.
Vodka was your mistress.
You cheated on me.
You couldn't give her up,
although you said you would.
I lay awake at night, consumed with her elixir.
I tired of competing for your affection.
Our passion divided us.
You had to leave.

When the moving crew came to pack up your belongings,
I sobbed rivers of tears.
One of the movers asked why I wept.
"He can't give up his mistress," I moaned.
He hated you.
I loved you.
The marble soap dish broke again.
This time I threw it away.
But I can't throw away my heart.

I'm constantly reminded of the thrills
that shot through my body
when your car pulled into the driveway,
the excitement that raged when our hands touched,
when our lips met.

Ethel Ann Shaffer

I still love you!
I still hate you!
Bastard! Liar! Cheater!
Do you ever think of me?

Chapter Four

The same day I sent the email, a response from Kurt arrived. Holding my breath, I read.

"Dearest woman,

"How interesting our exchanges have become lately. We are digging deep from our past and sharing it with each other. Vegas was a one-act play and its stars are now laying the groundwork for act two. In twenty-five more days, the curtain will rise once again to reveal a couple of Thespians, center stage, giving the audience what they want to see...a union. As I learn more about you, an ever sharper picture emerges to diminish the distance between us. Thank you for the personal touch, and I will await the honeymoon story. You know, I really like Wesley for having taken care of you, and may he bask in happiness all of his life. I feel reassured that you now have one love for me.

"Oh Ned, I am not sure about this fellow. I wish him no ill, but I hurt when I envision the struggle imposed upon you and the girls. I cannot imagine a man lifting an angry hand toward his wife. I tear up a bit picturing you and your daughters heading for the California refuge, and into the unknown. If this story was a novel, the reader might conclude that all turned out well when your journey ended at the Pacific shore. But no, more sadness would be your companion. But hey, the daughters grew up, you have grandchildren, a career, and you are still beautiful.

"Will. I like him too. I envy the guy for having had you as his wife. It's unfortunate that neither Will nor Wesley could find a way to hold on to you. I feel sad for those two men.

"You and me. I guess all men are different. I sense that during Vegas, you saw enough quality in me to proceed with, well, whatever will come next. What you saw is what you will get. In love, I like to attend to the small stuff. Over the years I have learned how to appreciate the female sensitivity. I had a lot of practice being married to Pam. Oh, she and I never so much as raised our voices to each other. Never had a serious argument. There was a lot of profound respect at work. Pam is gone and I want another woman … I want you! I don't know on what level you and I will be assigned, but let's give it lots of thought. I loved the way you held me off at Vegas. I'm not an aggressive guy with a woman, but I can read the signs. You have a lot to offer a man, and I only hope that time and circumstance will permit me to enjoy your being.

"I attend early church service, and this morning the Pastor asked all veterans to stand. Gosh, it was reassuring to hear the loud and extended applause for us. I take a great deal of pride from my military service. Wednesday is

Veterans Day. Kiss a veteran if you can find one. If not, wait until I arrive on the scene.

"Thanks for your wonderful personal story and add to it when something new arises.

"Sexual intercourse is a slight attack of apoplexy, if done correctly … Democritus."

"I love you. Kurt. P.S. Where are the panties you promised me?

Oh, yes, the panties. I had on a purple hip-hugger that I wiggled out of and sniffed before putting them in a 9 x 12 manila bubble envelope. I scribbled the address across the front, guessed at the postage, giggled like a teenager, and took the envelope out to the mailbox.

What a guy! Kurt could thrill me with his voice, and I couldn't wait to see him again. But I was starting to fret about his upcoming visit. Putting two passionate people in a small condo together can be both beautiful and dangerous. I want us to be ourselves, but I want us to feel comfortable with one another before having sex. I feel pressured and wonder whether Kurt feels the same way. My head spins with the proper Eva, the naughty Eva, the in-love Eva, and just Eva. Why am I questioning myself? Is it because I've been celibate for so long, is the age factor pushing me, did the short, beautiful time we shared together cause me to feel an urgency?

I emailed Kurt and asked if he's experiencing the same rollercoaster I am.

"One minute I think it's okay for you to stay at my condo, and the next minute I think you should stay in a motel." I thanked him for reading the newsletter and my writings and for the generous comments. "As I previously said, I'm impressed with the way *you* write. It's an unusual reporting style rather than just an email response. Where did you learn to write that way—from writing military reports? You could use your journals to write a book about your life. I'm sure it would be enjoyable with your unique childhood, your time in the service as a pilot, your job with the State of Ohio, your marriage, and beyond Vegas." I told Kurt he might not be hearing from me as often because I'm working on my novel. BOL. Your saucy Eva. Be sure to check your mailbox."

At our last writer's club meeting, I had told Ray, the editor of the monthly newsletter, the way I feel about Kurt. While working closely on submissions and editing, Ray and I have become good friends. His advice is not to be so quick in thinking my feelings for Kurt are love. "You don't know him very well as an adult," he said, "and I don't want you getting hurt."

"You don't understand," I replied. "It's a deep feeling, and Kurt feels the same way."

"Okay. Just promise me you'll go slow."

My daughter Susan called a few days later and asked if I'd mind if she called Wes, my former boyfriend and a real estate lawyer, because her homeowner association president was making off-the-wall decisions about things she thought should be voted on by the homeowners.

"Of course you can. He'll probably be glad to hear from you. … You know, it's been ten years since I've spoken to him." I swallowed hard and continued. "He didn't want to remain friends after we broke up. But it was probably the way I broke up with him."

Susan called him, and he was glad to hear from her and gave her the information she needed. She said he asked about me, and she told him I was fine and doing volunteer work.

I had always felt bad about the way I broke up with Wes and decided to call him to put things in order. He answered the phone. "Hi, I'm surprised you're still working," I said.

"I enjoy coming to the office every day. … How have you been?"

He sounded happy I called, and I told him that I'm fine, I'm retired, and I've accepted a volunteer job as a Commissioner for the Area Housing Authority.

"What does that entail?" he asked.

"We help low-income people find affordable housing, and we're turning a hotel into a housing project to provide more housing. I'm also seeing a lot of the United States by going to housing authority conferences, and I'm meeting lots of interesting people. Anyway, tell me about you and your family."

He said his daughter is married, and his son has his own business doing animation for television programs. I told him my granddaughter has her master's degree in psychology and is working on her dissertation for her doctorate; and my grandson is living with his girlfriend and her mother, who is elderly and overweight, and they take care of her and the house.

His phone beeped as we talked, and I said I didn't want to disturb him if he was busy. He asked if I'd like to have lunch with him Saturday. "Sure," I said. I knew Kurt wouldn't mind.

Wes called the next day and asked if we could make it dinner instead, and I agreed. I was a little nervous about seeing Wes after ten years, but it felt good to be friends again.

* * * * *

When Wes rang the doorbell, I invited him in. He looked the same as he did ten years earlier, except for more grey in his hair and a black and white peppered moustache. He hugged me and kissed my cheek. A warm feeling rushed through me.

We talked in the hallway for a few minutes and my cat walked out. That was very unusual because Moxie doesn't like anyone but me and usually hides from people.

"Beautiful cat," Wes said, and bent down to pet him. I thought for sure he'd get the usual hiss, but Moxie let him stroke his head. "What happened to Sasha and your black cat?"

I told him they passed away, and he said his dog had also died.

Knowing I like Chinese food, Wes had made reservations at The Plum Tree. We talked about our families and friends. I asked if he was seeing anyone special, and he said *no* but that he was dating. That's when I told him about Kurt.

Wes reminded me that since Kurt was part of my past, perhaps I was reading more into the relationship than was actually there. "Nostalgia does funny things."

"It's the real thing," I said.

"If it is, I'm happy for you."

I told Wes that I sent him a fax because if I'd faced him in person I might not have ended our relationship. His smile was wistful as he said, "I'm glad you told me that."

"I'm sorry about us," I said. "I felt we were growing apart."

"You shouldn't be sorry," he said. "It was my fault."

It felt good renewing our friendship and being able to confide in one another. But I was starting to get emotional. This was the person I'd loved for over twenty years, and he's still the same person. But I'm not. Lots of things had happened in the past ten years, and I knew things could never be the same between us. Not that Wes led me to believe he wanted to reconnect.

We were silent on the ride home. I guess we were lost in our thoughts. At least I was. Wes walked me to the door and stepped in behind me. I turned around, and he hugged me tight, brushing his lips lightly against mine. He said huskily, "I'll always love you."

"And I'll always love you," I replied. He then closed the door and left.

Picking up my cat, I sat on the sofa cradling him, and crying for what seemed like hours. Some of my tears fell on Moxie, but he didn't move. Then I dried my eyes while a million thoughts unscrambled in my head. There are many kinds of love. … the love I feel for Wes, my past love and dear friend, and the love I feel for Kurt, my new love.

I called Kurt the next day and told him about my dinner with Wes. He wanted to know how that came about; and I explained how Susan called Wes about problems with her homeowner's association, and he asked about me. "I called Wes back to put things in order between us," I said. "We talked on the phone for a long time but kept getting interrupted by clients, so Wes asked me to have lunch with him, which got changed to dinner."

"Did you resolve anything?" Kurt asked.

"Yes." And I told Kurt the gist of my conversation with Wes. "Anyway, we're friends again. You have to remember we were a couple for over twenty years and he's in a lot of my family albums. He was best man at Lexie and Stephen's wedding, and I was Maid of Honor." I told Kurt that Lexie and Stephen flew to California and were married at The Little Brown Church in Studio City where Ronald Reagan and Nancy had gotten married. "Wes and I share many good memories, and we were always there for one another."

"I could never understand why you two didn't marry," Kurt said.

"It's complicated," I replied.

"I rather like Wesley. He took care of you and treated you well. And as long as I'm the one you love, I don't care if you stay in contact with him. In fact, I'd like to meet him one day. By the way, give me some dates in December, sweet one. I can hardly wait to see you again."

"I love you, Kurt, and I'm eager to see you, as well. I'll email you tomorrow."

When I hung up, I felt like the luckiest woman in the world.

Checking my calendar the next morning, I came up with December 2 through December 7, 2009, so I emailed

Kurt the dates to see whether they work for him. Then I wrote:

> "Will you feel the same way about me after seeing me sans makeup and running for the bathroom? I'm thinking we'll be learning too much about one another too soon. Will this cool the romance?" I ended with, "ILUVM. Your impatient near virgin."

A response came a few hours later:

"My Dear Romantic Partner,

"Let's see. Where do I start today's edition of man to woman? I read your letters very carefully after I've copied them, and so I'll just start at the top of your last letter and work down. First, I'm looking forward to kissing you before all the makeup goes on. Your lips will still feel the same, eh? When you walk across the kitchen floor in your well-worn nighty, wearing those beat-up slippers, your voice will still sound the same … am I not correct? The brown eyes will still smile at me. Oh, the bathroom fox trot. Well, I can watch your boobs bounce. I see nothing but another successful encounter. Trust me, none of the above will cool our romance. You suggest we might learn too much too soon about one another? Nah! The Man is waiting just off camera. I dare say that if we got a glimpse of him, he might even nod his approval. But in these matters, I best defer to my woman.

"As to the December dates, they are fine. I can't wait to see you again. It's up to you if you want me to stay at your home or in a motel. You know what I'd prefer, but I'll be a gentleman in either case.

"Now, how do I see you? First of all, I knew you before I met Pam. Back when we were young, I thought of you as untouchable. A pretty thing not available to the likes of me. Small, soft spoken. A quick smile and then you were gone. From time to time over the years I thought about you more than I should have. Now you know. And yet, nothing could have separated me from Pam. My vision of you did not include that of a caregiver. Nor did I know how strong you are. I don't see much shyness in you, but it is not difficult to see your passionate side. Going back to college in later life really impressed me. You have a great deal of resolve. Dealing with two daughters, working hard, and trying to find a man who is worthy of you. Having said all that, there is still something about you I can't put my finger on. Perhaps it will come to me later. Be well, princess. INY. Kurt."

Just reading Kurt's email gave me hot flashes. Believe me, love is as rich at eighty as it was at eighteen. Maybe more so because you know what love is all about. I can't wait to hold hands with Kurt and taste his kisses again. I swear he's the best kisser in the world. But how dare he copy my emails. They were for his eyes only. I decided to write to him immediately.

"Dear Kurt,

"Shame on you for saving my emails. I'll have to spank you for being a naughty boy. And now that I know my emails may be saved for posterity, I'll not be so loose with my tongue.

"Well, I have to prepare for my writer's club meeting tomorrow. Just want you to be prepared for a spanking if you don't burn my emails. Vengeful Eva."

Chapter Five

As I drank my morning cup of coffee, I phoned my friend Carrie, who now lives in Michigan. She used to belong to the same writer's club I belong to until she moved. She and I have been good friends for over twenty years, and I want to tell her about Kurt's upcoming visit.

"I don't know whether he should stay at my place or at a motel," I fretted.

"If you check him into a motel and then get amorous, you could stay there with him. Doesn't that sound romantic?"

"Yes, but my practical side doesn't want him to waste his money. I have a spare bedroom, you know."

"Do you really think you'll be sleeping in separate rooms?" I heard her snicker.

"I'm not sure. Things have to be right."

"Things are right," Carrie said. "You're eighty and have been married twice. He's eighty-one and a widower. It isn't like you're both virgins."

"I know that, but I haven't had sex for ten years. And Kurt hasn't had sex for six years."

"Let him stay at your place and go at it," she said, laughing raucously.

"What if he can't perform? He is eighty-one."

"Didn't you say he stuck out like a gear shift when he kissed you by the shuttle bus in Vegas?"

"Well, yes," I harrumphed. "What's happening between you and your roommate?"

"Things are good, although she isn't into sex as much as I am. But I'm not pushing. She has a lot going on. She doesn't like her job, and her mother interferes in her life."

"If her head's cluttered, that may be the problem," I replied.

After hanging up, my decision was made. Kurt would stay at my place, and we'd play out our feelings. I got hot thinking about it.

I poured myself another cup of coffee and called Lexie. "How's the weather in Georgia?" "It's beautiful, Mom. Stephen and I are working in our yard and trimming trees and bushes. … I was just going to call you. There's a home for sale a couple of streets over, within walking distance from our home. It's a bank foreclosure, and there's one bid on it; and I know what that bid is. If you bid one thousand dollars higher, you'll probably get it."

"How many bedrooms and bathrooms?" I asked.

Lexie said it has two bedrooms and two bathrooms, and hardwood flooring throughout. "You can add a master bedroom and an adjoining bathroom since you'd be getting it so cheap."

I asked if she could send pictures of the house, and she said she would.

When I hung up, I thought about what she'd said. If I got the place for one hundred one thousand dollars, I could afford to add a master bedroom and bathroom. I knew I had to move out of the Village when I had my last asthma attack. Too much crop dusting and spraying going on here. Also, the homeowner association fees are more than my retirement income can bear.

I had lived close to my youngest daughter and two grandchildren all of their lives, and I had enjoyed it immensely. Babysitting my grandchildren was perhaps the happiest time of my life. We'd do something special at least once a month, and then they'd stay overnight. When they were toddlers we'd all sleep in my king-sized bed. When they got a little older, we'd start out together in my bed, telling scary stories. I'd usually start the story by naming the main character and who she or he lived with, and then I'd paint the hero in a corner. My grandson would take over and have to figure out how to get the hero out of that danger and make up more of the story and then point her/him in danger's way again before turning the story over to my granddaughter. What an imagination those kids had! We'd hike through the hills and roller skate at Balboa Park. But now my grandkids are twenty-seven and thirty-one and have their own sets of friends. I still see them, but not as frequently. Susan has been married to Rob for twelve years, and they seem happy. So, after much thought, I bid on the Georgia home even before the pictures arrived.

Kurt called that night to tell me he'd gotten the tickets for the December trip.

"Terrific!" I replied.

"And I got the much-anticipated package from you yesterday afternoon." I could hear amusement in his voice. "I tucked the purple panties in my pillowcase and slept like a baby."

"I probably should have a pair of your jockey shorts because I don't sleep well."

"I think you got mixed up and sent me your panties *before* you wore them," he said.

"No, I filled your request."

"Then you probably should have worn them a couple of more days before sending them."

"I didn't want to give you nightmares."

"Have you decided where I'll be staying?"

"You'll know when you get here." I told him about bidding on a foreclosure in Georgia.

"Sounds good. Georgia is about seven hundred miles from Ohio. We could see each other more often. … How do your daughter and grandkids feel about your move?"

"Susan and her husband live about an hour from me, but they're always on the move—to Vegas, the Laker's games, etc. We try to get together monthly, but it sometimes doesn't happen. I adore my grandkids, but they're adults and who knows whether they'll even stay in California? Marie, my granddaughter, graduated from UCLA and is starting her second year of graduate study at a private college to become a psychologist. She really doesn't need new patients. She can keep busy counseling her grandpap (my ex-husband), and his kids with his second wife. Two of them are in prison for killing a college classmate. But you know about that from reading the local newspapers."

It sounds like you've been giving this move a lot of thought."

"I have, although I still have unsettled feelings about leaving California."

Kurt gave me his flight information, and I wrote it down. "Well, sweetheart, I love you and look forward to seeing you in California, although I'll be calling you before then."

"I love you, honey, and can't wait to see you," I said.

The ten days before Kurt's arrival went slower than any ten days I ever experienced. But the day finally arrived, and I drove out of the Village and onto the 101 Freeway ramp. Turning the radio up, I sang along with "You're Always on My Mind."

As bad as traffic was, I got there fifteen minutes early and waited at the baggage claim. Spying the grey-haired fox about twenty feet from the baggage claim, I ran to greet him. And what a greeting! He grabbed me up in his arms, giving me the tightest hug. When he set me back down, he kissed me long and hard. It was as if nobody was in the terminal but the two of us.

We held hands and kept interrupting one another until his bag hit the turn-table. Kurt grabbed it off, and we headed for the parking lot. We kissed again, and as he pressed against me, I felt his manhood spike. Hmmm. Pretty exciting!

Placing his bag in the car trunk, off we went. There was little traffic on the way home, and I pointed out Westwood where I'd worked for eighteen years—"that tall building over there." I told him if we took the Santa Monica freeway we'd end up at the beach. "And that turnoff would take us to Beverly Hills," I said, pointing.

Fifty minutes later, I turned off the 101 Freeway ramp where a Marriott Hotel sat and drove on by. I caught a glimpse of Kurt's face in the streetlights, and he was grinning.

When we arrived at my condo, I pushed the garage door opener and drove in. Walking from my garage into the kitchen, Kurt looked around and said, "Very nice." He then asked where he should put his bag, and I said in the spare bedroom. His eyes darkened as he looked at me.

"I cleared space in that closet for you. But first, you must meet my beautiful cat."

"Moxie, Moxie," I called; but he didn't appear. He usually came to greet me as soon as I got home, but he must have heard Kurt's voice. I found him in my bedroom and carried him into the hallway to meet Kurt. His eyes got large and hateful. I asked Kurt to hold his hand out so Moxie could smell it. He did, and Moxie hissed at him.

"I don't think he wants to be friends," Kurt said.

"Give him time, and he'll make up."

"I'll give him as much time as he wants," Kurt replied.

I put Moxie back on my bed. Hmmm. That didn't go very well. I had imagined my two men really taking to one another. I remembered how friendly Moxie was with Wes, but he probably knew Wes presented no threat, while Kurt, with his stay-overs, would interfere with his life with his mistress. Smart cat. While Kurt hung up his clothes, I had a talk with Moxie. "I really like this guy and want you to like him, too. No more hissing, you hear?" Moxie feigned interest and then fell asleep while I talked to him.

"How about a sandwich?" I asked Kurt as I walked into the kitchen. He nodded.

After eating, I showed off my two-bedroom condo and the room I'd added on for an office. He said he really liked it, especially the large living room/dining room; and he asked if the skylight was there when I'd moved in.

"No, I had that put in. I bought the glass panes with white diamond-shaped figures in them, and then I had the skylight made to fit around the panes."

"They look like stars," Kurt said.

Walking back out to the kitchen, I made a pot of coffee. I said, "I love my kitchen. I recently painted it beige and installed beige floor tile."

Kurt's eyebrows shot up. "You're a handy lady to have around."

"You don't know just how handy," I said jokingly.

"I'm willing to hang around and see."

After eating, I poured glasses of wine, and we sat on the sofa, kissing and petting. Things were getting very hot. "Do you want to lie on my bed to get a little more comfortable?" I asked, trying to keep my voice calm.

"I feel sweaty from the flight. Do you mind if I shower first?"

"You really think it's from the flight?" I asked.

"Probably not," Kurt muttered, laughing.

I freshened up and put on a sexy nightie and robe and stood in front of the television, watching the news.

When I heard the exhaust fan go off in the guest bathroom, I yelled, "It's okay if you put on your PJ's and robe. We can watch TV in my bed until we get sleepy." I had unfolded the open-out couch in the guest bedroom and made it up, but that was probably a waste of energy.

My heart jumped in surprise and excitement as Kurt walked into my bedroom in the buff, posing like a muscleman. Wow! What a first act.

Walking towards me slowly, he unfastened my robe and dropped it on the carpet. My heart hammered. Oh, God, how I needed him to love me. His arms reached for me and tightened as they circled my waist. His lips caressed mine, patient at first, and then deep and possessive. He pulled away slowly and stared down at me. I saw a raw hunger in his eyes as he led me to the bed. "I love you," he murmured, pulling me close. I was smart enough to realize that some things, no matter how you fought them, were meant to be.

"You're so damned cute and tiny," he said. "But you're to let me know when I get out of line because I don't want to ruin our relationship. I'm crazy about you ... but I can wait."

The room was dark, and I could feel the heat of his manhood throbbing against me. Kurt groaned softly, and I whispered that I loved him. Then, suddenly, an irresistible passion swept over us with such an overpowering force, that neither of us could have stopped it. I gave myself to him completely, while he took me on a journey of undeniable love and passion that we both knew would change our destiny. We had crossed the bridge from uncertainty to a love that would bind us together, hopefully, forever. OMG. It was worth waiting ten years for this.

"I love you so much, Eva. Did I make you happy?"

"You were wonderful, Kurt. "I love you from the depths of my heart. And your lovemaking was as if it were my very first time. I never felt so loved."

"I feel the same way, Eva. We're very lucky to have found one another."

We slept all night in one another's arms and awoke in the morning full of passion and desire. I let my fingers trace his erection. His eyes were closed, and he moaned softly.

"You're getting very brave," he said, raising up and kissing me deeply.

"So are you," I murmured under his lips.

I could feel his penis grow. "Look how large it is, and I didn't even touch it."

"It's you, Eva," he said huskily. "After six years, I thought that part of my life was over. But you revived me."

"Aren't we the luckiest couple in the world!" I exclaimed. "I don't think many men your age can still perform, do you?"

"Age is just a number. I doubt that many women your age are still excited about sex."

"Well, I am, and your excitement just increases mine."

"Hold that thought," Kurt said. "I've got to go to the bathroom." As he tried to sit up, his hand pushed against my ribs. I immediately felt a pop and rolled over.

"Did I hurt you?" Kurt asked, standing up.

"My rib cage tells me a rib just cracked."

"Oh, no," Kurt said, kneeling next to the bed and cradling me.

"I'm sorry," Kurt said. "What can I do?"

"Just don't make me laugh. That's when it hurts the worst."

"I won't," Kurt said. "But shouldn't I take you to the emergency room?"

"They won't do anything. I had a cracked rib about a year ago when I was moving boxes, but never before in bed."

"Gosh, I feel bad. Are you sure nothing can be done?"

"I called my doctor the first time this happened, and he said to just take pain pills and to take it easy – that they no longer wrap ribs when they're cracked or broken."

"I'll be very careful from now on," Kurt said.

We both went to the bathroom and then slipped back into bed. We lay still for about an hour, completely sated. Kurt spoke first. "Your vagina is very small."

"And here I thought we were having foreplay."

"That, too," Kurt said, "but it took me a while to open you up enough to get in."

"If we keep playing in the evenings and in the mornings, I'll probably stretch so much you'll complain I need a vagina tuck."

"Never, sweetheart. We're perfect together." He breathed deeply and said, "Why don't you tell me about your honeymoon with Ned. I think I can take it."

"Tell me about your marriage and honeymoon first."

"Pam and I got married at the First Methodist Church in Tiltonsville. Her sister Deena and husband Ed were our only guests. After the ceremony, Ed drove us to Wheeling where we all had dinner; and then we got on a bus for Pittsburgh, where we spent our honeymoon. ... I didn't have a car."

"That sounds lovely."

"Ned and I had a large wedding – about one hundred fifty guests. My mother made my wedding gown, and Julie was my maid-of-honor. I had four bridesmaids. We had a sit-down dinner and an open bar at the Greek Hall. Changing clothes in the bathroom, we planned to drive to Little Washington to spend the night and to continue on to Niagara Falls in the morning. But when we got past Wheeling, Ned pulled off the highway onto a lonely road and told me to climb in the back seat. He said I was his wife now and he wanted me now.

"I pleaded with him to wait until we reached the hotel where we had reservations, but he wouldn't listen.

"You've put me off long enough," he said in his cocky manner, and he raped me in the back seat. Then he got mad because there was blood on the seat of the car. I certainly didn't enjoy my first sexual encounter. But I really enjoyed last night, my darling."

Kurt hugged me and kissed my eyes and nose and lingered on my lips. "It will always be this way, Eva."

"I love you, Kurt, and that will never change … but how about we get up and do some sight-seeing? Or should we spend the day in bed?"

"It depends on how your ribs feel," Kurt said.

Chapter Six

Kurt watched as I made coffee and lined up my morning pills on the kitchen counter.

"Geez. You take all those pills?"

"There are only six, and they work. So why not?"

"I guess," Kurt said.

Kurt poured the coffee and took the milk from the refrigerator. I set the Shredded Wheat on the table and watched Kurt sneak three pills down his throat. I didn't say anything, but I would certainly watch to see how many more he took in the course of the day.

I know how Kurt likes the ocean, so I planned a trip to the Santa Monica Beach. The day was a little overcast as we started out, but it seemed to clear up the longer we drove.

"How are your ribs?" he asked.

"I took a pain pill this morning; but what's the difference if I hurt in the car or at home."

"I'll leave that up to you, honey."

As we approach the beach, the first marker we see is the Ferris Wheel, a popular tourist attraction. After driving around for a parking space, a guy pulls out in front of me, and I take his space. Kurt and I walk hand in hand. Since a good many rollerskaters zip by on the walkway, the sand seems like a better walking alternative. We stop occasionally for Kurt to hang-walk on the bar sets. I'm usually energetic, but this cracked rib doesn't allow for any exertion. Kurt said he works out at a gym three times a week. No wonder he looks and feels fit. We laugh as we walk.

Strolling down the pier, we breathe deeply and enjoy the sea air and one another. We walk by a fortune teller's stand but decide not to have our fortunes told. We already know our future holds love and promise. We then stop for a couple of fish tacos. Since it's a little cool outside, we go inside and ride the carousel. The cool air finally urges us back to the car.

As we pull out of the parking spot, I mention to Kurt that I'd heard about an adult sex shop in Santa Monica, and I'd love to see what it has to offer. It didn't take much to convince Kurt, so we ask for directions and pull up in front of "The Pleasure Palace." As we enter, I'm surprised to see the many women in the store making purchases. We laugh as we look at the creams and jellies that are touted to make the sex more thrilling. Devices are on the shelves that say if men strap them to their penises, that would drive their partners crazy. I didn't want to go crazy. We then look at the dildos. One looks like a thermos bottle. I wince. Kurt picks up a slick purple dildo about five inches long and says he'd like to buy it for me in case I get the urge when he's not around. We leave the store with some tantalizing creams and a purple dildo.

In bed that night, I ask if Kurt wants me to bring in the tantalizing cream.

"Why not?" he replies.

I get the cream and climb back in bed, rubbing some of the cream on Kurt's dick.

"It feels good, but I was already in the mood."

"And look how greasy your dick is. I don't want that grease in me," I grimace.

"Hand me a Kleenex and throw that stuff away. All I need are a couple of kisses."

"Me, too."

Kurt and I then did what rabbits do best and climaxed rather quickly.

"Maybe that cream had some benefits to it after all," I murmur.

"I really don't want to climax quickly – I like to enjoy the feelings for a while. Maybe that cream would help ninety-year-olds; but I'm eighty-one."

The next day we drove up the cragged coastline through Ventura to Santa Barbara. I steered with one hand while Kurt held my other hand. We constantly touched one another. We saw a dozen surfers in their slick, black body suits riding the waves at Ventura. The waves looked majestic, yet angry, as the surfers struggled to stay on their boards. Kurt and I both love the ocean. He said he and Pam would spend a week every year in a condo at Myrtle Beach. "I'm looking forward to taking you to Myrtle Beach one day soon," he said.

Closer to Santa Barbara, we were greeted by hang gliders bobbing and ebbing gracefully overhead. The air breathed warm and windy as we rode along. I pointed out the steep landslide to the right of the freeway where a mother and her three daughters were buried and never found. "The husband and oldest daughter survived because they left to buy ice cream for the family."

"Terrible," Kurt muttered.

Stopping at a beach restaurant, we ate Shrimp Louie's with hot, crusty rolls and sipped Chianti with floating lemon and orange slices. The romantic setting was not lost on us—a couple of newbie lovers. We held hands across the table and gazed longingly at one another. As Kurt's eyes burned into mine, he reached over and touched my cheek. My body yearned with desire.

"Your skin is so soft," he said. "Just touching your cheek makes me want more of you."

I squeezed his hand.

"I've never made love so often in my life, and yet I want more," he said.

"Should we get a motel room and forget about the Santa Barbara Mission?" I teased.

He didn't respond.

"Did you hear what I asked?"

"Don't rush me. I'm thinking."

"Do you know what I think? I think we should see the mission and then head home."

So that's what we did. The Santa Barbara Mission, founded in 1786, is called the Queen of the Missions for its graceful beauty. It is the tenth of twenty-one Franciscan missions in California. In the front of the landscaped grounds sat a Moorish fountain surrounded by pepper trees. While walking around it, we stopped a half dozen times to kiss. Next, we toured the inside of the mission and sat in the chapel, marveling at the stained-glass windows and simplicity of the Stations of the Cross. Although Kurt is a Methodist, he said he's always admired the deep tradition of the Catholic faith.

I told Kurt I love visiting the California missions. "I'll never forget waiting for hours to see the swallows return to San Juan Capistrano on their designated return day. More people were in attendance than swallows as only a dozen swallows appeared amid cheers and claps."

Kurt laughed.

On the drive home, we were both relaxed and happy to be together. This was the third day of Kurt's visit and the first day we hadn't felt the urgency to copulate. It was incredible how well we knew one another in such a short time. That morning while applying eyeliner in the bathroom, Kurt stood behind me and watched. I didn't mind sharing the space at all. I recalled the hungry look in his eyes when he said, "I love looking at you in the mornings, especially after those dark brown eyes have a little paint on them."

"What about when they're naked?"

"That's a turn-on as well," he murmured. "In fact, your perfume turns me on."

I remember thinking how loved I felt. "I've memorized your many faces," I said. "I know when you're angry about something, and I know when you're aroused."

"Oh, so you know when I'm aroused, do you? Am I aroused now?" he asked.

"I'm driving, so it's hard to tell right now."

"I'm always aroused when I'm with you. You make me feel like a sixteen-year old in love for the first time," Kurt said.

I went on describing my man as I drove. "I know how your eyes change color with your mood. I know the feel of your square, resolute jaw, and the feel of your face beneath my fingers. I'm not sure what turns me on more."

"Do you know if you're in love with me?"

"I know that I'm deeply in love with you," I whispered, giving him a coquettish look. Just then my car's tires hit the berm of the road and I had to adjust the wheel to get back to the middle of the lane.

"Keep your eyes on the road, sweetheart. I'd like to enjoy a few more years with you."

That night after an early dinner, Kurt and I whipped out our cameras and snapped surprise pictures of one another. I took him sitting on the commode unrolling toilet tissue, and he shot one of me removing my bra.

We also positioned one another in sexy poses. Kurt shot me in the buff on my bed, posing like a pin-up queen on my tummy, with my legs stretched high. I snapped Kurt showing off his muscles in the doorway with his pecker peeking out of his robe. We snapped away, laughing uncontrollably. Later we wondered what we should do with the pictures. We wouldn't want our kids seeing them, but we weren't ready to destroy them. Kurt has two married sons; one lives in Utah, and one lives in Maryland.

Kurt took pictures of our feet with his phone camera. That's when I noticed the grotesque toenails on his little toes, which were very tough and thick. I also noticed how long his toenails were, and I offered to give him a pedicure. Of course, he took me up on it. I cut and filed his toenails, doing a little extra filing on his ugly little toenails, and then I snuck a bottle of red nail polish in the bedroom on the pretext that I had to have a warm cloth to clean up his cuticles. Painting all his toenails with quick sweeps, I was done in a minute. As he thanked me for the job, he looked down at his toenails with puzzlement. Then it hit him what I'd done, and he roared.

"Where's your polish remover?" he asked.

"I don't have any." Kurt didn't seem angry, and in fact, he flew home after his five-day visit with the nail polish still intact. He kept saying, "What in the hell will Joe say about this?" Joe and his wife Marla have been friends of Kurt's for years, but I haven't met them yet.

"Why does Joe have to know?" I quizzed.

"We tell each other everything."

"I think this is one time you might want to keep a secret from him," I murmured.

"You may be right," he said, grinning.

* * * * *

The next day we visited the Camarillo Library. It filled up most of the block. Although I'd lived in Camarillo for fourteen years, I hadn't been inside the facility. The pillars holding up the walls were made to resemble stacks of books, which Kurt captured on his camera.

That night Susan invited us up to her home for a barbeque. On the way, I explained to Kurt that Susan's first husband was Tom, and her second husband is Rob. When we got there, I parked on the street and we walked to the front door and pushed the doorbell. Susan opened it, and we hugged. I introduced Kurt to her, and they hugged. As we strode into the hallway, Susan's husband appeared, and Kurt put out his hand and said, "It's nice to meet you, Tom." Kurt mixed up the men's names and called the present husband by the first husband's name. Not missing a beat, Rob said, "And it's nice to meet you, Wesley." That broke the ice. Kurt met Brian and Marie, my adult grandkids, and we all had a fun evening. I'm sure Kurt got a better sense of me from my grandkids' tales about when I would babysit them.

My family was interested in hearing about when Kurt and I knew each other as kids. So Kurt told them about a summer day when he and Dick Thomas were playing ping pong in the basement of St. Joseph's Catholic Church, and I walked in wearing red shorts. He said Dick missed a couple of serves by watching me instead of the ball. We laughed a lot, and everyone seemed comfortable. I fleetingly wondered whether his sons would like me.

The next few days of Kurt's visit were very sweet, holding hands, soft kisses, deep kisses, long talks. He told me about writing in a journal since John F. Kennedy's death. He said he's long ago learned that if one needs to understand something, write about it. "Most people will just stew, or run around breaking up the joint, taking it out on the lawn tractor, or even a friend. Time and time again I've used my journal as a source of refuge. I simply sit down, think, and write. I always feel better." He said there's some risk in recording your deepest thoughts in a journal, remembering that sons and daughters will most likely read what you've written.

Kurt said that for him, he felt he should go as far as he dared, yet preserve the intent of the journal. "Keeping a journal," he said, "taught me that time slips by all too swiftly."

"I've always been sorry I didn't start a journal. Now I feel it's too late."

"Of course it's not too late, especially since you're a writer. It could prove very valuable in helping you remember events when you later look back on your entries; and your grand-children will appreciate your efforts. A number of times I almost ceased writing in my journal, but it's like a disease…it must continue."

"Are you writing about us in your journal?" I asked.

"What do you think?" he asked. "I'll savor reading about those events later."

It's hard to believe how well Kurt expresses himself. It's been my experience in the past, limited experience, that is, that if a guy is intelligent, he's a poor lover, or vice versa. The package deal had always eluded me… until Kurt. Did I ever hit the jackpot!! I would welcome an entire week in bed with him reciting poetry and massaging my breasts. However, this visit is for five days, and only one is left. His passion matches mine as we explore one another's bodies. I guess the Good Lord gave us extra time for being celibate for so many years. In any case, our ages don't hold us back. The pleasure is just as delicious and heightened when our bodies touch. Waking up, leg over leg, is pure ecstasy. Kurt said we should meet monthly, that he doesn't mind the flight to California, knowing what he's going back to. I gave him a hot and spicy kiss.

On our last day together, we visited Wanda in the nursing home, and Kurt cut Wanda's fingernails. He was such at ease with her, and she kept rolling her eyes when Kurt wasn't looking and giving me the eyes-up look that she approved of Kurt. Then we stopped by for Kurt to meet

Aunt Wilma. It took half an hour to find her as she wheeled around the facility, never staying in one place very long. A gentleman in the room next to hers called out, "You looking for Miss America? I think she's in the TV room with the doctor's brother." And that's where we found her. She and Armand seemed very intent on what the other one was saying. When my aunt saw us, her eyes took on a soft look and she smiled demurely. She told Armand she'd see him later as she honed in on Kurt. She loves men, and Kurt is a handsome man. Kurt pushed her wheelchair to the back patio, and we visited for an hour, drinking cokes and eating junk food from the vending machine.

Kurt was impressed with my aunt's agility and memory. "One hundred? Amazing." He said his grandmother lived to be ninety-eight and her sister lived to be one hundred three. "So we might be sharing a long life together," he said, taking my arm and leading me out of the facility.

The rest of the day was spent at the Camarillo Airport, a public airport located three miles west of the central business district. Kurt was looking forward to it because it housed a Lockheed Super Constellation airplane, a plane similar to one he'd flown out of the military base at Camp Cod, Massachusetts. It was a radar-equipped, early-warning plane that was on the airport ramp for display to the public. A guide took us on a tour of the airport, and he was surprised to discover that Kurt knew more about the plane than he did. In fact, he thanked Kurt for the information and said the people taking the next tour will be much more educated because of Kurt's imparted comprehensive knowledge of the "Connie."

I enjoyed visiting the museum as much as Kurt did and seeing the C-46 'China Doll,' an F6F Hellcat, and many more WWII airplanes, some of which are still in flying condition to this day. Kurt was quiet on our drive back to my condo, most likely enjoying the nostalgia of the day.

When we got back home and were settled on the sofa with glasses of Red Moscato wine, we talked about my projected move to Georgia. "Yes," he said, "you are going to walk away from friends and family. I've done that a couple of times, and it's not easy. But you have plenty of time to make new friends in Georgia. And don't forget it will be easier for me to visit you."

After we undressed for bed, I walked into the kitchen and caught Kurt downing three pills. "Aha, I believe you take as many pills as I do," I taunted.

"Probably," he said, grinning.

That night in bed, we turned our imagination loose and loved like this was our last night on earth. We simply could not get enough of one another.

At seven in the morning, I felt Kurt's skin whistle, as he jokingly called it, awaken me with rhythmic taps on my pubic hair. "You are very tight," he murmured. "Remember the artificial penis I bought you? I think you should put it in your vagina and leave it there until I return next month. You should be stretched by then."

"Hmm. Too cold and impersonal. Besides, it doesn't have balls."

Chapter Seven

The next morning, we got up at seven, yawned and stretched, and stretched some more. Neither of us had gotten much sleep with all the love shenanigans going on, keenly aware that we won't be seeing each other for another month.

I hurried into the kitchen in my long, animal-print Mumu, sans makeup, to brew the coffee, and I laughed out loud. Earlier I fretted about Kurt seeing me without makeup and with bedroom hair, and here I was, fretting no longer. Our love went deep, and it didn't need perfection. Wanda always said, "If you want perfection, you can find it in the dictionary." She's a wise lady, and I really enjoy her company. She'd had one son who choked on a cracker when he was two years old, and her husband died over thirty years ago. Her condo is several blocks away, but if I walk through the common area, I can be at her door within minutes. She's been in a nursing home because of a fractured femur, but she expects to be discharged soon.

I chuckle when I think about her telling me that she and her husband had made love in a canoe. She's ninety-six and quite savvy. We feel comfortable confiding in one another.

"Are we on schedule?" Kurt asked, walking into the kitchen and kissing me on the cheek.

"I think so. It only takes me twenty minutes to get ready."

"I'm ready now, but not for my flight home." He reached for me and folded his arms around me. "I've had a terrific time getting to know you and falling more in love with you."

We managed to eat, between kisses, and hit the freeway at eight fifteen for Kurt's flight at ten. "Plenty of time," I said, patting Kurt's hand. But after running into freeway traffic around the Westwood area, I started to sweat.

"Five lanes of traffic and none of them are moving," Kurt murmured.

"When we pass the Los Angeles freeway, traffic will open up." I wondered whether I should have allowed more time. I used to live in the Valley but now live another half hour north.

"I'll drop you at the terminal, and you can put your luggage in the overhead bin."

"Good idea," Kurt said. He paused as if deep in thought. "I can't believe how compatible we are." He grinned salaciously and put his hand on my thigh. Heat rushed through my body.

* * * * *

We arrived at the terminal at nine-forty. Kurt kissed my cheek and hurried inside.

I looked at my watch and decided to park my car and go into the terminal. I spied Kurt leaving the check-in counter. He said he'd missed his flight but another one would be leaving within a half hour. "It's okay, honey. How were you to know traffic would be this heavy?"

We kissed again, and he said he'd call when he arrived in Pittsburgh.

I felt exhausted and lonely as I drove back home, but I smiled as I remembered Kurt saying we are very compatible.

In bed that night, I slept on the side of the bed Kurt had occupied for five days. I could still smell his scent, taste his lips, feel the gentleness of his fingers. I could hear the guttural sounds he emitted when reaching that moment of no return; the way my hips matched his rhythm and rose to his thrusts; how I exploded in a sea of ecstasy beyond anything I could have imagined. Yes, our libidos are certainly compatible. But does that apply to our personalities?

I opened a paperback novel, prepared to read until Kurt's call. I'd started the fourth chapter when the phone rang. "It's your lover. I just arrived in Pittsburgh and will be heading to the parking lot to get my car for the drive to Ohio."

"It's good to hear your voice and know your flight landed in Pittsburgh safely."

"Just want you to know I had a terrific time and should probably buy stock in the airlines with my many planned trips back and forth to see you."

"I love you, Kurt, and miss you already."

Closing my book, I fell asleep before I could finish praying my rosary. I'd like to think the angels finished them for me. Yes, we were naughty, but we're single and not hurting anyone.

The next morning when I awoke, I went into my emails to see if one awaited me from Kurt, and there it was. He'd written it when he arrived home.

"Dearest Eva,

"I made it home in good shape. I lost only three hours. Please don't think that missing the plane was your fault. The five lanes of traffic just didn't move fast enough. And the guy at the check-in didn't cut me any slack; but rules are rules. Changing planes was no big deal. All in all, the airlines are doing a great job, but at times there are glitches.

"On the way home all I could think about was you. Gee, it was hard to say goodbye, but I hope it's not too long until we love again. Thanks again for the wonderful visit.

"It is now 12:20 AM and I must get to bed. I really enjoyed sleeping with you. It just seemed natural. Sleep well, my love, and send the pictures we took of one another asap.

"All my love, Major Kurt."

Return email from me:

"Dearest Major Kurt,

"I'm glad you got home with your sanity intact. Sorry about your delay—that's a negative of living in L.A.—traffic tends to control one's life. I tried to scan in the pics and run them out, but the paper was too thick. So I drove to Staples to exchange the paper and when I got back home I was too tired to deal with them; but I did take another look at them. I love them and can't believe we were so passionate, yet comfortable, with one another to take such racy pics. Such fun, as was your visit. I'm a branded woman now.

"Your sweetheart and lover, Eva."

"P.S. I think Moxie misses you. I know I do.

"P.P.S. It won't be long before I'll need new batteries for my new toy. JUST KIDDING."

* * * * *

I hadn't heard a word about the money I put down on the foreclosure in Georgia, and if I don't hear soon, I'll have to get another loan. So I called Lexie.

"It often takes time, Mom, but I think you should hang in there. I spoke to the real estate agent recently and she said the bank likes to do appraisals on all the foreclosures at once. As I said before, it's a very nice house and only a few blocks from Stephen and me."

"I'm thinking I should get Aunt Wilma settled in a nursing home in Georgia before I move and would like you to check out the two you mentioned. It's tough coordinating selling my home here and buying one in Georgia, plus getting Aunt Wilma moved."

"I know it is, but you'll get things done, Mom. You always do."

After hanging up, I thought about the projects I want to do before selling my condo. Replacing all light fixtures and installing ceramic tile on the bathroom floors. Since there are about six or seven condos similar to mine for sale in the Village, I want to make mine stand out.

I told Lexie that if the foreclosure takes much longer, I'll simply ask for my earnest money back and look for a home when I fly to Georgia with Aunt Wilma.

She's thriving in the nursing home she's now living in, although she was hesitant at first to move there. I'd told her it would be a temporary move, so she willingly went along with the plan. She'd ask occasionally when she'd be moving back with me, and the hairs would stand up on my arms as I'd make excuses. When she started having memory problems is when I moved her in with me. I was on the Ventura County Grand Jury at the time, but I had to resign because of the care Aunt Wilma needed. However, it didn't take long to realize that she needed more care than what I could physically give her. In fact, I was headed for a nervous breakdown six weeks after she moved in. She loved to take walks and promised to walk to the corner and return home. But she didn't return as promised, and I'd have to go looking for her. Once I found her in a neighbor's garage poking around among his tools. Another time she was headed towards the main street. I had a problem walking with her because of my bum knee, and I couldn't watch her constantly. And did she love to argue. When we turned in for the night, I'd ask her to turn off her bedroom light, which she'd leave on and read into the wee hours of the morning.

"What does it matter how long the light is on?" she'd argue.

"The point is that you stay up half the night and sleep all day. Then you don't want to eat when I do. You've got to get your days and nights back to normal."

She'd roll her eyes and mumble under her breath. This aunt has always been the black sheep of the family, not getting along with her brother (my dad whom I adored), nor her sister (my Aunt Mary whom everybody liked). I remember Aunt Wilma pushing me off her lap when I was five and she was visiting from California. She never liked kids and, thankfully, she never had any. She was always nasty to me, yet now I'm in charge of her welfare. Life sure tests us.

In Kurt's latest email he said he sympathized with me when thinking about my packing up my belongings. "I'm still unpacking boxes from my move a year ago," he said.

> "I must not need the items in the unpacked boxes because I'm doing fine without hem and don't even remember what's in them." He then said he'd be happy to help me pack and to shred documents on his next visit. "And how's Wanda and Aunt Wilma? I'm glad I got to meet them because now I'll know whom you're talking about."

> "I'm attaching pics of the outside and inside of my home. The dining room is the one without furniture. Since my kitchen is large, I gave the dining room furniture to my son Doug. Maybe one of these days you'll visit me, and I can entice you into my bedroom like you did with me. AYS. Kurt."

My reply email:

> "I haven't heard a word about the home in Georgia I bid on, so I'm asking for my money back. I plan to fly to Georgia to visit my daughter in a few weeks and I'll check out nursing homes for my aunt and also look for homes to buy. I probably won't move until the summer, but I'd like to get my aunt moved while she's still

strong enough to handle the flight. I saw her the other day and she had on the silver slippers I bought her for her birthday. She's so cute! She's also quite healthy, other than being somewhat forgetful. And believe it or not, she seems to be getting nicer.

"Yes, I remember coaxing you into my bedroom and having my way with you. So you can have a rerun. And definitely I'd like your help in packing and shredding papers. I think we could squeeze those things into our heavy petting schedule.

"Hope you are well and missing me. I'll be emailing you a copy of my writer's club newsletter. I have two articles in it this month: The President's Message, and one about the upcoming speaker. Ray is a terrific editor and is on top of things. But I need to cut down on my club responsibilities or I'll never get my new novel finished in my lifetime. ILUM. Eva."

Chapter Eight

I visited Wanda in the nursing home in the morning and found her sitting up in bed, listening to tapes of Jerry Vale. He was a popular crooner about the same time Frank Sinatra was popular. Since she's so enamored of him, I ordered a copy of his autobiography for her.

We talked about her nephew Mike who lives in Madison, Wisconsin, and who's been encouraging her to move to an assisted living facility near him and his family.

"Mike told me just yesterday that his mother, who is my deceased husband's sister, whom I like so much, will be moving there due to a decline in her health, and he said we could live in the same facility. He also said it would be nice having all the family living closeby."

"That's something you should give a lot of thought to," I said, "since most of your friends have either passed away or moved closer to their families."

When I was leaving, she said it sounds more exciting than living alone with caregivers to take care of her, and especially since I'll be moving. We hugged, and I left, thinking what lovely people Mike and his wife are to want to make their aunt happy and to make her life easier for her at this stage of her life.

When I got home, the following email was waiting for me.

"My dearest dark eyes,
    "It's been three weeks since I've seen you. Don't you think it's time I made reservations

for a return flight to California for a week? Remember, I'll need time to help you pack, make love, shred papers, make love, clean out your garage, and make love.

"I've had a headache this morning. Probably from drinking last night with Rocco.

"He was my neighbor before I moved across town, and we get together once a month and drink red wine. He and his wife are liberals, like you. We've managed to stay friends, although I've been a conservative all of my life.

"What's going on with Aunt Wilma and Wanda? I think I told you my grandma lived to be ninety-eight and would have lived longer if she hadn't eaten so much cheese and fried foods. Her sister lived to be one hundred three. So I figure I have a long life span, which I need since meeting you. We have to make up for the time we were celibates.

"How's Moxie? I thought he started warming up to me just before I left for Ohio. He's one beautiful cat. But so is his mistress. My mistress. ILUSM. Kurt."

I emailed Kurt back and said I appreciated being called a beautiful cat. He was befuddled until he re-read his email to me.

In my return email, I said that one week in January sounds good. I said I plan to fly to Georgia with my aunt and get her settled in a nursing home before putting my home up for sale, and in the same trip I'll check out homes to buy. I said I am unhappy with the delays in trying to purchase the foreclosure property and will cancel my bid and get my money back.

That night Kurt called, and I told him about my earlier phone conversation with Lexie in which she said several homes were for sale in her neighborhood. I also said I'd called the two nursing homes in Georgia that she'd recommended and requested brochures of their facilities.

Kurt agreed that Aunt Wilma should move to a nursing home before I put my home up for sale. "That will remove a lot of stress from you," he said. "And I can wait a few weeks, if I can stay at your place an entire week. Wow! Can I be master of the bedroom for that week?"

"Just so you don't get into kinky stuff, you can have that title," I agreed. "Say, where's the poem you're writing about our relationship?"

"I'm still perfecting it."

I told him about the conversation I had with Wanda about her nephew wanting her to move to Madison to be close to the family, and I told him that Wanda is seriously considering the move since her deceased husband's sister plans to move there. "Isn't that great?"

"From what you say, Mike and his wife sound like good people."

* * * * *

The brochures from the Georgia nursing homes arrived, and after a review of them, I called the administrator of Presbyterian Village to discuss moving my aunt there. She said the home would need a report of my aunt's health, a list of her prescriptions, and whether the doctor feels she can physically handle the flight. I said I didn't foresee any problems, so we discussed rooms and room rates. Because of my aunt's advanced age, I chose a semi-private room. I felt she would enjoy sharing her room, and in case she fell or needed help, a roommate would be there for her. Caroline, the administrator, said that semi-private rooms will be available sooner than private rooms, so I placed my aunt on a waiting list, pending the doctor's report.

I hung up and drove to the Oxnard facility where I spoke to the administrator there about my aunt's projected move. I also briefly spoke with her doctor about having her evaluated for the air flight and her health in general.

Within days, I got a report from Aunt Wilma's doctor stating she's in good health and takes a thyroid pill and a pill for her early dementia. He said he believes she can handle the flight without any problems. So I mailed signed copies of the documents and the doctor's original report to Presbyterian Village in Georgia. The ball was now in their court.

Kurt's email last night contained an attachment of pictures of him in sporting attire posing with a rifle. I don't like guns and don't approve of shooting animals as a sport. I emailed him, telling him how torn up I am about seeing this picture and that I hope the rifle is plastic.

I further said, "I can't wait until I can get back to writing my novel. As soon as I have things packed and have my home up for sale, I intend to finish it, hopefully, before my move. A book signing? I have to get it published first.

"I must go. I'm headed to Mass and then to see Wanda. You're my only love. Eva."

I got an immediate response.

"Dear Ms. Tiltonsville,
    "I'm not a hunter; never shot anything in my life except for a raccoon that had gotten into my house. I tried to catch him, but he was much too clever. It took me a couple of weeks to lure him into the garage. Then someone lent me a large trap, and I baited the inside with food. Several days later, I heard a scratching, scraping sound coming from the garage and I found the raccoon had been caught by several toenails and was lashing about in the cage. He was quite large and very angry. I managed to push the trap out of the garage onto my driveway. There was no way I could have released him without his attacking me, so I shot him. I felt very bad about that, but I had no choice. That was the extent of my shooting career, except for shooting at bottles. I hope I have put your mind at rest about my not shooting animals.
    "I have joined the Country Club and can't wait for you to visit so I can take you there. Since I don't play golf, my membership is strictly social. I plan to use it for treating myself and family to quiet meals. I really enjoy lingering over a good cup of java. This morning I had my usual eggs over medium-well, hash browns, sausage links,

and popcorn. Popcorn is always available for the golfers; and it smelled so good that I asked for a plateful. It tasted delicious with my breakfast. I've always enjoyed eating breakfast out. What do you like to do for breakfast, my sweet? Before I forget, Jon Ryan called and is driving to Tiltonsville to visit his sister and family this weekend, and he and I plan to meet for lunch. He always asks about you and is very happy we've found one another. It's been about three months since his wife passed away, and I can offer him a lot of advice in that area. AMLA. Kurt."

Kurt and I both treasure our friendships with our high school classmates and keep in touch regularly. Jon is one of our favorites, and I look forward to hearing about his life since his wife had passed. I know he'll get a lot of comfort from talking with Kurt. I often wonder why the Good Lord had spared Kurt and me and yet had taken over half of our classmates.

I chuckle when I recall Kurt telling me that he'd dated some of the most popular girls in high school. He said one of the rich ones dismissed him when she'd asked him if he planned to attend college, and he said he wasn't sure. And I couldn't believe my ears when he said he'd dated Anna Mae Kurtis, a tall, tough-looking gal who's a year older. "I thought you didn't have a car," I responded. "I didn't," he said. "We'd either walk or take the street car."

I hadn't realized Kurt was such a Casanova. I guess that's because I'd been wrapped up in Ned for my last two high school years. When Kurt asked me who I went to the prom with, I said Tommy Sloan. "The school wouldn't permit juniors or seniors to take outsiders to the Prom – not even former students, so I went with Tommy. He bought me a huge wrist corsage and we ate and danced together. Then I left to celebrate the rest of the night with Ned."

"That wasn't a very nice thing to do," Kurt said.

"Tommy knew that was my intention, but he wanted to go with me, anyway." I told Kurt that Tommy was a very good friend but always hoped for more. "I was always truthful with him, so I don't understand why you think that wasn't nice."

Kurt said he never liked Tommy. "We worked on the railroad together the summer before we graduated, and he always found some excuse not to work."

"Well, he was always very, very sweet to me. He attended our tenth class reunion with his girlfriend, a pretty blonde who had a small daughter. I heard they got married and moved to Arizona. It was nice seeing him after all those years and knowing he's happy."

Kurt didn't remember seeing Tommy at a high school class reunion, but he later recalled he hadn't attended that one because he was in the Air Force.

"Several of the girls I dated in high school have since passed away," Kurt mused. "Remember Shirley Jenkins?"

"You dated Shirley Jenkins? Unreal! You sure were busy and didn't even have a car!"

He said he and Frank Roman, a good friend of his, had been standing on the stair well on the second floor of the school when Pamela raced down the stairs. Frank said, "That would be a nice girlfriend for you." Kurt said he thought about it and then asked Pamela to attend the Prom with him. Their relationship simmered slowly with Pam sticking with him when he visited his mother and stepfather in Florida, and when he attended college. "She'd visit me at college, and I'd visit her in Tiltonsville. We dated five years before marrying. I don't think I ever proposed, but we talked about marriage and knew it would happen when the time was right."

"You made a good decision. Pam was a very nice person," I said.

Chapter Nine

The other day when I visited Aunt Wilma, I noticed that the small, red spot on her cheek appeared to change color, so I called her dermatologist's office for an appointment. On the appointment day, I drove to the nursing home and had an aide wheel my aunt to my car and help get her in the passenger seat. She'd just finished lunch and said her stomach was queasy. No sooner had I pulled the seatbelt across her abdomen that she heaved up her lunch. I grabbed the beach towel I carry with me and tried to catch the vomit; but I was too late. She'd upchucked not only on her blouse and shoes, but on my hands and long-sleeved blouse. We were running late, so the aide brought out wet towels, and we cleaned up my aunt as best as we could. I wiped my hands and spot-cleaned my blouse. We then sped off to the doctor's office. While sitting in the waiting room, I noticed food particles on my shoes. We didn't sit there long before we were whisked in to see the doctor. I'm sure the smell from the puke cut down on our waiting time.

After examining my aunt, the dermatologist, a young man in his mid-forties with thick grey hair and kindly blue eyes, said he was relatively certain the spot on Aunt Wilma's cheek was cancer. "Since it's small," he said, "I'd like to treat it with a salve." As he spoke, he wrote out instructions for the application of the salve on one of his prescription pads and handed it to me. "I'd like to see Wilma in two weeks," he said, walking us out of his office.

While I paid for the visit at the reception desk, my aunt sat next to me in a wheelchair, reading a magazine loudly enough for all in the waiting room to hear.

"**Cialis** isn't for everyone," she read. "Be sure to tell your doctor if you have heart problems or are taking any nitrates. **Cialis** is shown to improve erectile function compared to placebo up to thirty-six hours following dosage."

I was horrified and reached down to turn the page; but she pushed my hand away and kept reading, urged on by the laughter in the waiting room. I hurriedly paid the bill and pushed Aunt Wilma's wheelchair to the back of the waiting room while I searched for my car keys. All the while, my aunt kept reading loudly: "The recommended starting dose in most patients is 10 mg, taken prior to anticipated **sexual activity**." She put extra emphasis on sexual activity, and that's when I took the magazine away from her and pushed her to my car. I'm sure my aunt doesn't know what Cialis is, but I think the patients in the reception room did.

* * * * *

When I spoke to Kurt on the phone that evening, I told him about Aunt Wilma's upchuck experience and driving to the dermatologist's office smelling like vomit. "We didn't wait long before being ushered into the dermatologist's office. I think the smell got us in sooner."

"You'll have to remember that for her next visit," Kurt said jokingly.

"Yeah, I'll have to put some rotten meat in her purse in case she doesn't throw up."

"That might work."

I then told Kurt about the star my aunt was in the reception room, touting Cialis.

Kurt roared. "Your aunt is so funny," he said. "She reminds me of my Grandma Smootie, my mom's mother. She's tiny like your aunt and has the energy of a quarterback. One Christmas the family spent it together at Grandma Smootie's home. My Uncle Pete bought me a toy gun that you'd load with soft balls, similar to tennis balls; and when you'd pull the trigger, a ball shot out. I accidentally shot one that hit Grandma Smootie's leg. It didn't hurt her, but she scolded me for shooting the gun in the house, and as she grabbed the gun from me, one of the balls shot out of the gun and broke several of her Christmas tree ornaments. The look on her face was priceless; and it took a great deal of restraint for my family not to laugh."

"Is she the grandmother that always said, "That's what is it?"

"Yeah, she was so funny without trying to be funny, like Aunt Wilma."

"You know, Kurt, it's difficult for me to understand the emotions you must have been feeling with your mom leaving you with your dad's mother and having little contact with your dad. What I mean to say is that you didn't have a normal childhood, yet you turned out normal."

"I got a lot of love when I lived with my dad's mom and dad. I remember sitting on my grandpa's lap and of us talking about anything. When it would storm outside and the thunder and lightning flashed across the sky, Grandpa would take me outside, and we'd watch the elements go crazy. Grandma would yell for us to get back in the house, but we'd laugh. Grandpa and I were very close, and I took it very hard when he died. But my grandma was a very affectionate person. We'd go to the movies together; and I had a good many cousins to play with."

"I think you turned out so great is that you were loved by the relatives you lived with."

"I'm sure that's it. When I was about to start my junior year of high school, my Aunt Thelma and Uncle Pete asked me to move in with them. That's how I ended up at Tiltonsville graduating with the class you were in. I already had friends in Tiltonsville from staying with my aunt and uncle during the summers, so it was a natural move. I feel very fortunate to have had two home towns: Brookfield and Tiltonsville."

"Do you still have friends in Brookfield?"

"Yeah, I do. I don't see them often, but we keep in touch by phone. Say, I got the package of sexy pictures you mailed me of our romantic tryst. They are great and came just in time. I'm meeting Jon at Bob Evans Restaurant tomorrow and have picked out several pictures to take with me. I know he'll like looking at them."

"I've always liked Jon. We were in the same Catechism class at St. Joseph's when we were kids. He came from quite a large family. I remember his mom and dad and Jon and his brothers and sisters filling up an entire church pew. Be sure to tell Jon I send my love."

* * * * *

When Kurt called the next night, he told me about his visit with Jon. They hadn't seen one another since graduating high school. Kurt said Jon was taller than he'd remembered, over six feet and very lanky, with a newly-sprouted moustache and beard. His wife of fifty years died three months ago, and Jon struggles to get on with his life. He's happy about Kurt and me hooking up, and Kurt showed him the pictures we'd taken when he visited me in Camarillo.

"You didn't show him the picture of me in my nightie, did you?"

"You were fully covered," Kurt responded.

"What about the picture of you in your robe with your pecker hanging out?"

"I forgot to remove that picture, so I guess he saw that one, too."

"Now he knows just how close we are," I said.

Kurt howled.

Since Kurt's wife passed away just over a year ago, Kurt said he informed Jon of the feelings he could expect to go through before things got better. Kurt said they sat in the restaurant eating and peeing, drinking coffee and peeing, and reminiscing for four hours.

"I think I told you five of us hung around together when attending high school, and Jon was one of them. We were good, solid guys. No drugs or booze. I asked Jon why he didn't go to college after high school since he was salutatorian, and he said he was burned out. But after working his first job at the supermarket in the meat department and getting one cold after another from carrying racks of meat back and forth to the freezer, he said he headed for college. He got a degree in liberal arts and taught math at a high school in Cuyahoga Falls until he retired."

"It's a shame how we lost touch, but we had separate careers at different parts of the world." He sighed. "Jon, Dick Thomas, and I are the only ones left of our group of five."

"I always liked Jon and wondered why he never attended any of our reunions."

"He had four children and said if the reunions hadn't been held on the July 4th weekends, he would have made them; but the family always held get-togethers on that weekend."

"I'm glad we're back in touch and look forward to seeing him when I visit you."

"Oh, you're planning to visit me?"

"You bet I am. Any objections?"

"Not a one."

No sooner had I put the phone down than it rang. It was the administrator at the Presbyterian Village Nursing Home in Georgia. "We have a semi-private room for Miss Wilma, if you're interested. The price is $6,250.00 a month. That includes room and board, showers and personal attention, medication dispensing, all activities, laundry, and housekeeping."

"That's fine," I said. "I'll make arrangements for my aunt and me to fly there next week, and I'll mail you a check in the morning."

After checking airfares, I found out that if reservations are made two weeks in advance, airfare is much cheaper. But paying room and board for two facilities would cost more. So why wait?

I made reservations to leave the middle of next week, and I called Kurt to tell him.

"And what about my visit to California?" he asked. "I planned to see you in January."

"You can still come in January. I'll only be gone five days. That will give me sufficient time to get my aunt settled in. Lexie lives about two miles from the nursing home and she promised she'll visit Aunt Wilma weekly. She and Aunt Wilma have always been close."

"Okay then. I agree it's probably a good idea to get Aunt Wilma moved before you move. I just wish I could help you with your aunt's move."

"It's no big deal. I made a red-eye flight in the hopes my aunt will sleep."

"Good luck, darling, and remember that I love you and am looking forward to our visit."

The next day I drove to the nursing home in Oxnard and told Aunt Wilma of my plans. "Am I going to live with you?" she asked.

"You'll be living in a really nice nursing home until I can get moved, and then we'll talk about it." I told her again that Lexie lives in Georgia and will be visiting her. She smiled as we sorted through her clothes and packed her suitcase. Earlier I had seen her roommate wearing one of her dresses. My aunt didn't particularly like the dress, so it didn't matter. As I was cleaning out her nightstand, I noticed she had over a dozen small packets of strawberry jam lined up in the dresser drawers, plus silverware which I retuned when I left that afternoon.

The night of our flight, my deceased friend's daughter Carol drove me to the nursing home in Oxnard to pick up my aunt. We then headed to the Los Angeles International Airport. On the way, my aunt read the freeway signs to

Carol. When we arrived at the airport, Carol parked temporarily and placed our two bags at the curb. We hugged and kissed, and she said she'd pick me up when I returned. A wheelchair was waiting for my aunt, and an airport employee pushed my aunt's wheelchair to the gate while I walked alongside. We were early and sat next to a young mother with a beautiful, chatty two-year-old daughter who entertained us until we boarded the plane. I hoped to sleep on the plane and was sure my aunt would, since she was one hundred and had been active all day. That wasn't the case, however. She kept unbuckling her seat belt and trying to get out of her seat the entire trip. "You must stay in your seat," I scolded her.

"Look at all the people walking up and down the aisles. I want to do that."

"Somebody would have to push you in a wheelchair, and nobody is available to do that. The people walking in the aisle work here. Everyone else is asleep. Aren't you sleepy?"

"Where are we going?" she asked for the fiftieth time.

I dozed off several times but was awakened by Aunt Wilma trying to crawl over me.

I was exhausted when the plane finally landed, but my one-hundred-year-old aunt was wide-awake. An airport employee was waiting for her with a wheelchair, and we made our way to the baggage claim. The employee helped us get outside with our bags, and it was only a matter of minutes before Stephen and Lexie pulled up at the curb and got us and our luggage inside their car. Since traffic was heavy in the loading zone, we welcomed one another once settled in the car. Aunt Wilma pointed to the plastic bags that covered the back seats and back doors of the car, and she snickered. She didn't realize the plastic was there in case she upchucked.

It was 7:10 a.m., and we decided to eat before checking Aunt Wilma in at the nursing home. She ate a hearty meal of scrambled eggs, bacon, potatoes, sliced tomatoes, and her usual warm glass of milk. She attributes her longevity to drinking three glasses of warm milk a day and exercising. While she was a nanny for the movie star, Robert J. Wagner, and his sister, when they were twelve and thirteen, respectively, Mrs. Wagner told her she could swim in their pool; and Aunt Wilma did so several times a week. Then when she moved to Leisure World in Laguna Hills, she swam in the community pool there. I remember taking long walks with her at Leisure World and thinking how physically healthy she was for her age. She's still healthy, but dementia is slowly diminishing her thought process.

After lunch, we took a tour of the nursing home, which looked like a college campus with a brick façade and beautifully landscaped lawns and flower gardens. Aunt Wilma's semi-private room was quite large with separate closets for her and her roommate, and a dresser and nightstand for each of them. A window overlooked one of the flower gardens. Her roommate, Rita, was a pleasant lady in her sixties who loved to watch football from the TV in her room. She welcomed Aunt Wilma warmly. Nevertheless, that night Aunt Wilma got very agitated and wanted to leave. I guess it finally hit her that she was in unfamiliar surroundings. My daughter suggested I hire a private nurse to sit with her throughout the night to calm her anxiety, which I did. That seemed to work, and the next morning the nursing staff spent considerable time spoiling her and making her feel comfortable. I was told that one of the female residents holds the title of oldest living resident, being one hundred one years of age – one year older than Aunt Wilma. "She has advanced Alzheimer's and isn't as social as Wilma," Rita said.

The next few days passed swiftly as I spent time with Lexie and Stephen at the nursing home visiting Aunt Wilma in the mornings and house-hunting in the afternoons. I viewed the house I'd put the deposit on and was told the present owners couldn't be found, thus halting the bidding process; so I got my earnest money refunded.

While in Georgia, Kurt and I spoke several times over the phone. I voiced my disappointment about not finding a house to buy.

"You have a lot of packing to do, so buying a house now might be a little premature," Kurt said. "Also, you haven't listed your home yet."

Kurt was right. Selling my home and buying a new one needed to be coordinated so I wouldn't be paying for utilities and property taxes on two homes. Putting Wanda's affairs in order was also a priority. Kurt and I finalized plans for him to join me in Camarillo when I returned home. "A week this time; right?" Kurt asked.

"Perfect, if you help me pack and shred papers."

Chapter Ten

A lot of things were happening at the Writer's Club where I was serving as president for a second time. I appointed a committee that was working on amending the by-laws to define the offices and to clarify which offices would be elective or appointed. That was taking up a large chunk of my time. However, I welcomed Kurt's upcoming visit for pleasure and diversity.

* * * * *

On the night of Kurt's arrival, I dusted the furniture and changed the bedclothes. Then I drove to the Los Angeles Airport. Kurt's flight arrived at eight in the evening, and I was standing at the baggage claim when I spied him. *What a distinguished-looking gentleman*, I thought. My heart raced. As Kurt kissed me and held me tight, I could feel the tremors flowing through him. When he released me, he said how lovely I looked … and sexy. I felt his buns while he grabbed his bag off the moving platform. He grinned widely.

Walking to my car, we bumped rumps and held hands. We mouthed our love for one another and stopped to kiss along the way. Kurt commented about the warm, breezy night. "In Ohio when I left, the weather was fifty-two degrees."

"On the drive here, the outside temperature registered seventy-five."

"Nice," Kurt replied. "I hope it stays this way because I'd love to re-visit the beach."

"And how about the 'Pleasure Palace?'"

"I don't think we need anything to enhance our love-making, my dear. I'm ready now."

"Well, you'll have to wait because this parking lot is just too public."

We joked and laughed and kept lusting after one another all the way to Camarillo. When I pulled into the garage, Kurt commented about the heap of files and papers stacked up on the garage floor.

"Do you want to start shredding papers tonight?" I asked.

"No, I want to start shedding clothes tonight."

So we did. And after our feverish love-making session, Kurt tried to make up with Moxie, but he got a few hisses and decided to let Moxie do the making up.

Moxie, looking smug, cozied up to me on the couch while Kurt and I watched the news and ate raisin bran.

* * * * *

The next day Kurt felt lazy from the time change and suggested we spend the day attacking the pile of papers on the garage floor. While I pulled more papers from the file cabinets, Kurt fed the papers into the shredder. As he shredded, I saw him holding back some papers. "Do you mind?" he asked. "These are photocopies of you."

"Not at all," I smiled. "They're probably pictures of my travels with the Area Housing Authority. Are other people in them?"

"Yeah, but I only want those of you."

After a couple of hours of shredding, Kurt and I needed a break, so we drove to Home Depot for a new supply of boxes. While there, I asked a salesgirl where the patching plaster was. Leading us to the site, I picked up a can of patch to fill in the nail holes where pictures had been removed. She asked if I needed a tool to apply the patch. "No, I like to use my finger."

She replied. "My dad always uses his finger."

Kurt whispered to me, "If her dad had used his finger, she wouldn't be here."

No matter how I tried to suppress my giggles, they wouldn't stop. The salesgirl walked away, shaking her head.

After picking up a half dozen boxes, we left, still laughing.

I love Kurt's sense of humor. And I love looking at his profile as he sleeps next to me. He usually awakens before I do, and I saw him one morning with his camera, snapping pictures of me. He said he never saw anyone look so pretty the irst thing in the morning. That floored me but proves that love is blind.

Later in the evening we had dinner at Ottavio's Italian Restaurant where we enjoyed a crisp Caesar salad and combination plates of spaghetti and ravioli. We toasted our relationship with Merlot and kisses and had Spumoni ice cream for dessert. It's rare to find Spumoni in supermarkets, except for holidays; and I love Spumoni. Ottavio's serves it year-round.

We left the restaurant and drove to Old Town Camarillo where we walked the streets window-shopping. Street lights were lit up at every corner.

That night at my condo, we found Moxie sleeping on Kurt's jeans that he'd thrown on his suitcase. And from that day on, he and Kurt began their relationship. While I cuddled Moxie and loved on him, Kurt roughed it up with him. One of their favorite games was boxing. Kurt would put his hand out quickly, and Moxie would throw a paw at it. Kurt would change hands, and Moxie would change paws. This went on about five minutes, with Moxie totally engrossed. When Kurt walked away, Moxie quickly threw a last punch at Kurt's rear end with his paw.

Every time Kurt walked past Moxie, Moxie would take his boxing stance and wait for his buddy to spar with him. I happily watched as my two favorite males finally bonded.

Kurt confessed he'd never been around cats before but feels they are more independent and even smarter than dogs.

A few days later, Kurt and I drove to my daughter's home for lunch with the family. My granddaughter pulled a microphone from her tote bag and plugged it into the TV. She said when we are done eating, we'll have a sing-a-long. Passing around song books, she said to pick a song to sing. She then brought up the song on the TV. The device not only played the tune, but it displayed the words and notes to follow along. She said a monitor would grade our performance.

It was such fun to hear my grandson belt out a rock-and-roll song with a voice much deeper than his speaking voice. The monitor gave him high marks for keeping in tune. My son-in-law rendered a love song in which he gave it his all. He was shocked when the monitor gave him low marks. The family wasn't shocked, however.

Kurt, with the deep, newscaster's voice, had difficulty carrying a tune and also got low marks that left him puzzled. Marie, with her soft voice, earned a high mark; and Susan, whom I rarely heard singing around the house when she was growing up, rendered a lovely version of 'Sentimental Journey,' and got an 'excellent' rating. I, who don't like to brag (not frequently, that is), also scored an 'excellent' rating with 'Please Release Me.' My grandson asked when Susan and I would be heading for Nashville.

We tired of the sing-along, and my granddaughter asked if anyone wanted to drive to Vasquez Rocks. When my grandkids were teens, we'd go there for picnics. On one occasion, I remember leaving our picnic basket and lawn chairs in the care of a young couple who offered to watch them. When we returned, our basket and chairs were gone, along with the young couple.

Kurt, a former geology major, expressed interest in seeing Vasquez Rocks, and I wanted to go again. The rest of the family opted to stay at home, so it was just Kurt and me, with Marie driving. It took about fifteen minutes to get there, and when we pulled into the park, Kurt expressed awe at the massive rock formations that were a natural formation of sandstone rocks uplifted in prehistoric times. They comprise 932 acres of rock formations, named for Giburcio Vaqquez, one of California's most notorious bandits, who hid in the rocks to elude capture.

Marie said that many hit movies, television shows, and commercials were filmed here. Some were *Bonanza, Big Valley, For the Boys*, *In the Army Now,* and *Planet of the Apes.*

Kurt and Marie climbed the rocks while I sat on a large rock taking pictures. I couldn't participate because of a knee I'd injured while roller-skating with my grandkids twenty years ago at Balboa Park. I was surprised to see how aggressively Kurt climbed the rocks since he's fifty years older than Marie. However, he'd been a runner and never drank booze or smoked.

During Kurt's visit, we not only packed pictures and books and cleaned out file cabinets, but we also found time to walk the beach in Ventura and to enjoy a fish platter at the Ventura Pier. Kurt remarked that although the Pacific coastline is rugged and more beautiful than the Atlantic coastline, the beaches aren't as white or pristine.

Another event that Kurt enjoyed was attending a writer's club meeting with me and meeting our speaker, Burt Prelutsky, a Los Angeles Times opinion writer, who had written a book that Kurt bought and had autographed titled, *Liberalism: America's Termites.*

My best friend Nancy, an author of thirteen children's books, had talked her husband into attending the meeting, and I'm sure that helped make Kurt feel more comfortable. Kurt and Brad really hit it off, which made me happy as Nancy is my best friend.

Kurt is one great companion, and he says the same about me. We're never at a loss for words. We both enjoy reading the *Wall Street Journal* and keep current on world affairs. We like discussing articles we've read and exchanging opinions. Since he's a conservative and I'm a liberal, our discussions do get heated. He said he and Pam never had an argument. We have at least one a day, but that doesn't diminish our respect or love for one another. I'm sure much of the dissent is charged by the abusive conduct I suffered during my marriage to Ned. My self-esteem at that time was zero, and since regaining it, I plan to keep it; and if that means arguments to have my opinions validated, so be it. I also taught my daughters to stand up for their rights.

When I was around five or six, I had a lot of vim and vinegar. When my parents scolded me for something that I felt was unwarranted, I wouldn't cry—I'd run away from home. I don't remember how many times I did that as a child. I'd usually pack fruit, maybe a peanut butter and jelly sandwich and head to my girlfriend Linda's house. She was two years older and always glad to see me. Sometimes her older sister Genevieve would join us, and we'd sit on Linda's bed and talk. I'd tell them my problems, and the two of them would act like therapists and poke around in my head to find out why I was feeling bad enough to leave home. Repeating the problem never seemed as bad as when it originally occurred; and I'd go home and sneak in the back door and climb the stairs to my attic bedroom. I wouldn't come down when mother called me for supper. I just ate my sandwich and orange. I don't know how she knew I was home. I bet grandpap told her because he also had an attic bedroom.

I remember my friends saying how I made them laugh when I was a little girl. I also remember having lots of friends and always being picked first when choosing up sides for games. But that all changed when I married Ned. I still had lots of friends, but Ned kept me isolated from them. When Rosemary asked me to be maid of honor at her wedding, Ned said I should refuse because she nor her fiancé asked him to be in their wedding party. "But she's my best friend, and her fiancé is having his best friend be his best man."

"Well, it makes me feel crappy, and that's that!" he shouted.

I'll never forget how sad Rosemary was when I told her, but she knew Ned and I were having problems, and I'm sure she put things together. When I divorced Ned, I moved to California, and Rosemary started writing to me. She and her husband flew out twice to visit me.

Kurt was born under the same sign as Ned. Both are Leos, and both are into telling jokes and making people laugh. In fact, I used to be quite a joke teller, until I met up with Kurt and he took over that task. I think that's their only similarity, but since my relationship with Kurt is new and blinded by love, I'll just have to pay close attention to see that I don't lose my identity again. Although I'm head-over-heels in love with Kurt, I have to be myself.

For Kurt's last night in California, I made a pot roast with potatoes and carrots. He'd told me early on that this is his favorite meal. *Every woman knows that the way to a man's heart is through his stomach, via his crotch.*

After a sumptuous meal, accompanied by a Grey Riesling wine, we settled on the couch for a little petting and discussion about the future. We both said we'd like to live in the present, just enjoying one another's company. Kurt voiced his excitement about my moving to Georgia. "Do you realize how close Georgia is to Ohio? We can see each other more often, if you'll let me stay longer than a week at a time."

"We'll see."

"I'm committed to this relationship," Kurt said, "and I hope you are, as well."

"I'm committed. But I'm of the opinion that if these feelings are as strong in a month or two, you should put a ring on my finger to show that commitment."

"No problem, sweetheart," he said, locking lips with me and awakening my sensuality.

"Would you like to pick out the ring?"

I smiled. "No, I'm sure you'll do fine."

Kurt beamed.

And I felt good speaking up about wanting an engagement ring. I knew I would feel better having my fiancé stay at my home rather than my boyfriend.

I rarely expressed my opinion when married to Ned because he didn't care what my opinion was, and if I disagreed with him, an argument would ensue with him getting physical and pulling my hair or putting his hands around my neck and applying pressure. If I fought back, which I often did, I'd end up with bruises to explain. One day my mother-in-law saw them, even after I'd applied makeup to my neck, and she insisted on knowing how I got the bruises. She was very sad that I was getting the same treatment she'd been getting from her husband. Although I pleaded with her not to speak to Ned about it, she must have, because Ned made sure no bruises were evident on my face or neck after that. My mother-in-law and I were very close, although Ned was her only child. I always wondered why Ned didn't try to stop the abuse his mother suffered at the hands of his father. Instead, Ned learned how to be an abuser.

I find it odd now that my role in my first marriage defined my role in any succeeding relationships. Or maybe it wasn't odd at all, I reasoned. It most likely was a growth issue and a desire to be happy. Yes, I'd grown a lot since my divorce from Ned, and I vowed I would never let anyone put a hand on me or disrespect me again. My opinions and happiness do matter.

I remember submitting to Ned in the bedroom, never voicing my desires; and he never asked. I also learned from that marriage if you didn't express your desires, you'd never get them.

Kurt broke into my thoughts. "Can you believe we've been seeing one another since last October?"

"Do you recall who said 'I love you' first?" I asked.

"I did, on our third date in Las Vegas."

"I'll never forget that trip. It was magical; although I think I fell in love with you through our emails. You were so funny and vulnerable. And I loved your quotes from Mark Twain."

"I have to admit, I have a book of his best quotes."

"I wondered how you could remember them. But don't you think that was deceptive?"

"I'm confessing now," Kurt said, laughing.

We laughed and joked into the night. After the late news, Kurt suggested we shower together. He stood up and pulled me to my feet. "I want everything at once," he said. "I want to look at you, touch you, and taste you. And I want to be inside you already."

As I undressed, Kurt watched my nipples harden, and he hadn't even touched them yet.

I was amazed at the size of his pecker as we entered the shower, and I hadn't even touched it yet. We gazed at one another in awe. There was such a naked desire in Kurt's look as we soaped one another with our hands.

"Tell me what you want—what feels good to you," Kurt said huskily.

I couldn't believe what I was hearing. My lover wants to please me. "For starters, you can kiss me."

"We should have turned the furnace off," Kurt said. "I'm hot hot."

"I did turn it off."

I thought about the ways to a man's heart and decided through the pecker is a more intimate, exciting way.

"You want me?" Kurt asked.

"Is the Pope celibate?" I asked, curving my body into his.

"Then let's go to bed and finish what we've started. And you can tell me what you want me to do to please you."

I shivered, anticipating what was to come.

Kurt followed me into the bedroom and kissed me, deeply, making me feel his urgency, and making me want him more. And then he was looking down at me with such raw emotion that I wasn't even aware that he'd made his first tentative entry. It was the withdrawal that thrilled me, and the second thrust.

"You're still very tight. Haven't you been using the artificial penis I bought you?"

"No, I wanted to wait for the real thing."

I witnessed his smile, gleaming through the dim light of the bedside lamp. I waited until I heard a pattern of repetitive breathing, and then I slipped out of bed and removed my poem, "Childhood Friends," from my writing folder and placed it at the bottom of Kurt's suitcase. When he gets home tomorrow, he'll find it and be pleased that I'd taken the initiative to get my poem to him first.

The week Kurt spent here was pure heaven. I can't help wondering, though, whether we're not placing too much emphasis on sex and not enough emphasis on how compatible we are in other areas. Oh, well, our love is new, and we need to take advantage of the intimacy and passion for as long as it lasts.

Chapter Eleven

The ride to the airport was uneventful, and I got Kurt there in ample time. The drive back to Camarillo, however, was another story. Evidently an accident had occurred because an ambulance, two police cars, and a firetruck whizzed by as I sat in stalled traffic.

I was exhausted when I pulled into the driveway. After hugging Moxie, I changed into a robe and went back to bed. After sleeping a couple of hours, I reached across the bed and patted the place Kurt had owned for the past week. I felt loved and lay there enjoying those feelings.

Kurt is great fun and makes me laugh. He says I make him laugh. He has a knack of putting captions on cartoons that is hilarious. Picture a court jester's neck in a guillotine with the court adjutant ready to drop the blade. And Kurt's caption: "The jester dared to goose the King."

My forte is writing humorous essays. I'm told my funniest ones are about my making inanimate objects animate. One contest winner is about my seventeen-year-old fridge whom I'd befriended, and who has outlasted my marriage by four years. He's always glad to see me and lights up when I open the door. He runs day and night without any breaks.

I spend entire weekends at the computer, writing into the wee hours. Kurt was a pilot and spends hours at his computer watching planes take off and land. Ho hum. He probably feels the same about my writing. I watch CNN and he's glued to Fox News. I wonder if trouble is ahead.

Kurt is very savvy about the planet and its resources; and he loves to quiz me about the types of clouds, why the seasons occur, carbon dating, rock formations, tectonic plates and their movement. His information is endless and interesting. But I don't enjoy these quizzes. It's not *my* thing--it's *his* thing. Geology was Kurt's college major and the only class I got a C in, although I still graduated magna cum laude.

Kurt said he and Pam never argued. That's difficult for me to buy since knowing Kurt. Perhaps he didn't quiz Pam, or perhaps she played along with him. Kurt and I have our share of arguments, but I believe they're healthy. What better way to find out about one another? As in our case, after the argument is over, Kurt hasn't changed my mind, nor have I changed his mind. But the possibility was there that one of us might have. Another thing to recognize is that we both have gleaned a better understanding of the other side of the issue.

Reading about the Civil War and biographies about the signers of the Declaration of Independence are what Kurt enjoys. He's fascinated with Thomas Jefferson's intelligence and insight. I like reading biographies and autobiographies about Supreme Court Justices, Presidents, movie stars, and famous people. We both like history. I related a report I'd written in high school about Ulysses S. Grant, whose given name was Hiram Ulysses Grant, but which he changed because of the teasing he got when he initialed documents as HUG.

The phone rang, interrupting my meanderings.

"Hi, Sweetheart. I'm in Pittsburgh and will get my car from the parking lot and head for St. Clairsville. How was the traffic on the way home from the airport?"

I told him about the accident and sleeping for a couple of hours. "I bet you're tired, as well. How is the weather?"

"A hell of a lot colder than in California. I'm glad you talked me into wearing a jacket. Just wanted to say I love you and will call you when I get home."

"Look in the bottom of your suitcase. I tucked something in there for you."

"Can I put it under my pillow?"

"If you like."

"Love you again. Bye, my lover."

When Kurt called later that evening, he'd read my poem.

CHILDHOOD FRIENDS

Childhood friends never stray far from the heart,
even though they may build their destinies
miles from their beginnings.
The threads that bind such friendships,
no matter how wispy,
keep the memories alive that were
there when those pals parted.

No deeper bond than childhood friends exists
unless kin-to-kin or lover-to-lover.
Who else knows our past and loves us
because of it or in spite of it?
Who else knows how we became who we
are and will remain to one another?

Absolutely nothing can be more sublime
than for childhood friends to bypass
time and fall in love like we did.

"Your poem moved me, and I was really impressed with its professionalism. Wow! I'll treasure it, my darling. And be on notice that you'll be getting my poem in a day or two."

We talked about a meet-up in Georgia for our next get-together so that I can look at homes. I also need to see for myself how Aunt Wilma is adapting to her new surroundings. Kurt said he'll drive to Smyrna so we can have access to his SUV during the house-hunting process.

"I am so looking forward to seeing you again, and in a vacation setting this time," Kurt said. "Every time I see you, I feel our relationship gets deeper. I can't quit thinking about you."

"What about Moxie. Do you ever think of him?"

"Yes, I do. I think we bonded my last visit."

After hanging up, I turned on my computer and read my emails. One from Ray popped up. "We haven't talked for a while. How are you and Kurt getting along? Is he still visiting? I chuckle every time I think of the day we first met while attending a meeting to put the San Fernando Valley Writer's Club back together. I almost choke when I think of what the Central Board President said when he spied you in the audience. 'Goodness gracious, is that you, Eva? I'm glad to see you – it's been a good many years since we were on the Central Board together. Are you going to help put the club back together?'

"Since we were seated next to one another, I introduced myself, and we've been friends ever since. I appreciate your critiquing my novel, the monthly newsletter, and all the other stuff I write. Anyway, just thinking about you and hoping things are going well with you and Kurt."

I emailed him back telling him that Kurt flew back to Ohio this morning and that we'd gotten a lot of document shredding done. I told Ray how I appreciate his friendship and emotional support.

Ray is one terrific writer and he's become one of my best friends. He encourages me in my writing projects, and he's editor of our writer's club monthly newsletter. Ray writes several columns, short stories, poetry, you name it, and all he writes is thoroughly enjoyed by the members. He's written several books, and I've critiqued them all. Not much to critique because his writing is flawless. Ray is our only club member who is also a member of Mensa. My projects are writing a monthly president's column and usually how-to articles about points of view, characterization, and query letters. We exchange four or five emails a week. He's also a song writer and is putting together an album. He has a lovely singing voice, sounding a bit like Engelbert Humperdinck. I am totally crazy about his first recording, 'I want to be the One.' I asked him to send a copy to Kurt, and Kurt said it sounds like he wrote it for you and me.

The next morning when I went into my emails, I found Kurt's poem.

TWILIGHT LOVE

My lady true and ever fair,
Where have you been?
No dreams of me were ever there,
Other loves you sought to win.

Oppressed by him whose child you bore,
To other climes you fled.
Mother's instinct would insure,
Child's fortune be not dread.

Denied anew for wedded bliss,
Resigned to thrive alone.
Yet, search for love still in her kiss,
Is Kurt the one to take her home?

Grant me haven in your bosom warm,
Words of solace whisper there.
Listen to the heart within me storm,
Feel the quickened pulse now we share.

Even as our love is new,
Silent shadows call,
HIS mercy blesses all that's true,
In our life's ceaseless pall.

I read and reread the poem and found hidden messages. 'Is Kurt the one to take her home?' really touched me. My lover had come through with a lovely, meaningful poem, and he'd made himself vulnerable; and that's what love is all about.

Chapter Twelve

It was a cold, rainy evening when I arrived at the Atlanta Hartsfield-Jackson Airport. Kurt told me it was his second run around the airport in his SUV when he spied me by the curb with my olive-colored suitcase, all bundled up in a heavy down jacket. Parking at the curb, he jumped out of the vehicle and kissed me soundly. He then helped me into the SUV and placed my suitcase in the backseat.

"I'm so glad to see you!" he said excitedly. "Did you have a nice trip?"

"It was great! And it's so nice to see you. But this weather is the pits."

"This is January in Georgia. If you bundle up warm like you are, it's not so bad."

"Where are we staying?"

"At the Marriott, close to the airport. I made reservations for two nights only in case we don't like it there. I can't believe we'll have five days together, although I was hoping for more."

"I still have a lot of work to do at my condo, and I need to stay focused right now."

"One thing I know, we'll be sharing the future together." Kurt reached over with his right hand and clasped mine. "What kind of a spell have you cast over me? I can't wait to feel my lips on yours and to sleep next to you again."

"I feel the same way," I said, squeezing his hand.

"And how is that little guy, Moxie?"

"Rachel will be spending an hour with him twice daily, but I don't think she's a cat lover. She watched him before, however, and he was okay; and that's the most important thing. I just wish I could have had someone like Donna to love him and play with him."

Why don't you ask Donna?"

"We had a falling out that I sincerely regret."

"Do you want to tell me about it?"

"Another time, okay?"

"Sure," Kurt replied.

"I spoke to Lexie before leaving home, and she wants to meet in the morning instead of tonight. I'm glad, since my flight was late, and I knew we'd both be tired. How was your drive from Ohio?"

"It was very long – seven hundred twenty miles. The next time I'll break it up and stay overnight about half-way."

"That's a good idea. You know, Shelly, the real estate agent I met when I was here for Aunt Wilma's move, has scheduled appointments to see three houses and one condo." I paused, thinking about my aunt and watching the windshield wipers sweep the raindrops off the glass. "Maybe we can pay Aunt Wilma a quick visit after house-hunting. I'm anxious to see her."

"I know you are," Kurt said, "and I am, as well."

Since Lexie knows the neighborhoods, she'll be house-hunting with us."

"How about Stephen?"

"He has to finish up a construction job in Atlanta but expects to get off early to have dinner with us. You'll like Lexie and Stephen. They are down-to-earth people."

* * * * *

When we arrived at the Marriott, Kurt parked under a streetlight. "So a thief will think twice before stealing my SUV in plain sight," he said smugly.

"Now, that's a good idea," I said, getting out of the car. The rain had lessened to a drizzle, but I still pulled my jacket hoodie over my head.

Kurt grabbed his suitcase and mine out of the backseat while I carried my overnight bag and purse and followed him to the front door of the hotel. He opened it and said, "Follow me. Our room is on the second floor, close to the elevator."

The room was large and beautifully decorated. The wine-colored draperies and wine velvet bedspread were tasteful, as were the teak furniture and scenic wall paintings. Dropping my overnight bag and purse, I pulled off the bedspread from the king-sized bed. "I always worry that someone's semen is on the spread," I said.

"Those are my exact thoughts," Kurt said, scooping me up in his arms and placing me in the center of the bed. After some passionate kisses, Kurt pulled away and looked at me while his eyes danced with devilment. "Would you like to have dinner or continue making love?"

"Let's eat first and make love later. I actually feel like a light meal, maybe breakfast."

"Sounds like a plan." Placing my jacket across my shoulders, he led me out of the room.

* * * * *

At the restaurant, we enjoyed scrambled eggs and corned-beef hash. Then we went back to our room where we cuddled and watched TV. It wasn't long before I felt

Kurt's arm fall from my shoulders and saw his head slump back into the couch cushions. He'd been up since four this morning in order to hit the road for the seven hundred plus mile drive from Ohio; and I felt pretty dipsy from the three-hour flight and the three-hour time change. So after the movie ended, I stealthily slipped off the couch and walked to the bathroom for a quick shower. As I soaped my back, a naked Kurt walked in. My heart lurched, but my body didn't respond. I was just about to tell Kurt how tired I was when he said, "I'm beat. Why don't we finish our shower and hit the sack? Unless you have other ideas."

"No other ideas. Why should you be pumping while I'm sleeping?"

"How can I pump without a pump?"

I couldn't stop laughing. My man must be very tired to pass up a make-out session.

* * * * *

In the morning, after a quickie, we dressed, brushed our teeth, and walked to the parking lot to retrieve Kurt's SUV. He reached in his pocket for his keys, but they weren't there. He panicked and went through all of his pockets. No keys.

Maybe you left them in the SUV," I said.

Walking up to it, he said, "Here's hoping." He then tried the door and it opened.

"Geez," he said. "The keys are in the ignition. How in the hell did I do that?"

"You were tired last night, that's how."

"And to think the SUV is still here. Very weird. I'm surprised someone didn't steal it."

"Me, too."

We got in the SUV and drove to The Cracker Barrel where we were meeting Lexie for breakfast. She was already there, and I introduced her to Kurt. After we were seated and had ordered, Kurt told Lexie about leaving the keys in his SUV.

"You were really lucky," Lexie said. "That Marriott is in a very bad part of town and cars are constantly stolen from there. Most likely yours wasn't stolen because the keys were in it and it was under a street light. Some thief probably thought, 'This has got to be a setup, it's too easy, and I ain't takin' any chances of goin' to prison.'"

Kurt laughed so hard he started choking on his coffee. He said he paid for two nights, so we'd have to stay tonight, but we'd move to another hotel in the morning.

Arriving at the first house a little early, the three of us viewed the outside of the property. The house was a red brick bungalow with an olive front door with a long, oval cut-glass design in the center. It made a very nice appearance. However, a church and parking lot were adjacent.

Shelly arrived shortly, and after greeting one another, she showed us the interior which had recently been remodeled; and the floor plan was lovely. However, I couldn't get past the activity that would take place at the church grounds.

The next viewing was a two-story condo in a good neighborhood, which had been updated. But I didn't want a two-story.

The next house had three bedrooms, two baths, a large sunroom, a large side porch, and a cellar. Living alone, I didn't vision going down to the cellar, so I crossed off this house.

The last house, beige brick with dark red shutters, had a two-car carport attached. The main entrance had a small brick porch and brick steps that fanned out at the ground level. The curb appeal was lovely. Another entry was from the side door off the carport that opened into the kitchen. The kitchen cabinets and appliances were old, but after walking through the house, I could see myself living here. It had hard-wood floors, crown molding, and a certain charm that appealed to me. It had two wooden sheds in the back yard which sat on an acre of land.

Shelly told us the property had been vacant for three years since the owners died; and she was sure the children of the deceased, who now own the house, would reduce the price. It needed quite a bit of work in the kitchen and bathrooms, but the house overall was structurally sound. The front door led to a wide foyer and hallway closet. The kitchen was large and could be utilized as a kitchen/family room. The living room was long and would accommodate my dining room furniture at one end and my living room furniture at the other end. Kurt liked it and also saw the possibilities I did.

Shelly quickly wrote up an offer that was fifteen thousand dollars lower than the asking price and sent it by fax to the sellers' real estate agent. She included a forty-five-day escrow to give me time to sell my home, and she put a deadline of noon tomorrow for the sellers' response. She winked as she got in her car. "Keep positive thoughts," she said.

"I will, and thank you very much, Shelly. You found the right house for me."

"You happy?" Kurt asked.

"Yes, but I'll be happier when it's a done deal."

"Since it's only three o'clock, we have time to swing by the nursing home and visit with Aunt Wilma before dinner."

Lexie said she'd pass and let us have some alone time with her.

Kurt put the nursing home address in the GPS, and we got there in ten minutes. As we drove along the winding road to the entrance of the main building, we passed a lovely man-made lake. Kurt mentioned that the buildings and grounds looked like a college campus. I had thought that when I'd moved Aunt Wilma there several months ago.

As we entered the nursing home, a few patients and guests were seated on couches in the large reception room. They smiled and nodded as we continued on toward the elevators. "Aunt Wilma's room is on the second floor, and so is the social room/dining room, which makes it convenient for her to be back and forth from her bedroom. They call her Miss Wilma here."

When we got off the elevator, I punched in a security code, and we entered the memory care section. My aunt's room was the second room on the right. When we walked in, neither she nor her roommate was there.

We found Aunt Wilma in her wheelchair in the social room watching television. She didn't see us until we spoke her name, and then her face lit up like a flashlight. I bent down to hug her and so did Kurt. I asked if she remembered

Kurt, and she nodded. I told her we'd be here for a few days, and her face glowed. Kurt pushed her wheelchair to the side of the room where there were a couple of empty chairs. We sat, and I held her hands while we talked. Roy, a friend of hers, came by in his wheelchair and introduced himself. He said Miss Wilma reads out loud to the patients. I laughed, thinking about her reading the Cialis article in the doctor's office in California. One of the nurses later told us that Roy is a West Point graduate and had lost his wife recently. Another gentleman, also in a wheelchair, smiled and waved to my aunt.

My aunt told us she likes the place and the food and has made good friends, especially with her roommate, Rita. She wanted Kurt to meet her, so Kurt pushed her wheelchair over to Rita, a few feet away, who was looking out the window watching the geese glide by on the lake. Rita, also in a wheelchair, was sixty-five, suffering the effects of a stroke, and spoke haltingly. She seemed very protective of my aunt and acted like a doting daughter which Aunt Wilma loved. Rita was divorced, and her only son had died recently.

That night Kurt and I met Lexie and Stephen for dinner at a barbeque restaurant. Stephen and Kurt liked one another immediately and seemed to have a lot to talk about that Lexie and I started our own conversation that excluded them; and they didn't even notice. We overheard bits about the house Stephen was working on in downtown Atlanta and how the building supplies and tools would be stolen during the night by thieves breaking windows to gain access. "The building contractor finally had to hire a night watchman," Stephen said.

Stephen said that after this job was finished, he wouldn't be taking another one in downtown Atlanta. We overheard Kurt talking about his days as a pilot during the Vietnam War. Lexie and I smiled at one another conspiratorially.

Chapter Thirteen

Since Stephen doesn't work on Saturdays, he and Lexie took us to the Atlanta Zoo where we saw our first Panda. She looked cuddly and adorable, romping around with her mother. We then spent considerable time in the reptile room, gazing at the various snakes. It was both repulsive and fascinating to see these slithering creatures up-close in their habitat. The zoo wasn't as large as I'd expected, and we were done viewing the animals by eleven o'clock.

We left the zoo and were having lunch at a nearby café when the call came in. Shelly said that the sellers had accepted my offer and the escrow terms. "The next move," she said, "would be an inspection of the property." Since we'd be leaving in a few days, Stephen said he'd find an inspector to examine the property and write up a report. Stephen was in the contracting business, so I breathed a sigh of relief.

Stephen then asked if we'd be interested in seeing the Civil War Museum and the Cyclorama, a three-dimensional panorama-in-the-round of the Civil War with emphasis on the Battle of Atlanta. Kurt, being a Civil War buff, wanted to see it. When we arrived at the theatre, we sat in the second row, middle of the aisle. Kurt's head bobbed from side to side as the stage moved slowly, exposing the bloody soldiers at war. "It's very realistic," he said, absorbed in the action. After the show, he and Stephen spent considerable time in the Civil War Museum while Lexie and I sat outside on a bench talking.

I asked Lexie what she thought of Kurt, and she said he seemed very nice, and it must be a plus having known him before. I expected more, but she'd just met him a few days ago. I was happy, though, that Kurt and Stephen were hitting it off.

It was a most enjoyable day with us finishing it off by eating at Lexie's favorite Chinese restaurant. The owners remembered that Lexie liked the dumpling plate with a few substitutes, and since I love dumplings, I ordered the same dish. The guys ordered seafood platters. We enjoyed plum wine with dinner and discussed the home I'm buying. Stephen said he'd be glad to hire contractors and oversee the renovation projects. He'd recently installed a tankless hot water heater in his and Lexie's home and said he'd install one in my home.

* * * * *

Kurt had gotten us reservations for the last three days of our stay at the Double Tree Hotel, which was across the street from the small mall that housed the Chinese restaurant. Since it was still raining, he and Stephen headed for their cars while Lexie and I waited under the awning of the establishment. Kurt showed up first and opened the passenger door for me, goosing me while I climbed in. I turned and caught Lexie laughing.

"Shame on you," I said. "Lexie saw that."

"She must know we're sleeping together," he said, "so what's the big deal."

* * * * *

We checked in at the Double Tree and walked down the hallway. "I got us a suite," Kurt said. "I hope you like it. There's room for us to chase one another around."

Kurt opened the door and ushered me in, setting the suitcases in the bedroom.

I looked around at the roomy suite which was decorated with ornate baroque furniture and mid-century paintings. I then opened the bathroom door. "There's a big spa/tub in here! And do I feel like relaxing in it!"

"Go ahead. I'll watch the news and take a shower after you're done."

As the bath water ran, I brushed my teeth and pushed my hair away from my face. I dropped my hand in the water. Hot. Just the way I like it. I must have soaked for half an hour, enjoying every minute of it. The rain in Georgia was a cold rain that made my bones and joints ache. Not a good sign. But Lexie assured me the rain never lasts long and isn't usually this cold.

When I came out, Kurt said he liked my clean, scrubbed look.

"Now it's your turn," I said, pulling down the bedspread and getting comfortable in bed.

"Don't fall asleep. I'm in a very amorous mood," he said.

"So don't spend all night in the shower. And make sure it's not a cold shower."

Kurt laughed as he pretended to smuggle his pecker out of the room, reminding me of a joke he'd recently told me. An old English baron who rarely got stimulated at his elderly age, awoke one morning with a huge hard-on and quickly summoned his servant, Master Gibbs. "Should I summon Mrs. Hartfield?" Gibbs asked. "No, no," said the baron. "Fetch my baggie tweeds. I'll smuggle this to town." Kurt's accent as he told the story made it even funnier.

The rest of the story: A family friend happened to go into the bathroom when the baron was toweling off, and the baron grabbed a piece of toilet paper to cover himself. Madam Hatcher looked at him and said, "Every time I think of Peter Piper's pecker peeking out of that piece of paper, my pussy puckers up and I can't pee."

* * * * *

When Kurt walked back into the room with tousled hair, smelling of after-shave, my heart raced. He must have caught me gawking and smiled shyly.

"My dear," he murmured, "come closer."

As I approached and stood in front of him, naked, I could smell traces of soap in the heat of his body, and I could feel his pecker surge. I kissed him lightly on the forehead. "Hold that pose," I said. "My bladder is screaming. I'll be back before you can say, 'Peter Pecker picked a peck of pickled peppers.'"

"I think it's Peter Piper!" Kurt shouted, as I closed the bathroom door.

* * * * *

The room was dark when I returned to the bedroom. A small glimmer of light escaped between the draperies where they met in the middle. I didn't know what to think as I climbed in bed and nuzzled my head against Kurt's neck. He reached out and enclosed me in his arms, kissing me gently, then wildly. He is absolutely the best kisser in the world. Hitching my leg over his, I could feel his remarkable organ. Then I hitched my leg a little higher on his thigh. His erection brushed my knee, and I slid one hand over his taut belly and then down to the thatch of dark hair at the base of his pecker. He made a sound in the back of his throat and mounted me, sliding his rigid organ inside me. It fit perfectly, and it knew exactly what to do.

"Have I pleased you, my darling?" Kurt turned the bedside lamp on and gazed at me.

"I can't believe how you thrill me. I wonder whether other eighty-one-year-old gentlemen can still perform."

"If they have an eighty-year-old Eva, they can," he smiled. "You do this to me." He sucked in his breath and said, "And I don't believe many eighty-year-old women even want sex."

"Well, I do, and I'm glad we can still enjoy it together." I ran my tongue across my dry lips. "How long do you think this is going to last, Kurt? Twenty years? I'd be happy with twenty, wouldn't you? Do you think you're up to making love to a nympho for twenty years?"

"I wouldn't count on it, honey. That would put me at one hundred one."

"OMG. I was just thinking. If I didn't have my hysterectomy, you could probably knock me up."

"No, no, honey." Kurt laughed. "I think all your eggs must be rotten by now. And if I have any sperm left, I'm certain they've forgotten how to swim."

"Well, I'd be delighted if you could still make me laugh at one hundred one. Can you promise me that, Kurt?"

"Yes, I can promise you that, Eva. And I can also promise you that I'll always love you."

We fell asleep in one another's arms, whispering love snippets to each other. Before drifting off, I remember thinking how loved I felt.

* * * * *

Our last three days were spent visiting Aunt Wilma and getting familiar with Smyrna; and what we saw, we liked. Smyrna is part of the Atlanta metropolitan area, located about ten miles from Downtown Atlanta, population estimated to be 51,271 as of the 2010 census.

Lexie took Kurt and me on a tour of City Hall, the public library, several parks, and a Civil War Monument. Kurt was enthralled by the history of Smyrna. Two Civil War battles occurred in the area, the Battle of Smyrna Campground on July 3, 1864, and the Battle of Ruff's Mill the next day. The area's businesses, homes and 1849 covered bridge (since rebuilt and still in use today) were burned by Sherman's troops. The covered bridge sits about a half mile from the house I'm buying; and I'll be crossing it to get to the nursing home.

Known as the "Jonquil City," it derived its name from the thousands of jonquils that flourish in gardens and along the streets in early spring. Yes, I could imagine myself living here, working away at my computer, a Mint Julep within reach. I didn't know anything about Mint Juleps except that Scarlet in *Gone with the Wind* drank them.

"Can you find out how to make Mint Juleps?" I asked Kurt.

"You bet," he responded.

We climbed back into Lexie's car, and she slowly drove past the nearby Bell Bomber plant that produced B-29 bombers during World War II, and which was reopened in 1951 by Lockheed and became a catalyst for growth. Since Kurt was a pilot in the Vietnam War, he was interested in viewing the plant and possibly volunteering to restore some of the older planes that were housed in the yard. He had told me recently that he and four friends were given permission to move a Lockheed 233 aircraft and to restore it at a small airport in Harrison County, Ohio, about fifteen miles from Kurt's St. Clairsville home. He said he recalls that restoration project with nostalgia. After sanding and painting for several hours, he and his friends would stop and have lunch at one of the restaurants close by and shoot the bull about their years in the service. His voice got soft. "Two of those friends are now deceased."

* * * * *

That night, alone in our hotel suite, Kurt and I discussed my move to Smyrna. "The first plus is that you'll be within driving distance, albeit seven hundred miles away," he said. "And from my experiences living in Selma, Alabama, while I worked at the Craig Air Force Base is that southern living is easy and slow-paced, and you'll find that the townspeople are friendlier than northerners, very helpful and very receptive. Frankly, I can't say enough good things about southern culture."

"If half of what you say about the South is correct, I'm sure I'll fit right in."

Chapter Fourteen

I've been back in California for a week, missing Kurt, and have embarked on refinishing the dark oak kitchen cabinets with an almond color paint that matches the appliances. The balance of working with my hands and my brain unstresses me and makes me happy.

Kurt said it's been cold in Ohio, so he's staying inside, trying to get caught up on some reading material. He said he only ventures out to have lunch or dinner with Joe and Marla.

In his recent email he said,

"As I walked near my street, I noticed how beautiful the night snow looked under the lights. This prompted me to send you the poem written by Robert Frost. There's nothing quite like the sound of fresh snow crunched under foot, the stillness of the cold evening air, and thou. You must visit me when the snow is on the ground, my darling.

"Yesterday in the bookstore, I found something I think you'll like. I'll send it to you soon. I'm also writing another poem for you. I have several books of poetry, and over the years I've learned that a good poem is short and to the point. I've tried to read some longer poems but lose interest. It has been said however, that a poem is never finished. I thank my eighth grade teacher, Mrs. Orlando, for getting me interested in poetry. One day she told the class that each member had to memorize a poem and recite it in front of the class. I chose 'To a Waterfowl,' by William Cullen Bryant. Over the years my sons would ask me to recite the poem, and I did many times. Not long ago, I tried to recall the poem and was forced to relearn the end of the poem. Have you ever read, 'Elegy Written in a Country Churchyard' by Thomas Grey? His is some of the finest poetry ever written.

"I am still reliving the last time we were together – it was so perfect. I had wondered whether I could still enjoy love-making as an old guy. But I need not wonder any longer. For at least thirty seconds, I didn't know where I was. I was actually out of my head for a short time. I'd never experienced such a strong climax. Thank you, my dear lover. I love the way you love. I think we make a great team. Just thought you might like to know.

"I am saddened by the passing of two more classmates. I get the idea that our union is good for the class of 1947. Like keeping it in the family. To answer your question about your having male friends, how can a man or woman avoid having friends of the opposite sex? I have female friends, so there you are. Just so the guys remain friends only.

"I had thought my libido would go to sleep during our long separations, but that's not the case. You opened me up again and now you must accept what I have to offer. ILOU."

My return email:

"Depends on what you have to offer. You mention the snow. I'd like to experience it again, but not for three months. I just hope it doesn't snow in Georgia.

"Ray and I met for breakfast and talked about the future of our writer's club. He's such an interesting guy with crazy wild hair and thick round glasses. He's quite an intellectual, however. We've become good friends and email one another several times a week. He writes quirky articles, like I do. He wrote a series of 'Letters to J' that are captive. I'm moved by the way he expresses his love for Jennifer. He's putting the letters in book form and will publish them. He's worried how his wife will feel since the letters are about a woman he was in love with before meeting her. He said he may use a pen name for publication and thinks his wife might go along with that. He said he's looking forward to my critiquing it. We also discussed the projects I'm working on, a romance novel and a coffee table book. I told Ray you're interested in poetry and are a good writer yourself.

"I plan to visit Wanda this afternoon. She's excited about moving to Madison. I think she's looking forward to living close to her sister-in-law again. I understand they used to be good friends, and it was she who introduced Wanda to her brother.

"I can't offhand recall any of Thomas Grey's poems, but I'm sure I've read some of them. Have you read any poetry by James Wright from Martins Ferry, Ohio? One poem is: 'Autumn Begins in Martins Ferry, Ohio;' another one: 'In Response to a Rumor that the Oldest Whorehouse in Wheeling, West Virginia has been Condemned.' If you haven't read them, I'll scan them in and send them via my next email.

"My libido has started screaming. I thought you should know. Just remember that you are a bachelor no longer. You belong to me. ILU – Your naughty Eva."

Kurt wrote:

"Dear Sunshine,

"I have heard of Martins Ferry's native writer James Wright but have not read any of his works. Please copy me in. You sure have your plate full these days. I wish I could assist you in some way. If you think of anything, let me know.

"I plan to visit my son Doug and his wife in Maryland this weekend. The trip is about six hours. I'll probably stay about five days and will call you from there. I'm anxious for you to meet them. And when can I visit you again in California, my sweetheart? How about a week in February that includes Valentine's Day?

"I've been looking at you in the black bra and red scarf you sent me, and it really gets my motor running. I have to say I have never known a woman like you. You are bright, and yet sensuous. I have noticed how you can discuss business one minute, and the next it is about pleasure. How did you achieve those skills? Yes, you will be commander in chief as to the kitchen and those recipes, and I will take care of bedroom recipes. Now and then you may contribute. I love you, you little love creature. I must go now, and good luck with your woman-about-town activities. I love your energy, baby. AML, Major Kurt."

Kurt and I had gotten back into our routine of emailing one another daily since returning from Georgia. As we learn new things about each other, we fall deeper in love.

I finished my painting, showered, roughed up the cat, and was on my way to see Wanda. As I approached her room, I heard Jerry Vale singing "Have You Looked into Your Heart?"

Wanda looked pale as I bent down to kiss her. "Turn off the boom box so we can talk," she said. She wore two hearing aids and said they probably need cleaning because her hearing is getting worse. I told her I'd take them to her audiologist's office. Pulling a chair close to her bed, she and I talked about her health and possible move to Wisconsin.

"My nephew's wife Sally has been calling me weekly to check on me. She seems like a caring person and said there's a very nice assisted living facility a block from their home. I was wondering whether you could check it out to see what kind of a place it is."

"I'll be happy to do that," I said, taking the slip of paper from her that the faclity's name and address were on. We then talked about the Georgia facility where my aunt lives, and I told her that Aunt Wilma and her roommate have become fast friends, eating at the same table and watching Rita's television in their room. The staff and residents are all friendly and Aunt Wilma said she likes it there and feels safe there.

Wanda voiced her concern about making new friends. I leaned over and took Wanda's hands in mine. "You are much more outgoing than my Aunt Wilma, so people will flock to you."

"You think so?" Wanda smiled; and I saw some of the concern fade from her face.

Wanda wanted to know how Kurt is and how we're getting along. She and her husband were high school sweethearts and married young. She loves to talk about the crazy things they did. "He taught himself to play the guitar and made up tunes to play for me," she said. "He was so tender and loving. He's been gone twenty years, and I still think about him every day."

I dropped off Wanda's hearing aids and was told they'd be ready in the morning.

When I got home, I picked up the package from the mailbox. It contained pictures of Tiltonsville: my old home, the firehouse, library, and St. Joseph's Catholic Church. They brought back warm memories. A book of Mark Twain's favorite sayings was also in the box. I would check out his quotes in the future. After removing

everything from the box, Moxie jumped in and took a nap.
I wished Kurt had put his after-shave lotion on the items.
I'll have to request a postcard drenched in his after-shave
for Moxie to sniff.

I recalled last Christmas when my elderly neighbor
Tom wanted to know what my favorite cologne was, and I
said Chanel No. 5. On Christmas, Tom handed me a bottle
of White Musk. I must have looked puzzled because he
said, "I hope you like White Musk as the Channel No. 5
was more expensive." I laughed, thinking how honest old
people and children are.

After he left, I sprayed my shoulders and wrists with the
cologne but didn't like the smell on me and set the bottle
on my dresser. When I walked back into the bedroom, an
hour or so later, the bottle was on the carpet and Moxie
was snoozing next to it. Evidently he liked the smell and
claimed the White Musk for himself.

I checked my email after dinner and was glad I did, as
one awaited me from Kurt.

"Dear Georgia, Georgia,

"Nowhere do I find, just an old sweet song
I've got Georgia on my mind.

"Have you heard Willy Nelson sing Georgia?
I've heard it many times and still don't know
whether he means a woman or the state of
Georgia. Many arms reach out to me, many
eyes smile tenderly, but in my dreams I see her
coming back to me.

"Fear not, fair maiden. I have no other loves.
I have never been so intimate with a woman, and

I dare say it will get better. You are a powerful attraction in my life, and I value that very much. I often re-read our emails, and I notice that as time wears on, they have gotten warmer and warmer. Except for an occasional reunion dance, we've not had any physical contact, and we've not seen one another for many years at a time.

"When I learned of your second divorce, my thoughts of you had not changed my perception of an unusually beautiful woman living at leisure in the hills of Southern California. And I let it go at that. After we started our email contact, I wondered where in hell are all the great guys that she could have at the snap of her fingers. After all, the beauty was still there. So what does Eva do? She turns to an old school chum twenty-three hundred miles away, living in a small town. Eva, my dear, if you were looking for a change of pace, with a country bumpkin, you sure got one.

"Perhaps you are returning to your roots, and I happen to be in those roots. I am happy that you and I finally got together after sixty-two years. I love telling the story about you and me. It gets strong reception by all. The money … well, I do not consider myself wealthy, but I have enough for us to do about anything we want. Perhaps you should write a book about rejecting wealth for a country bumpkin.

"I am all set with airline tickets for February. I have the feeling you're taking good care of me in these matters. Did you know that Dolly Parton has two swollen legs? Yep, went right up to her chest. I'll bet her husband has his hands full with her.

"Your Wright poems didn't show on my screen. Please send them again.

"The realist always falls in love with a girl he has grown up with, the romanticist with a girl from 'off somewhere." (Robert Frost)

"I have joined a gym about ten minutes from where I live and have been going pretty much every day for almost three months now. Great way to spend a winter afternoon. A lady at the gym is a former weightlifter and has been teaching some of us how to use the equipment properly. When I see you, I will demonstrate the proper push up. Our lady muscle mechanic told me to find a book dealing with basic body building. Will you still love me when only my muscles are hard? My dork is a muscle, you know. A muscle that seems to react when you come near me. The first night we slept together, I had a difficult time sleeping. Seems I didn't have enough skin left to close my eyes. I am now so strong, I can make love to you holding you in my arms standing up in a hammock. Do you realize that it is only sixteen more days until we meet again? I have never wanted a woman so badly. Do you plan to stay in my life? If not, I will sell the hammock. Good night and try to dream about me. Till death do us part. Your lover."

I answered Kurt's email that night.

"Dearest Muscle Man, I'm glad you joined a gym. It will keep you out of trouble. And keep the hammock.

"I can't believe how racy our love has become and how it has kicked up in intensity. I can't imagine a life without you. I really enjoyed looking at the pictures of Tiltonsville. It brought back fond memories. I'd love to walk the streets hand-in-hand with you, hopefully, in the near future. It's still a little unreal that we've found one another after all these years. And thanks for the Mark Twain book.

"I'm wearing the sweatshirt hoodie you sent me. It feels great in this nippy weather. Yes, the weather gets cool in January. I'm waiting for you to warm me up.

"Ray, my writer friend, sent me an album of songs he's written. They are so beautiful, and he's making you a copy. They are also romantic. Makes me think of you and me.

"Since the weather is a little cool this time of year, you should pack some sweaters.

"Nancy and Brad have suggested going to the Magic Castle while you're here. I'd gone there soon after moving to California, where I saw Walter Matthau performing magic tricks. Right after that, he became a popular movie star. Magic Castle has several rooms where magicians perform. The food is good, and the place is charming. Just give me the nod, and Nancy will make reservations.

"I'm glad you're in my life, Major Kurt. Every time I think of you, I smile, which is often. This time you're going to get a hickey that lasts from Valentine's Day until Christmas. How about one on your wiener? ILU. Your Sexy Senior Senorita."

I sent the email, watched "Accidental Tourist" and wrote a chapter. It was twelve o'clock, but I wasn't sleepy; so I checked out my email. A new message from Kurt appeared.

"Dear Miss Fantastic,

"The hickey you put on my lower right shoulder has disappeared, but I'm sure you'll fix that. A hickey on my wiener? Never had one. This might require three people: me, one to stretch it, and you to apply the artwork.

"I think we're both well-rounded. We like the finer things of life like books, poetry, art, good food, and family. Then there is the sex. You excite me no end. I hope in the not-too-distant future we'll have the opportunity to spend an extended period of time together.

"The Magic Castle sounds good. Let's cover as much ground as possible in these next few years. Many times I've thought how much fun it would be for you to visit me in our old hunting grounds. We could drive to Tiltonsville as lovers, for a start. I have a very nice queen-sized bed from where we could plan our operations. Think about it. This letter will be short as I'll be leaving for Maryland in the morning. I'll call you from Doug's place tomorrow night at seven your time. Until then. I love you. Commander Kurt."

Chapter Fifteen

I got up early and started rolling beige paint on the kitchen walls. It contrasted perfectly with the almond cabinets and appliances. By noon my hands started hurting, so I wrapped the brush and roller in tin foil, and I headed for the shower. As I toweled off, the phone rang.

Lexie asked if I'd heard anything about my escrow. I said I hadn't but wasn't concerned because I actually need the forty-five days to be here to conduct the May meeting of the writer's club, and then I'll move. I said I plan to fly back for the June meeting, which is my last one.

"No problem," Lexie said. "It's just that Stephen wants to remove some diseased trees."

I told her she'll probably have to sign escrow papers for me and that I'll send a power of attorney to allow her to do that. She agreed and said that they'll be glad to have me near them. "Do you realize everything is cheaper here? Seniors over sixty-five don't pay school taxes."

We talked about what needs to be done at the Smyrna home and what I'm doing to spruce up my Camarillo condo. "You amaze me, Mom. I hope I have your energy when I'm your age."

Lexie said Aunt Wilma is fine and enjoying the entertainment the facility provides every Friday afternoon. "It's so good that Stephen and I both go. Last week three women with fabulous voices sang oldie tunes, and a gentleman accompanied them on the piano. One of the women had been crowned Ms. Senior Georgia and sang a Patsy Cline song, 'I Fall to Pieces.' Every time she sang the words 'I fall to pieces,' something fell off her, such as her shawl, her wig, false teeth, fake arm. When the song ended, she hobbled off the stage to thundering applause."

"Weren't you in the Ms. Senior California contest, Mom? Isn't that the one you placed third runner-up in?"

"I was, but I didn't sing. I read a humorous essay."

After hanging up, I finished my coffee and drove to the audiologist's offices for Wanda's hearing aids and then delivered them to her. Wanda said her doctor took chest X-rays because she's having difficulty breathing. While pulling a chair next to the bed, a nurse came in and handed me a surgical mask. "Better put this on. We've had some flu encounters."

After placing the hearing aids in her ears, Wanda said she's hearing much better.

I told Wanda I think she's sick a lot because the hospital sends patients recovering from diseases and illnesses to this nursing home, so there's a lot of interaction with sick people. "Other nursing homes care strictly for the residents of the home—no intermixing of sick patients."

When Kurt called that evening, I told him about my visit with Wanda. He said, "You mean she's serious about moving to Madison? What changed her mind?"

I said that her husband's sister plans to move to an assisted living facility near her son; and since Wanda has always been fond of Lily, she's counting on their being friends again.

"Tell me how your visit with your son and his wife is going?"

Kurt said he's having a good time and that he'll drop some pictures in the mail for me. "We went to a party tonight that Barb's boss hosted. Lots of good food. I'll have to work extra hard at the gym when I get back home."

"I think I'm getting another cold; I've been sneezing all afternoon." I told Kurt about the sick patients Wanda's nursing home is accepting for treatment and rehabilitation and that's why Wanda is sick, and I always have a cold.

"You better take care of yourself, my lovely, because I'll want to kiss you when I arrive, and I don't want your cold. Can you give it to someone else? I reckon you can show me a few more places before you relocate. The sight-seeing has been enjoyable. And our sexual encounters are flawless, we talk freely, love to hold hands, and we both are seeking cultural experiences. We need to touch more skin and find out more about one another. So far I love what I see."

"Oh, yes. I sent you a card the other day. I liked the message. Did you get it?"

I said I hadn't.

"Know that I love you, darling, and I'll call you tomorrow."

I sat on the sofa with Moxie, pondering our conversation. It was full of love and promise, but I felt it a bit odd that he didn't say Doug and Barb want to meet me, or that he spoke to them about our relationship. Our love seems as strong as ever, but something is missing. Oh, well, he'd just arrived that afternoon. Perhaps he didn't get a chance to tell them about me.

The next morning the mailman brought the card. A picture of an old guy cutting the lawn was on the front, and inside were the words: "I like you better than beer on a hot summer day."

It was a cute card. I'd cleared the day to work on my novel, and as I was finishing Chapter Twenty, Kurt called. I said I got the card and that I love him more than licorice. I said something in the card mentioned a loving Dad, and I told him that the card fit him perfectly and it also fit my wonderful Dad. "Because of him and my grandpap, I thought all men were nice; but I found out later that wasn't true, except for you, that is. As to our ages, there are advantages to being eighty, like not wondering what your boyfriend will look like when he gets old."

"Or not wondering whether your wife will look like her mother."

"If that's the criteria, guys should have been pounding on my door. My mother was very pretty. Did I ever tell you my dad was Chief of the Tiltonsville Volunteer Fire Department for about ten years when my brother and I were kids? When the whistle blew at a time other than nine in the evening, Dad would jump into his old pants and was gone."

"Uncle Pete belonged to the fire department, but I don't know whether it was when your dad belonged. They must have known one another. My uncle was born on June 18, 1903."

"That's when my dad was born. Isn't that crazy?"

"I'm sure they didn't know this," Kurt said.

"I thought it was funny that you said you pee-a-lot. Information about regularity is especially important at our age. In fact, I think you should know I crap twice every morning." Kurt roared. "I'm of German royalty, and we don't crap."

"I've always heard the German elite are full of shit."

"Is this my little Eva, or is someone else on the phone with us?"

"I'm multifaceted. Is this the first time you've noticed?"

"I guess I didn't pay attention to the signs earlier."

"I'm actually trying to determine whether we're compatible. I'm starting to read our astrological signs in case they reveal things about us that we don't know and should know. Nancy Reagan followed hers religiously and didn't let Ronnie set appointments if the signs weren't lined up. And look at the long life and great marriage they had."

"I've never studied the astrological signs, so I can't say whether they're accurate. I usually follow my gut."

"I used to do that. But now I look at both sides of an issue first and then follow my gut."

"You're one of a kind, Eva, and one of the most interesting women I've ever known. Don't change, my darling. I still savor those pic-taking scenes at your place in December. Wasn't that fun? I've never done that sort of thing with anybody before. However, I don't know what to do with those pics now. I can't cut them up, yet I wouldn't want my sons to see them."

"Let's just enjoy the pictures. I think we'll be around for at least another ten years."

"As good as we're both feeling, I'd say we have another twenty years together—maybe longer since we're energizing one another."

I told Kurt I'd refinished my kitchen cabinets and am now painting the kitchen walls. "I plan to put my home on the market the end of March."

"Sounds like a good plan. But I don't like you working that hard."

"It's no problem because I enjoy renovating homes." I told him about Susan and I buying a home together about twenty years ago that she and the grandkids lived in for two years. We painted the inside and outside and did some redecorating, mostly in the kitchen and bathrooms, and we each made a profit of $29,000. She and her fiancé bought a large home together, and they each put in $29,000 for a total down payment of $58,000. They lost it when the 1991 earthquake struck which did so much damage to their house that they just walked away from it."

"How sad. Couldn't they have fixed it up and then sold it?"

"It would have cost more than the $58,000 they'd invested in order to repair the damage, and they would still have a mortgage to pay off."

"I guess it makes sense to walk if you still have a hefty mortgage."

"I won't worry about earthquakes in Georgia, but that state has lots of tornadoes."

"I wonder if they sell tornado insurance in Georgia?" Kurt asked.

"I'll find out soon enough," I replied.

"Well, lover, I'll hang up now. I must spend time with my kids. Sleep well. I love you."

* * * * *

While sipping my coffee the next morning, I thought about my phone conversations with Kurt while he's been visiting his family. It's obvious that our connection is deep;

but it bothers me that he doesn't say his kids are eager to meet me or that they send their regards. I should perhaps consider that they might not be curious about me and have decided that they aren't interested in meeting me. I hope that isn't the case, but what other explanation can there be? Time will tell, I mused, and I'd just have to be patient and see what the future unfolds.

Chapter Sixteen

Kurt called every night when he was in Maryland. Last night, Kurt said he'd head back to Ohio in the morning. I wrote him a note and enclosed a new love poem, 'Master of My Heart.' I love Kurt's poem, 'Twilight,' and hope he'll get a tug of emotion when reading this poem.

After copying James Wright's two poems, I put them in the packet. It's interesting to read poems by a local poet about his take on local events and familiar sights and then compare your sense of the same events and sights, which can be entirely different. It's no wonder eyewitness testimony about the same incident often differs.

I also enclosed a recent picture of me with my daughter and granddaughter. Since Kurt had met them, I thought he'd enjoy the picture. I hope the pictures he sent of his youngest son and wife would show up in today's mail. He said he'd mailed them several days ago.

I told him my sore throat had gotten worse and that I'd started taking Echinacea and Golden Seal, a non-prescription medication that usually helped if I started taking it early enough. "In any case, I'll be well by the time you make it to California."

"Do you think you can rope me and ride me and stay on me for longer than twenty minutes?" I asked. "I'm glad you're working out so you can keep up with me. Remember, it's been my pattern to associate only with much younger guys. In your case, however, I made an exception because of your searing kisses and tight abs.

"The only way you'll get me back in snow country would be for you to do all the things you fantasized about me doing for you. Even with all that, you'll have to up the ante. You forget that I'm not the little innocent Eva Sandor any longer—I'm a sophisticated lady who drives in the fast lane. Which one do you love, Cowboy?

"I'm also eager to visit you in Ohio, but when the weather gets warmer. I'd love to go to Wheeling Park. A couple years ago when I was in Ohio, I saw an albino alligator at the Wheeling Park Zoo. His alligator eyes were mesmerizing, and he almost taunted me into his cage. Gotta go and clean the house. AML. Your California flower."

When I got to the mailbox, the mailman was there. I handed him my packet, and he handed me some junk mail along with a letter from Kurt. I hurriedly walked back home and opened the letter to find a picture of Doug and Barb along with her adult daughter, and a few other pictures taken at the party. Kurt said Doug had married Barb when Laura was only three years old, and she's now twenty. She looks a lot like her mother. Pretty, with soft features, black hair and blue eyes. Kurt said Doug is six feet one, a large guy with bulky shoulders and big hands. His head is shaved, as Kurt had mentioned. I think Doug looks good with the bald head. *So this is Kurt's family.* I look at the pictures again. Doug resembles his mother, I think. I remember Kurt saying that although he and Pam had tried to bond with Laura, she always held herself aloof from them. He said that Doug is very jovial and well-liked by his colleagues.

Laura had a pensive look on her face, and Barb wore a half-smile and looked approachable. I look at the pictures taken at the party with Kurt holding a glass and mingling. *A good-looking stud.* I place the pictures on my dining room table and read Kurt's letter.

"Dear Chocolate Eyes,

"I hope your cold is gone and that you're done painting. Wish I could have been there to help. But I will help you with whatever when I see you in February. A whole week? I must be growing on you. The 'Magic Castle' sounds like fun. Hell, just being with you is fun. What do you get by crossing a rooster with an owl? You get a cock that stays up all night. (This is your stand-up comedian speaking.) (Now, this is your lover speaking.) What do you call a Jewish homosexual? He-blew. What do you call an Irish homo? Gay-lick. What do you call a Chinese homo? Chew-man-chew. I just can't help it.

"I'm almost finished with Burt Prelutsky's book, *Liberals: America's Termites.* I like his style of writing, but I'll have to seek out a book that counters Burt's views.

"Our time is ever closer, and the fever increasing. Have you noticed the unusual intensity of heat between us? It will last, my love. Until tomorrow.

"Ready to go, Cowboy Kurt."

I giggled as I placed the letter back in its envelope, and I look at the picture of Doug and Barb again. They are a good-looking couple, and I can't wait to meet them.

* * * * *

Nancy, my BFF, had called last night to see if I could meet her for lunch today, and I agreed. I needed a break from my painting project.

I brushed my hair, applied lipstick, kissed my cat, and was on my way. Nancy and I are meeting halfway between our homes at the 'Spitfire Grill.' When I arrive, Nancy is parking her car, and I pull up alongside her. About five feet five, she has an athletic build, and short, sassy, reddish-brown hair. Her hazel eyes are both expressive and playful. She looks like someone's best friend. We hug and joke as we enter the restaurant.

Nancy is a good friend and shows it. When I was elected president of our club this second time, Nancy accepted the office of treasurer, one of the most difficult offices because of the spreadsheets and having to report income and expenses to the Central Board.

After making changes to the by-laws, our discussion turned personal. I told her of my deep feelings for Kurt, and she said she and Brad think Kurt is a really nice guy and they're happy for us. She'd gotten the tickets to the 'Magic Castle,' and she expressed sadness that I'd be moving; but she understood my wanting to live closer to my oldest daughter.

She said her daughter Kaye and her husband would like her and Brad to move to Northern California to be closer to them, and she and Brad talk about it frequently. "But when we think about leaving our church and our friends here, it's a tough decision. Eventually, we'll move up to Northern California," she said wistfully.

Nancy asked if there's a writer's club in Atlanta, but I said I thought it was closer to Augusta. "I'll have to check out how far it is as I don't like driving farther than ten miles."

"I don't, either. Now, tell me about your house," she asked.

"It's a three bedroom, two-bath brick home with hardwood floors throughout. And it's on an acre of land with a large fig tree and blueberry bushes." I pulled out a picture to show her.

Nancy said it looks like a charming ranch-style home.

Our get-together made for a very pleasant day. On my way home, I stopped at The Home Depot and bought chrome handles for my kitchen cabinet doors.

That evening I sent Kurt a short email thanking him for the pictures of him and his son and family. I said he'd described them very well, and that Kurt looks like a hunk. I said I'd bought chrome handles for my cabinet doors that my handyman would install. "I have other plans for you." I told him about meeting Nancy for lunch and said Nancy and Brad think he's a nice guy. I told him that Nancy got tickets for the Magic Castle and that my poem follows. "I hope you like it. Well, I better close now. Moxie is enticing me to play with him. ILU. Eva."

MASTER OF MY HEART

You are the master of my heart
Methinks we'll never, ever part
My love for you is like fine art
I'm your Bacall, you're my Bogart

You're quite accomplished—first-class
The jokes you tell, I can't surpass
Just treat me tender, do not harass
Or you won't know what hit your ass

My dreams came true, you're the guy I adore
You're all I want, and even more
I don't care if you're rich or poor
And to think you were the boy next door

Your kisses cast me under a spell
They're sweeter than creamy caramel
Without you I'm only half a shell
Together we're hotter than a day in hell.

After having my morning coffee, I turned on my computer and found an email from Kurt.

"Dear Hungarian Gypsy:
"First, I love your poem, 'Master of My Heart.' I labeled it and put it in a file cabinet next to my desk. It's a very moving poem, and

I appreciate it. Also, thank you for the picture of you, your daughter, and granddaughter. Now I'm in love with three women."

"As to both Evas, I love them both. And I'll have little trouble roping and riding you. But for only twenty minutes? I'm sure you'll reconsider after the twenty minutes are up. I'm doing fifty push-ups a day and am going back to the gym today. I have never had such upper-body strength than I have now, and I intend to squeeze the sophistication out of you, and you'll ride in the slow lane hereafter. Thanks for the Richard Wright poetry. I found the pieces interesting and weird, knowing some of the sites he wrote about.

"I got home to four inches of snow with another three inches to come. I love to arise to snow and cold weather in the mornings. I like to hop in my 4-wheel and go for coffee and a breakfast roll. Winter lets us know who's boss and there's nothing we can do about it.

"But not liking snow country? Come on, you pussy cat. I don't know how much longer I can take this long-distance relationship. I need you now. Till death do us part. P. S. I know we talked about you being in charge of the kitchen and me being in charge of the bedroom, but I've changed my mind. You are in charge of the bedroom. ILUL. Kurt."

That P.S. got my blood boiling, and I sat down at my computer and wrote:

TOP SECURITY – NEVER TO BE
RELEASED TO VIRGIN EARS

"Dear Major Miller:

This letter is to put you on notice that if you fail to carry out your duties as you were elected fairly and judiciously to be Boss of the Bedroom, you will be furloughed for 60 days from Madam Sandor's queen-sized bed and enrolled in Salsa Dancing Classes.

1. It is unconscionable, after receiving such a high honor, that you are now asking to be relieved of that duty, and with no explanation. Sir, as a former Major in the Military, you must realize you do not have the authority to change your orders once they have been published.

2. How can you expect a 118-pound lady with a 1-ounce vagina to maneuver you around the bed, especially when she's already on guard keeping the cat out of the bed?

3. How many jobs can you expect this tiny, almost virgin, to take on when you have one job, to make her climax?

4. If you will remember, the first time you were on duty in Camarillo to please Madam Sandor, you were very careless and cracked one of her ribs. That dereliction of duty is in your personnel file. She has asked us to remind you that you are a 180-pound sex-

starved tiger in the bedroom, and she is but a lonely, misunderstood nymphomaniac.

5. Also in your personnel file is a letter from Master Moxie that he wasn't given the proper treatment that royalty of Himalayan descent should receive while you visited.

6. Madam Sandor's main concern is that she wouldn't be able to lift your legs and put them around her neck, which is a routine act of love-making.

7. Madam Sandor is further concerned that if she were to do so, your legs would be so heavy that she would either end up with a broken neck or your pecker would be permanently embedded in her face.

8. I am sure you know, and we are totally convinced, that Madam Sandor is a lady with the highest of reputation and social graces but she'd like to be a slut in the bedroom with you, Major Miller. So go for it and quityourbitchin, you horny bastard. General Petraeus."

I couldn't stop laughing as I signed it General Petraeus and pushed the Send button.

* * * * *

That evening the following email arrived from Kurt.

"Your letter about bedroom propriety is well received. Please forgive me for attempting to delegate my responsibility in this matter. In the military, one could delegate authority, but not responsibility. You seem to have learned this somewhere, quite to my surprise. OK, command reverts back to the Major. Your letter is the funniest piece of writing I have read in a long time, and I laughed till my pecker hurt. You have a unique way of displaying your intellect without damaging the relationship. Physically, I can win every time, but intellectually, that will be a battle.

"I visited Joe and Marla today. Marla and Deena thank you for copies of your novel, and Marla was happy you signed her copy. Joe and Marla are superior people and I'm fortunate to have them as friends. They are looking forward to meeting you.

"I have a feeling Wanda will move to Madison and live happily ever after. I enjoyed meeting her. What a mind for ninety-six, and such an upbeat attitude.

"I will call you tomorrow evening, and I'll also write you another love poem. Sleep well, my darling. The only man you'll ever need. Kurt. P.S. URTSLAIT."

I spent the next day putting together Wanda's income tax papers as she'd asked me to do and I delivered them to her accountant. She'd given me a Power of Attorney several years ago when she'd had an emergency appendectomy, and she wanted me to keep it.

I drove to the nursing home, and Wanda thanked me for taking care of her income taxes.

She said her cold is about gone, and her doctor told her she'll most likely be released within a month. "So, I've got to make my decision soon where I'll be living," she said reticently.

Chapter Seventeen

I'd just finished washing my hair and decided to call Lexie to ask about my aunt. She answered on the second ring and said Aunt Wilma is fine, except for her hearing.

"That's why I quit calling her," I said.

"She's happy, so don't worry about her. The activities director has devised a game for the wheelchair patients that Aunt Wilma loves. They all sit in a circle in their wheelchairs and take turns bouncing a large ball to one another. Aunt Wilma always catches the ball and bounces it within reach of another patient. Then once a day an aide has her walk up and down the hallway with her pushing her own wheelchair which helps with her balance and confidence."

"I'm so glad she likes the activities."

"Before I forget, Reggie. from Williams Home Inspection, finished the inspection. He spent three hours and listed nineteen items that need replaced or serviced."

"I just hope the seller fixes everything."

"I'm sure Shelly will work it out," Lexie said.

"Not to change the subject, but I have a feeling Kurt will give me an engagement ring for Valentine's Day."

"What makes you say that?"

"His past couple of emails have mentioned a ring of fire, which is out of context with what he's talking about."

"Do you plan to give him a gift?"

"I wish I could think of something funny to give him."

"What about a toe ring?"

I thought about his painted toenails and laughed. "Where would I get one?"

"At any novelty shop. I've seen expandable ones on elastic."

"That sounds perfect. I'll look around."

I told Lexie that my kitchen cabinets are done and the almond color of the cabinets matches the appliances perfectly. "I'm making café valances now to hang over my kitchen windows."

"You're so good at decorating, Mom. I'm sure your California home will sell fast."

"How are Kurt and Moxie doing?"

"Moxie warmed up to Kurt since Kurt spars with him. He even sleeps in Kurt's suitcase."

"Stephen rode by your Smyrna house the other day and identified the trees that are diseased. One is a pecan tree."

"Oh, no. I absolutely love pecans."

"You can always plant another one. We can hardly wait for the escrow to close so we can start cleaning up the yards. The house has been vacant for three years and needs a lot of work."

"I appreciate everything you and Stephen are doing."

"Of course. Stephen wants to remove the stove and shut off the gas at the main line. Then you could go all electric. Let us know if that's okay. I gotta go and make dinner. Love you."

I decided to work on my novel, but I checked my emails first. One was from Kurt.

"Today my brother Richard called to say that he and his wife Sharleen will be driving from Pennsylvania to visit me tomorrow. Richard is actually my half-brother. I also have a half-sister

Frieda. My parents divorced back in 1931, and later dad got remarried and had Richard and Frieda. When my brother and I were born, our father wasn't ready to be a father. In later years, he found the handle and went on to be a great dad to Richard and Frieda. Son Doug and wife Barb are at their cabin now, and I'm trying to contact Doug to see if he can meet an uncle he's never seen.

"Over the years I saw little of my father, but I visited him when I had the chance. He passed away in 1970, and his second wife is also gone. The song of time is sweet to ponder. Get your affairs in order, honey, and let's start living fast and hard, preferably together. 'Time goes, you say? Ah no! Alas, time stays, we go.' Austin Dobson."

My response:

"Dear Silver Fox,

"Thanks for the info about you. How else can I find out about my guy's early life? I look forward to receiving the pics of your family.

"After being so protective of my vagina, I hop into bed with you on our fourth date. Never been sorry; but it's more than the sex, my dear.

"One side of me enjoys manual labor, like painting and decorating, and the other side gets totally absorbed in writing. Then my third side loves to connect with people—I guess it's my nurturer side, and that's why I enjoyed being a hospice volunteer. Did I ever tell you I'd been born with a veil on? That happens in only one in a million births. Dr. Slenitzar told my mom that and also said I could end up being a psychic. Isn't that wild? If I were psychic, I wouldn't have picked the men I did. In the past, that is.

"I think I told you my mom came from a large family – five boys and three girls. Since Mom was the eldest daughter, she had lots of chores to do for her siblings. She told me she only wanted one child and was happy when my brother arrived. She said I was an accident, and she laughed. I hope she was joking because she was a good mother. She made me gorgeous clothes from patterns that I chose; but she rarely showed affection. I think it's a generational thing. holding one's self aloof.

"As for my Smyrna home, Lexie said the inspector is a friend of a friend of Stephen's, and he even listed the furnace, which is twenty years' old. I don't think the seller will pay for a new one since it's putting out heat.

"I have to sign off to prepare for our writer's club meeting Saturday. Our speaker sent a list of requirements for his presentation. Long tables for people to write on, a power-point set-up, and a large screen. I sent the requirements to Ray. Besides being editor of the newsletter, he's also the moderator for our presenters. This week it's

Dan Poynter, the guru of self-published books, so I imagine we'll have a huge crowd.

"I love you like crazy. Your feral cat."

In the morning, the following email arrived from Kurt:

"Dear Ms. Kitty Poo,

"I enjoyed your newsy letter and was surprised to hear there are three people living in your body. Ye gads, you mean I have been trying to satisfy three women?

"Yes, we came together on our fourth date, but it wasn't as if we were strangers. Since the time you came of age, I waited sixty-two years before enjoying your womanhood; and I must confess it was worth the wait. There is more than sex about us, but I am so eager to make love with you again. No woman has thrilled me like you have.

"So you were an accident, eh? I guess I was too. My parents didn't get married until after I was conceived. Right from the git go, I was an aggressive sperm. The second that my father released me, I headed for the egg. I made my way down the canal, past the left ovary, and under something that seemed to look back at me. I thought I was lost, but then I saw all the other sperm rushing in a different direction, and then I knew that it was they who were lost. I hit the egg wiggling flat out and dug in for the next nine months. I often wonder what happened to all of my fellow sperm.

"At this point in life, there isn't much left to complicate matters. No young children, we're healthy, no debt, decent income, grew up together, and ready for that final relation-ship. Since I've rediscovered you, I'm in splendid repose. Do with me what you will.

"You asked if I had worked while I lived with my aunt and uncle. Yes, I worked at the Belot Block Co. on three different occasions. That job gave me my first experience at working the midnight shift. It also taught me that I'd damn well get my act together if I wanted to avoid the drudgery of life. I respect anyone who works, no matter what the job may be, but young Kurt harbored other ideas. I also worked in the Yorkville Steel Plant for almost two years in the clerical end of things before going to college. Yes, it was my uncle who got me the jobs, but I did the best work possible.

"Since the time I was five years old, I wanted to be a pilot. I don't fly much anymore, but aviation will never get out of my blood. The first aircraft instrument I learned about was the altimeter. This tells the pilot how high he is off the ground. One day in grade school, I asked my teacher what the altimeter would do if I landed on a high mountain. 'Would it go back to zero?' She didn't know but promised that she'd find out and tell me. She never did get the answer for me.

So, there you have it. Airplanes are in my blood. Next time I'll have to tell you about the plane I built.

"I'll call you tomorrow evening. Sleep well, my dear. AYS. Kurt."

My response:

"Dear Love-of-my-Life,

"Have I told you how I admire your tenacity for knowing you wanted to be a pilot and made sure it happened? We come from similar backgrounds and have the same passion for love and life. But the main turn-on for me is the way you make me feel.

"Bye now. I'll tell you about the seminar later. Funny stuff about your pushy sperm."

After reviewing Wanda's water bill, which was very high, I walked through the back lawns to her home. Water was dripping from a broken pipe in her main bathroom. I called a local handyman who came in half an hour and fixed it. He suggested pulling up the wet tile and replacing it. He also said her condo needs painting and new appliances and that he'd prepare an itemized statement of labor, material, and new appliances, and leave it in my door.

When I returned from running errands, I found the estimate and drove to the nursing home. I brought Wanda up-to-date about getting the pipe fixed and handed Wanda the itemized list that the handyman prepared. Wanda sucked in her breath as she reviewed it and approved of installing new tile in both bathrooms only, saying she wanted to sell her condo 'as is.'

I said she'd probably get more money for her condo if she did the repairs and purchased new appliances, but she shook her head. I slipped the estimate in my purse in case a potential buyer would like to know what renovations would cost. Then I headed back home.

I was just finishing dinner when Kurt called. He said he mailed the pictures of his half-brother and his wife. "The visit went very well. Doug just missed meeting his uncle for the first time when he and Barb had to start back home early.

"Richard and I have our father's voice and sense of humor. Years ago my father told me his land was so poor, when the crows flew over, they carried their own nap-sacks to survive. Our father died when the second stroke took him down."

"I'm glad you had a nice visit," I said. I told him about Wanda's broken pipe and the handyman's suggestion to upgrade her appliances and to paint the interior of her condo. However, she wants to sell 'as is'."

"She'd sell it much faster if it's in good condition," Kurt said, "but it's her decision."

"I love your poem, 'Master of My Heart.' It told our story in a very funny way. Kudos to you, Eva. I'm also starting a new love poem for you. And I have a present that you'll like, but I'll bring it with me when I see you. Since we got together, I'm more aware of my writing and reading efforts. You are doing this guy a lot of good in life. Thanks, little one."

"You're welcome. Since you've been working out at the gym, I've been working out with five-pound weights and jogging on my treadmill. I find it boring, but I feel it's important to challenge my heart. But that's a task you should assume, don't you think?"

"I'd be delighted to take on that chore."

"Also, I don't want to get stuck with doing everything in this relationship – we need to balance out the work. Think about it. Do you prefer cleaning the bathrooms, mopping the kitchen, or shaving my legs?"

"Shaving your legs just might turn me on, so I'll take that task. Also, I could unfasten your bra and help you out of your panties. If you can think of anything else, pile it on me."

I could tell Kurt was enjoying this banter by the lilt in his voice.

"Do you realize the countdown is getting near zero, and I'll soon be able to hug you?"

"Oh, by the way, could you send me a moustache of some of your unwanted hair? I think that would be so neat."

"Sure can. And can you send a postcard soaked in your after-shave lotion for Moxie?"

"'ll mail it tomorrow, and I'll finish my poem tonight. Sweet dreams, honey. I love you."

Kurt would be here in three days, but we continued to email one another. I sent him one thanking him for the pics of his half-brother and wife. "I see no resemblance, but you say you both got your dad's sense of humor. So glad you did because you keep me entertained."

"Too bad Doug didn't get to meet his Uncle Richard. I love hooking up with relatives and old friends. Don't you wonder how I'll fit in with your sons and their wives? I can report that two mothers-in-law and I have been very tight. Wesley's parents also approved of me. They were lovely people, and I considered them family.

"I'm so glad you survived the war, Major Kurt. The Lord kept you alive for a purpose. Just hope you can survive our relationship. If so, I'd like to write a book about our love: 'Falling in Love after Eighty?' 'I Knew Her Before She was a Nympho and Stole My Heart,' 'We're Seniors, Crazy in Love, and I Have a Cracked Rib to Prove it,' or 'Last of the Red Hot Lovers.' I need a title before writing, so help me out."

Soon after sending my email, one arrived from Kurt saying he likes 'Last of the Red Hot Lovers.'

Since it was still early evening, I drove to the novelty shop on Poinsettia Drive to look for a toe ring. Sure enough, they had one that absolutely fit to perfection the one I had in mind for Kurt. It had fake sparkly sapphires all around a piece of glass that looked like a diamond. It was hooked to a piece of elastic. I recalled having an elegant velvet ring box at home and this $5.99 toe ring would look very expensive in it. I also bought a cute valentine and laughed heartily as I walked out of the novelty shop.

Chapter Eighteen

It had rained last night, leaving a gloomy overcast appearance that transcended into my thoughts and feelings. The kitchen was cool, and I pulled my robe tight. While sipping my coffee, I thought about my relationship with Kurt. It seemed natural and right, but I couldn't help wondering how his sons felt about me. Kurt's response when I asked was to say they were loyal sons and would accept me. Duh. He never said they were curious about me or wanted to meet me. Since we're not planning to marry soon, I tried to shrug off my trepidations.

As far as my family is concerned, they like Kurt; but I know they'll feel better by my having a ring on my finger to assure them that this isn't merely a shack-up relationship.

I was relatively sure I'd be getting a ring for Valentine's Day since Kurt had said he had a present for me that he knew I'd like.

Placing my cup in the sink, I thought I'd better get busy on the moustache Kurt had requested. Standing over the toilet, I cut pubic hairs and placed them in a paper cup. To my surprise, some hairs were about three inches long. That was great since I wanted to make a nice, full moustache for Kurt. Sifting through my office drawers, I found a two-inch wide package of scotch tape that was sticky on both sides, and I shaped a piece of it into a grand, curved moustache. Next, I placed lots of the public hairs on the scotch tape and pressed them firmly in place. I held the moustache over my lips and stood in awe. I wasn't sure whether Kurt was expecting hairs from my head, but I knew he wouldn't be disappointed with this moustache.

Wrapping tissue paper around the moustache, I put it in a business-size manila envelope, scratched Kurt's name and address on it and ran to the mailbox. The mailman was pulling away, but he stopped to get the envelope. Taking the mail from the box, I trotted home.

The brochure arrived from the Madison Assisted Living facility, and after reading it, I drove to the nursing home to review it with Wanda. She was sitting up in bed and excited to see me. I read portions of the brochure to her.

"Sally said there are different levels of care, and I may start out at Level 3 rather than Level 1, and that would be fine. Sally also said there are lots of activities for wheelchair patients. And the facility has entertainment every Friday like at your Aunt Wilma's facility."

"The place sounds lovely," I said.

"You know, Eva, I walk daily using my walker, and I feel stronger every day. I won't be in this wheelchair forever."

"That's such good news, Wanda. And look what else I have for you," I said, handing her a thin, glossy book.

"My goodness. An autobiography of Jerry Vale. You know how I love him." Her eyes twinkled as she thanked me.

"He's my favorite singer, also. I got his book for myself and plan to read it tonight."

I told Wanda that Kurt will be visiting over Valentine's Day, and that I'm very excited about the prospect of seeing him again. "We'll stop by for a visit while he's here."

"You two seem so right together," she said.

I told her about my plan to give him a toe ring, and we both giggled.

When I got home, Moxie was sitting on a kitchen chair. I petted him and gave him a plate of Fancy Feast chicken cat food. Then I warmed up some left-over bean soup and cut myself a thick slice of French bread. After dinner, I checked my emails and found one from Kurt.

"Dear Miss Jefferson County,

"While I write these letters, every now and then I sneak a smell of your perfume. Your sweet face comes into view instantly. You must send me another hanky soaked with your perfume because the one I have is about void of scent.

"Did you crap twice this morning? I must get a picture of this operation. Then my scrapbook will be complete. Giggle, giggle. You are a complete woman, you are.

"The countdown is getting near zero, and it will be nice to hug you again. Your panties are in my pillowcase, under my head. I wonder how many guys keep their lover's panties so close. I peek at your drawers every morning. What a way to start the day.

"I ran into your friend Grace at Mehlman's Cafeteria last night. After she told me who she is, I remembered her. She said your friendship has been ongoing since you were both in junior high. She thinks a lot of you, my dear.

"I'm really looking forward to seeing you and loving you.

"Tons of love. Starving Major."

My response.

"Dear Hungry One,

"I'm happy you got to spend time with Grace. We go back a long way. She's the friend who told me that Ned cheated with her sister. She has two daughters about the same ages as my daughters, and they took tap-dancing lessons together as children. I visited with her eldest daughter a month before she died, and I'm thankful for that. She was forty-seven when she died of cancer. How sad for a child to die before a parent.

"I got the Inspection Report on my Smyrna home. There are nineteen tagged issues, but the seller agreed to fix all of them. What a relief! Lexie said there's no popcorn ceilings. I guess nobody noticed until yesterday.

"Lexie and Stephen can't wait until the escrow closes as they want to remove a pecan tree in the backyard that's diseased and leaning towards the neighbor's house. The neighbor is so appreciative, he's going to help. I'm upset because I love pecans.

"Lexie plans to prune my bushes; she learned how from a neighbor who is a master pruner. My daughters are so clever and resourceful, I'm constantly amazed.

"Well, I've got to close and finish getting ready for the meeting Saturday. We're having an open discussion before the speaker makes his presentation. We'll discuss what the members like about our club and what we can do to improve upon to help members market their works. My sinuses are still plugged up, but the show must go on.

"Remember, next week you'll be arriving at U.S. Airways Terminal 'N' like in Nike.

"I love you bushels. Your sophisticated pussycat.

"P.S. I looked at the pictures of your bedroom again and don't see a bulge in your pillowcase. So, where's the proof my panties are in there? I must say it was very clever of you to put my picture in a frame and place it on your dresser before you took the pic of your bedroom. Very clever indeed. AML. Your Eva."

I was still at the computer when Kurt's email arrived.

"Dear Miss Sophisticated Kitty,

"Okay. I understand that I will report to Terminal 'N.' But what is this Nike stuff? If you are going to pal around with this old military guy, you need to be familiar with the military alphabet. In the case of 'N,' it is November, not Nike. Cheez! I am Tango Sierra, and you are Echo Alpha. When radio communications are bad, using the phonetic letters usually saves the day. I had to use this form of communication many times.

"I got the pictures of your writer's club officers, and they are really good. You look beautiful, as usual. Boy, that blond-headed vice president sure is tall.

"As you and I march on together, you will probably learn more about me, and I about you. My Uncle Pete would often tell people that I'm a very good young man, which made me feel as if I was really wanted. So, here's to Uncle Pete. He was the supervisor of the Tin Line at the Yorkville plant. He was an excellent man, and I still miss him. He and Aunt Thelma didn't have children of their own, so I served in that capacity with pride.

"Yes, your panties are in my pillow – they are too small to make a bulge in the pillowcase. But something else bulges when I touch them.

"Good news that the repairs on your Smyrna home will be absorbed by the seller, and that you don't have to deal with scraping popcorn off the ceiling. Too bad about the pecan tree; but my nuts are healthy and available any time.

"I hope you have a good meeting tomorrow, and I look forward to holding hands with you very soon.

"Love in the rain. Tango Sierra."

After reading the email, I closed my eyes and relaxed a minute. In a few days, Kurt will be here. I struggled to put thoughts of him on the back burner while I reviewed the agenda. Our members have a lot to discuss before Poynter gives his two-hour presentation. He's considered the guru of self-publishing and is in great demand, having published fifty books.

Before going to bed, I sent Kurt an email, telling him to be on the lookout for his moustache. I also asked him what his favorite foods are. I mentioned that I make a killer chili, barbequed ribs, and bean soup. I said I was hitting the sack early because I need to be alert for the meeting tomorrow. "I love you more than Chianti," I wrote, and signed it 'Echo Alpha.'

The next night, after the meeting, Kurt called. He said he'd bought a new color cartridge to print the photos I'd sent him several weeks ago of the two of us. He said he'd attach a copy as a background page on his computer, put one in his car, one in the rec room, and one in his bedroom. "I sure do look forward to receiving your daily sugar reports. Keeps life interesting."

"I also love receiving your emails," I replied.

"Say, better hold off on the bean soup. A guy and his wife are sitting on a train together, when all of a sudden the man in front of them farts. The man with his wife gets to his feet and says, 'How dare you fart before my wife.' The other guy says, 'How did I know your wife wanted to fart first?' Heh, heh, heh. I got a million of them. You cook it and I'll eat it."

"That is a funny one. I'll have to remember it."

"Now for a downer. Yesterday morning I watched a car burn while I sipped my coffee, looking out the window at Panera's. I could see that the damage would not buff out. Hey, a burning car in these parts is big news."

"You sure live the good life," I remarked. "I usually make myself a small pot of decaf and eat oatmeal with raisins and nuts every morning while relaxing in my robe and slippers. If I had a goodie every day, I'd be a roly-poly."

"No, you wouldn't. I'd work it off of you. Heh, heh, heh."

"Earlier this morning Doug and I enjoyed breakfast at the club. He's home this weekend for deer hunting. I talked to him about you. Doug and Ron are okay with anything I do. They are good sons."

"That's good to hear," I said. But my inner self got annoyed. I don't want his sons to just be okay with my relationship with their dad. I want them to accept me for being a good person. I wondered whether Kurt told them anything about me, such as raising two daughters by myself that turned out very well. Or of my putting myself through college when in my fifties? I wonder whether Kurt painted a picture of me that would help them like me? I wonder whether they are curious about me. All I ever get from Kurt is that they are okay with the situation. I guess it's possible that Kurt just wants us to meet and hopes we all get along.

As I was busy musing, Kurt kept talking. "On the walking track at the gym, I come up with good ideas for poems. Poem-writing is such a wonderful outlet. 'When lovely woman stoops to folly and finds too late that men betray.' That's the first line of a poem, 'Lovely Woman,' written by Oliver Goldsmith. The poem is so true to life."

"Did I ever tell you that I entered a poem in Eddie Lou Cole's poetry contest, and I won a 'Golden Poet Award,' and I was promised a trophy if I attended the convention set in Florida? The title of my poem is 'Together.' It's about a wart I had when I was a young girl."

"Funny you should mention Eddie Lou Cole. I also entered a poem in her contest years ago titled 'Meadow Sentry.' I'd love to read your wart poem, and I'll send you a copy of mine."

"That's a deal. By any chance did you have to pay for a copy of the poetry book before your poem would be published?" I asked.

"Yes, I did. That kind of put a damper on receiving the award, didn't it?' Kurt asked.

"Now to bed, my darling. Tomorrow is the final day for me to organize my trip plans. Sleep tight. A lot of long nights may be ahead for us, if we're lucky. Just call me Sleepless in St. Clairsville. I love you more than dark chocolate."

* * * * *

The next evening, Kurt called. He said he wished he'd made his flight reservations earlier so he could have attended the meeting. "Remember when I attended the writer's club meeting when Burt Prelutsky was the speaker, and I bought his book?"

"Yeh, how could I forget. He's a conservative and very opinionated." We talked a while longer and affirmed our love. Kurt said he'd email me tomorrow.

After hanging up, I looked for the poetry book, 'Quiet Thoughts,' that contained my submission. I found it on the bookshelf by my computer desk and scanned it into my computer.

TOGETHER

Ever since I can remember,
We have been together
Sliding down the cellar door,
Dancing on the kitchen floor,
Sharing secrets, being clever,
We have been together.
Now I am a woman grown
With desires of my own.

No longer can I tolerate
A friendship that is second rate,
One-time pebble, now turned stone
Around the neck of a woman grown.
I wonder why I vacillate
The fate of this unwanted mate?
It's time I cut this kinship short.
Wouldn't you, if it were your wart? … Eva
    Sandor

As soon as I finished scanning it, I emailed it to Kurt
and asked him to email his entry back to me. How much
fun is this, reliving childhood memories with the boy next
door?

Chapter Nineteen

While checking my emails in the morning, I found a short message from Kurt thanking me for my poem, 'Together.' He said,

> "As I read it, I pictured a little girl sitting on her porch writing what she felt. The wart can symbolize many things, like a man you want to rid yourself of, a car that never starts, herpes, gas, or a leaky bladder. A good poem should urge the reader toward original thought, and that's what you did. Thanks for the poem, little one.
>
> "Following is my poem that had won Honorable Mention in Eddie Lou Cole's contest years ago. It's about an old car I once saw abandoned somewhere. I often wonder if these old vehicles feel any pain while slowly going back to rust.

MEADOW SENTRY

Lonely, poised near barn or tree,
The banished coupe abides.
Willing yet a friend to be,
Wheels mired too deep and rusting sides.

Here and there on the wasting car,
Time failed to claim its prize.
Bits of chrome and sun conspire
Casting wonder to the meadow lark's eyes.

The Last of the Red Hot Lovers

Like as not, a yawning hood,
Invites a would-be crafter
To tap and tinker as he would,
Restore the motor's laughter.

Not far away sits a mighty Brougham,
Windows painted with October frost.
On this chill morn, no favorites shown,
For our little coupe, no beauty lost.

Young hands once urged her steering gear,
Long since silenced with age,
Our coupe one last tender word to hear,
Amid nature's ceaseless rage.

Just a final cruise, oh could it be,
Over sunny roads, through storms so fierce
Head lamps lighting the path to see
Again the darkened night to pierce.

But silence, yet our coupe endures,
Safe in beds of weed and flower.
Meadow sentry, fate insures,
Inspiring now with poetic power … Kurt Miller,
     1990

"I wrote another poem, 'Autumn in Prose,'
which I'll send along when I find it.

"Church, sex. and age. It has been a long
time since I've felt this great physically, and
I savor the thought of entering into a physical
union with you. Never in my wildest dreams did

I ever expect to hear ES say she loves me. This all seems like a dream, but I prefer to think it all started in Tiltonsville so long ago. I'm sure that there are church people who would caution us to forget about sex. But in the calendar of life, you and I are approaching midnight. We still have some wine in our cups, and we need to drink it all very soon. This is the way I feel about it, and I sense that you do, too.

"You're a strong Catholic woman, and no doubt have thought a lot about us. But the die has been cast.

"Next Sunday, do you want me to attend church with you? It's been a long time since I attended Catholic services. When I was in college and starting to read about the world, I came to the conclusion that in many ways the Catholic church stood between communism and us. I grew up in a Catholic community and lived one block from the Catholic church. I can still hear that bell.

"Oh, I love your small handwriting. It is so you. Good night, girlfriend. LYB. Kurt."

Kurt probably hadn't received the moustache yet, although I hoped he'd get it before leaving. He'll be flying into LAX a day before Valentine's Day and had asked me to make reservations at a nice restaurant to spend that special time together. I was getting excited to see him because I hadn't seen him for a month.

Since starting our journey together, I can't get enough of Kurt. He says the same about me. Although we're seniors, we feel like teenagers in love for the first time.

I re-read Kurt's poem and decided to email him this morning.

"Dear Poet Laureate,

"I read your poem and could see that battered old car from the images you used to describe it, rusting away in a lonely area by a barn. Rather sad, isn't it?

"It takes me forever to do the smallest of chores because I feel your presence and get lost in romantic feelings. I can only imagine what will happen when we kiss again.

"Yes, my love, I also believe our romance started in Tiltonsville when we were children, and that theme runs throughout the special poem I'm writing for you.

"I'm so excited you want to attend Mass with me. I'd also like to visit your church with you. When I visit, will I have to stay at Mote Six?

"I better sign off and get busy with my list of chores. I'll believe you really love me when you help me clean out my garage. BOL. Eva."

I'd just turned off my computer when Nancy called and asked when Kurt was flying in. I told her he's flying in Monday evening, and the next day is Valentine's Day. I said I'd made reservations at a restaurant in Newberry Park for Valentine's Day. I asked if she and Brad are doing anything special, and she said they're joining another couple for dinner. I told her that Kurt and I were looking forward to attending the Magic Castle with them.

"And remember," Nancy said, "on Sunday afternoon we have tickets to see 'Always,' a play about Patsy Cline. The last time Kurt was here, we only got to see him at the writer's club meeting and out to dinner once. I hope he's here longer this time."

I told her he'll be here a week, and said, "He wants to attend Mass with me, and he wants to hit the beach again. The weather in Ohio this time of year is rainy and cold. But other than that, we'll be free to visit and do things with you and Brad."

"How great he wants to attend Mass with you. I'm so glad Brad turned Catholic. I didn't push him into it, either. One day after Kaye was born, he said he thought it would be best if we were the same religion so she could have stability in her religious life. He'd been attending Mass with me for about two years when he decided to convert; and remember, Brad's dad is a retired pastor of the Baptist church. In fact, he was still a pastor there when Brad converted to Catholicism. Brad's folks didn't make a big to-do about it, which was nice."

"I think it's important to be the same religion if you have children, but since our children are adults, I don't think it matters that much. I'm definitely going to remain a Catholic, but I don't mind attending the Methodist church occasionally with Kurt."

After we hung up, I cleaned out a file drawer of Leisure Village papers, stacking them in the garage. The stack keeps getting taller and taller. I have to step over them to walk to the mailbox, where I found the usual bills, along with a manila envelope from Kurt. It contained pictures of the cabin his son owns at Piedmont and some pictures of Doug, Barb, and Kurt having lunch on a pontoon. I studied them skeptically.

A note from Kurt said Dennis from our graduating class had passed away. He said over half of our class had died. "We're lucky to be alive, healthy, and have one another," he'd written. "Looking forward to seeing you soon. Your lovestruck boyfriend. Kurt."

I emailed Kurt one more time that night.

"Can't wait for your flight to arrive tomorrow. I'd love a kiss at the airport, on the street, and in the car. Too bad Moxie can't drive.

"I'll meet you at the baggage claim again. It will take about fifty minutes to drive back to my home, depending on traffic, and we may want to stay up a while talking and maybe just sleep next to one another in the buff.

"I appreciate your sweet offer to help with household chores, but this visit I'd only like to get my old files shredded and then spend the rest of the time doing fun things.

"After sending this email, I'm going to unload a couple of drawers for your clothes. Moxie wants to know if you'll sleep at the foot of the bed while you're here.

"P.S. My libido is starting to talk to me after years of silence.

"P.P.S. Thanks for the pictures, but who's the hunk with the young couple? AML."

After two hours of CNN, I got a shower and washed my hair. While it dried, I checked my emails one more time. Glad I did as there was an email from Kurt.

"My Hungarian Rhapsody,
    'Her eyes are songs without words: Scott.'
"When we were together last month I had asked if you remembered that birthday party at Dorothy Pete's house in honor of her birthday. You seemed to have forgotten all about that little event until I reminded you.
    Then you thought you had remembered. Be honest. Did you remember? As I recall, the idea was for the lights to go out, at which time the boys would grab a gal to smooch with. I grabbed you. Do you realize that perhaps I was the very first boy you ever kissed? I remember this clearly as if it happened yesterday. But, sigh, you felt hazy in your recollection. I was always easy to forget anyway. You said we were playing 'Spin the Bottle,' and my spin landed in front of you. Since it was so long ago, I may have forgotten the game, but I haven't forgotten the kiss. I have always associated you with Tiltonsville. 'My lady true and ever fair, where have you been?' Tell me where you have seen this line before. The image of you walking past my house wearing those red shorts will always stay with me.

"Yes, when you are here with me, we can attend my church. No, you will not have to stay in Motel Six. You will stay in Motel Sex, right on Martha Drive. The room service is superb. Mirrored ceilings and secret cameras everywhere.

"Today I purchased some quality travel luggage from my AAA office. I bought a full-size bag and a carry-on bag. At least now I will be in style. I might become a frequent flyer, depending on how frequently you want me.

"I have a great joke to tell you about 'frequently.' The morning after a young couple's wedding night, the new husband asks his wife: 'How often would you like to have sex?'

"'Infrequently,'" she replies.

"'Is that one word or two words?'" asks the husband.

"My moustache arrived today, and I look like royalty with it on. However, those curly hairs have me thinking this royal moustache didn't come from your head tresses. No matter, I love it, sweetheart. Sweet dreams. Until tomorrow night. ILU. Your guy."

Chapter Twenty

It was close to eleven o'clock when Kurt and I got home from the airport. Moxie ran to greet us and started smelling Kurt's shoes. Kurt patted him on the head, and Moxie purred loudly. I looked at Kurt, and he smiled. "I really like your cat."

Kurt wrapped his arms around me. "I'm sure it's been a long day for you," he said, nuzzling his head in my hair.

"It's been a long day for you, too," I replied.

When we finally broke apart, I asked if he'd like a bowl of cereal, and he nodded.

As we ate, we talked and kept interrupting one another. We always have a lot to talk about, usually our classmates we've been in touch with, and those that have passed away. Kurt said he sees Vince and Alice at McDonald's. "They meet three or four friends there every weekday morning and have breakfast together, and I stop by occasionally to chat."

"I haven't seen Vince in years. He was a basketball star, remember?"

"Vince always asks about you. He's looking forward to your visit to Ohio, and so am I. You know I'm crazy about you and want to see you more often."

"That will happen when I move to Smyrna."

"I certainly hope so. I don't know about you, but I'm getting sleepy. Kurt yawned and said, "I have to admit, I snickered when I read your email about sleeping naked next to one another. But that sounds perfect to me right now. We can always light a fire in the morning."

"Do you think we might shower together without getting overly excited?" I asked.

"We could try." Kurt laughed.

* * * * *

I was already in the shower, enjoying the warm spray when Kurt joined me. He kissed me lightly and then more forcefully while the water rushed over our faces and between our legs.

"This is so sexy," he murmured. "And remember, I may be tired, but I'm not dead."

Feeling his erection pressing against my mid-section made me swoon, but I tried not to show it. It had been a long day, and by keeping our passion in check tonight might produce even more excitement in the morning.

* * * * *

"After a night of tossing and turning in the nude next to one another, I awoke to a light nudge by a hard object. Sunlight spilled through the windows, and provocative green-blue eyes stared at me. Kurt's cock was so damned hard, he could have pounded nails in the woodwork with it. But he chose instead to use it to tantalize me and heighten my first climax.

Kurt said he didn't need any foreplay. "Looking into your smoldering dark eyes is all that I need to complete my journey. By the way, Happy Valentine's Day."

"The same back to you."

Kurt asked if I'd made dinner reservations, and I said I had at a great restaurant in Newberry Park.

"This is our very first Valentine's Day together," Kurt said, pulling me close.

"And it's such a lovely, sunshiny day, we better get up and do something."

"We already did," he murmured.

* * * * *

We lay in bed a while longer, planting kisses on one another. We decided to spend a leisurely day at Ventura Beach. It was a little cool, but exhilarating, as we sat on beach chairs we'd brought with us, watching surfers glide by on the waves. Then we walked along the beach, swinging our joined hands in the breeze, stopping to kiss. "You are the best kisser in the world."

"That's because of my partner," Kurt replied.

"Isn't it wonderful to be in love at our age?" I asked.

"It's wonderful to be in love at any age," Kurt said. "And to think it's with a classmate. How crazy is that?"

"After living over half of my life in California, I end up with a home-grown Ohio boy. That's what I call crazy."

"I love the beach," Kurt said. "Pam and I used to drive to Myrtle Beach every year for a week. It's so relaxing. I look forward to taking you to Myrtle Beach."

"I'd like that. I used to bring my grandkids here and we'd walk the beach looking for seashells. I still have a bag of unusual seashells at home tucked in one of my dresser drawers. I didn't know what to do with them after I got them home. I still have a bag of black sand that I brought back from Hawaii about twenty years ago. The black sand and seashells would make a nice planter for my front porch, but it would probably get stolen. When I lived in Van Nuys, I put an orchid plant on my front porch, and the next morning it was gone. In fact, when I lived there, my home had been burglarized twice.

"You weren't home when you were burglarized, were you?"

"No, I was at work both times. I think the burglars knew that and felt safe robbing me because two empty coke cans were sitting on the coffee table, wiped free of fingerprints. The first time I was burglarized was a week after my Beagle had died. Nobody would have tried to rob me when he was alive. He'd sit in the den window sill and show his teeth when anyone stepped on the front porch."

"I felt very violated. The thieves took all of my medications and even my Beagle's medications. I think they were more interested in the meds than they were in my jewelry, although they got a lot of it." I paused to wet my dry lips. "I was so angry that I wrote an article about the burglary and sold it to the 'Los Angeles Herald Examiner.' They're now defunct. That was my first published article I got paid for."

"I'm proud of you for turning a bad incident into something positive."

"I was worried for fear of retaliation after the article had been published because I wrote about the ineptness of the police. You see, I didn't write the article right away as I was busy on another project; and in the meantime, I received notice from the police department that a showing of stolen jewelry would take place on a certain date and that I should appear with a copy of my police report. When I arrived at the police station, a long line had already congregated; but only ten people were admitted in at a time. About a dozen tables with jewelry sealed in plastic bags covered the tables, with two policemen in the room guarding the loot and socializing. All admittees walked around the room, looking intently at the jewelry. As I looked closely at a ruby ring, one of the policemen asked if I wanted him to take it out of the bag so I could view it more closely. I said the more I looked at the ring, I didn't think it was mine. 'Are you sure?' he asked, like he wanted me to take it."

"A few minutes later, I passed a table that had no bagged jewelry on it, which struck me as odd; and as I walked by the policemen, I heard them discussing how this bagged jewelry could possibly have been stolen a second time with them in the room. It was an aha moment that I inserted in my burglary article."

"Was this incident ever written up in the local paper?" Kurt asked.

"No, it wasn't, except for my mention of it in my essay. I don't think the police wanted anyone to know about this jewelry stolen a second time under the policemen's noses; do you?"

"It's actually funny."

"Yes, but you can see how I'd be worried about revealing their blunder in my essay, but nothing came of it. My handyman changed the locks on my doors, and life went on as usual."

"How did they get in?"

"They jimmied the lock on the living room sliding door that led to the back yard, and I had a devil of a time getting it repaired."

"Didn't you say you were burglarized twice?"

"The second time I had a warning. As I pulled into my driveway after work, I saw my Chihuahua and my black cat lying on my front yard, and the fence gate was closed. I hurriedly unlocked the front door and ran into the house with the pets at my heels. The burglars must have run out the back glass sliding door because it was wide open. My sterling silverware and small appliances were stacked on the dining room table, but nothing was missing. I must have scared away the thieves."

"That was gutsy of you to enter the house, not knowing if the thieves were still in there."

"I realized that later. I called my handyman first and then called the police, who came and dusted my furniture with a silver dust but only found palm prints, and they didn't track palm prints locally at that time. My handyman changed the locks again. This second time, I think a small person went through the doggie door and opened the door for the burglars because a woman's nylon stocking was sitting on the stoop outside the doggie door."

"Very scary," Kurt said, "but I have to admire how you handled yourself."

"Thank you. I realize now how my Beagle had protected me. Both of those incidents happened after he died. My Chihuahua was no guard dog – she was probably glad to be let out of the house. She and her cat buddy were having a grand time rolling around on the front lawn."

"Large dogs, or even ones the size of a Beagle, can dissuade burglars," Kurt said.

We were silent for a while, just enjoying one another's company. Then Kurt spoke.

"When I think about it, I don't mind being eighty-one as long as I'm healthy."

"I can vouch for your health," I interjected. "I think we're both in good health because we never drank, smoked, or abused our bodies in any way."

I wonder how many of our classmates are still alive?

"I have a group picture of our class in Ohio, and I check off the ones that have passed away. But I'm sure I missed some of them," Kurt said.

"When I go back to Ohio, I try to see the classmates that still live in the area," I said. "And I think it's great how you still keep in touch with your friends from school."

"Look who's talking. You're constantly telling me of someone you've called or has called you, and look how many miles away you live."

"You know what I think? I think we should get our stuff together and head back to Camarillo. I don't want to be late for our Valentine's Day dinner."

"Me, either," Kurt said. "I have a card and gift I want to give you before dinner."

I didn't mention the card or gift I'd gotten him.

When we got home, Kurt showered in the guest bathroom, and I leisurely soaked in the tub in the master bathroom. I dried myself, applied makeup, and put on my little black dress that emphasized my curves. Finding my dangling rhinestone earrings I usually wear with this dress, I put them on; and voila, I was ready. When I walked into the living room, Kurt was seated and looking very handsome in a white shirt, red tie, and a black and grey-checkered sports coat.

"My you look yummy," I said, eyeing him up and down.

"You look ravishing," he said huskily, handing me a huge card with a verse saying 'I love you' with other rhyming sentences. Seating himself on the sofa, Kurt pulled me down next to him. "I hope you like your gift," he said, removing a small, velvet ring box from his jacket pocket. He opened the box, revealing a 2-carat diamond solitaire.

My eyes teared up.

"With this ring, I commit myself to you and vow to love you forever. You are and will be my last love. I hope you feel the same way." As he spoke, he placed the ring on my finger.

I just stared at it, watching it sparkle. "I vow to love you forever," I said.

We hugged and kissed and promised to be faithful to one another.

It was a glorious moment, and I remember wishing we would feel like this for the rest of our lives. But why wouldn't we?"

"I didn't get down on one knee and ask you to marry me, but I'd be open to that in the near future," he said. "I love only you."

"I love you, and I love my ring. Let's enjoy one another and live in the present."

"Agreed," he said. Love radiated from his eyes.

"Now let me get you your card and gift." Getting up, I hurried to my bedroom and came back out with the card and gift. "Open the card first."

He read the mushy card about how I loved everything about him. He then pulled me down on his lap and gave me a warm, wet kiss. "You better quit that or we'll never make it to the restaurant." Smoothing my dress, I handed him his gift.

He took it from the box, admiring it. "I'm not sure what it is."

"It's a toe ring."

"It sure sparkles. Is that sapphires and diamonds?"

"What do you think? Only the best for my fiancé. Let's wait until after dinner before you put it on; okay? I don't want you spending time removing your shoes and socks right now."

Chapter Twenty-One

When we arrived at the restaurant, we are seated at a back booth in front of a lit fireplace. The ambiance was very romantic, which matched our mood. While sipping Merlot, we talk about our engagement and my move to Georgia.

"I don't think I told you, but I got a small loan from State Farm so I can pay cash for my Smyrna home without having to sell my Camarillo home first. That gives me peace of mind that the escrow will close on time."

"That's great! But if you find yourself running short of money, I can help you out."

"Thank you, Kurt, but I think I'll be okay now."

Kurt reached over and squeezed my hands.

"I already spoke to Lexie about giving her my power of attorney so she can sign the closing documents."

"It will be heaven having you live closer to me," Kurt said warmly.

"It's exciting for me to start a new life in the South and to be able to see you more often."

"Do you mean that?" Kurt asked, surprised.

"Of course."

"Then why do you limit my visits with you in California?"

"I have so many loose ends to tie up with Wanda's illness and completing my last couple of months as president of the writer's club that I don't even want to think about having to sell Wanda's condo; but who else is there?"

"I wish I could help you," Kurt said, patting my hand.

"You are by being patient and loving."

"You thrill me, Eva. I think about you every day."

Later that evening after we'd disrobed, I brought Kurt's toe ring into the bedroom and examined his toes. "My, your toenails are long. Why don't I trim them before putting the ring on your toe?"

"Would you do that for me?" he asked.

"Let me get a towel to put under your feet to catch the toenails." I hummed a tune I'd heard earlier in the evening as I hurried into the bathroom. Taking the nail clippers and fingernail scissors from a drawer, I put them in my left robe pocket; and I put the pink nail polish in my right robe pocket. Grabbing a hand towel from the counter, I hurried back into the bedroom.

"All ready," I said, walking over to Kurt. He was stretched out in the nude, his head on my pillow. Raising his head, he watched as I took the clippers and scissors from my robe pocket.

"Raise your legs while I place the towel under your feet," I ordered.

"Tell me when you're done," he muttered, closing his eyes.

In between the clipping and cutting, I managed to polish his toenails without his noticing. When I was done, I turned the nightstand light low and kissed my fiancé full on the mouth. It was a very sensual kiss and left us both spinning. Then I placed the toe ring on his toe and told him he was marked forever. He picked up his feet and looked at his toenails, but since the light was dim, he didn't notice they'd been polished.

"Very nice," he said, "and thank you for the ring. It feels very comfortable. Should I wear it with my shoes on?"

"Absolutely. You'll get used to it."

"I hope so. But at the moment, I have other things on my mind." His voice turned low as he said, "My heart is clamoring to pleasure you...now."

As he spoke, I felt myself shivering with anticipation. Sliding his open hands down the inside of my thighs, I heard my voice cry out. Slowly and deliberately, he touched my vagina with his fingers, moving them ever so gently. He then massaged my clitoris, making it bloom. My whole body arched.

"Are you getting close?" Kurt murmured.

"Yes," I whispered. "And if you want to join in, you better do it quickly."

And so we lay there, shuddering, while Kurt rolled his body over mine.

The next morning I awoke to shouts of "No, she did it again!" ringing in my ears.

"What did I do again?" I asked.

"Don't act so innocent. Look at these toenails!" Kurt jumped out of bed and stood, staring at them.

"They look so nice you should be thanking me."

Kurt rolled his eyes and climbed back into bed. He placed his arms around me, stroking me, cuddling me. I offered my mouth, and he took it. Threading his fingers through my hair, he started kissing me wildly, as though lovers meeting for the very first time, although we'd just made love last night. In a frenzy, I gave Kurt a prominent hickey on his neck. I had tried to suckle one to his forehead, but his skin was too taut there. I probably could have put one on his nose as he was completely absorbed in the heat of the moment.

Kurt's hands skimmed over my body, causing shivers of passion to surge through me. His touch was as I'd remembered: intoxicating. With each stroke, my body ached for more. How thrilling was this? To wake up in the morning with my nipples hard and my body yearning for whatever passion my lover has to give me.

"You want me as badly as I want you?" he asked.

"More," I murmured.

And so we re-enacted the events of last night and then fell into a deep sleep.

* * * * *

The week flew by. We went to the Magic Castle with Nancy and Brad, had a delicious steak dinner, and saw three different magic shows. At the last one, Fredrich, the magician, had a deck of cards in his hand and asked Nancy to come up on stage and to select a card from the deck. She did so, and Fredrich immediately put it on top of the deck, face down, which he then placed on a small table in front of the audience. Nancy returned to her seat.

Next, Fredrich asked for a volunteer to come on stage with him. A young lady in the back stood up, and Fredrich asked her if she had a cell phone. Answering in the affirmative, he asked her to join him on stage. He then asked her to phone one of her friends that wasn't in the audience. When her friend got on the phone, Fredrich tapped the card on the top of the deck several times, and then he asked the young lady Sarah to ask her phone friend what she thought the card was. Sarah said the friend thought the card was a Jack of Spades. Fredrich picked up the deck of cards from the table and turned over the top card and revealed it to the audience. It was the Jack of Spades. Nancy and I looked at one another, stunned. Brad and Kurt had puzzled looks on their faces, and the audience went wild. Soon after, Fredrich completed his magic show.

On the drive home, we discussed the various card tricks, and we came up with lame, slight-of-hand solutions; but no one had an explanation for the correct card identified by a non-audience member by phone.

It was an enjoyable evening, and it pleased me immensely to see how easily Kurt had fit in with my friends, although this must have been the fourth or fifth time we'd all gotten together.

As Brad pulled into his driveway, Nancy asked if we wanted to go in for a nightcap; but since it was late, and we still had a half-hour drive to Camarillo, we thanked her but declined.

"We're looking forward to seeing you two for the play about Patsy Cline Sunday," Nancy chirped, as we said our goodbyes to her and Brad and climbed into my car for the drive home.

Kurt told me how much he enjoyed my friends. "They are first-class people," he said.

* * * * *

During this trip, Kurt and I visited the Camarillo airport again. Kurt said he'd joined the Camarillo airport club but had his money returned because the club had disbanded.

"They just didn't have enough members to keep it alive," he said. "How sad since it's a great little airport."

We spent another day at the Ventura Beach, this time closer to the souvenir shops that we sauntered around in, buying a few T-shirts and marveling at the seashells and junk that customers were buying. We ate at a Greek restaurant, a first for Kurt, and probably the last, he informed me. Although I love Greek food and think this restaurant has the best lamb kebobs and cucumber salad, Kurt was not in the least impressed. He said he doesn't like Indian food, either, and that is also one of my favorites. However, I think I may extract a promise from him to try one of my favorite restaurants one night when he's particularly horny.

Kurt treated my family to dinner at the Outback Steak House one evening, and I showed off my engagement ring. "It's lovely," Susan said, with Marie nodding her approval. Later in the evening, we started bickering in front of them, and Kurt smiled shyly and said, "We're getting so familiar with each other that we're starting to insult one another."

My daughter Susan roared. She told Kurt, "I was wondering how my mother would act around you, and she is herself. What you see is exactly how my mother is." Kurt responded that he loves me this way.

We managed to get in a visit with Wanda at the nursing home, and I showed her my engagement ring. She oohed and aahed about it. Kurt clipped her fingernails as he had done on an earlier visit, and she thanked him profusely.

She said she'd be released in two weeks and asked if I could spend some time with her after Kurt leaves to discuss her possible move to Madison. She said her nephew's wife

Sally regularly sends her cards and pictures of the family, and she's getting excited to meet them and to see her sister-in-law again.

"I'm happy to hear that, Wanda. We can call Sally and coordinate your move with her."

Kurt said he thought Wanda was making the right decision.

"When do you think you'll be moving?" she asked me.

"I plan to put my home up for sale next month and, hopefully, I can move in May."

"Maybe I can put my home up for sale the same time, using the same broker?" she asked.

I told her that would work out great!

* * * * *

A day before Kurt flew back to Ohio, he attended ten o'clock Mass with me. We sat in the first pew because we're both starting to have hearing problems. One of the reasons I love the Catholic Church so much is because of the homilies that I apply to my everyday life, and which I think about and try to live by. Kurt asked what I thought about him accepting Holy Communion, and I told him I thought it was fine. "Don't we recite in the Nicene Creed that we believe in one God and one baptism?" Kurt had been baptized, although not in the Catholic faith; but that wasn't distinguished in the Nicene Creed. So we both accepted the host and thanked God for our blessings. It was a special moment, acknowledging one God together.

We decided to have breakfast after Mass at Coco's and then relax at home until we meet Nancy and Brad at the El Portal Theatre in Burbank.

"Always," a play based on the life of Patsy Cline, provided nostalgia with its romantic tunes. A lead role, that of Patsy Cline's friend, was played by Sally Struthers, who added a very funny touch to Patsy's story. The play was excellent, as were the soulful vocals.

After the play, our foursome ate at a Mexican restaurant a few blocks from the El Portal Theatre, not knowing it was Brad's birthday. He tipped us off when he ordered a ninety-nine-cent strawberry dessert "for my birthday," he said. We all wished him a happy birthday and ordered the strawberry dessert, as well; but Brad, lucky guy, got the last one. Of course we offered to pay for his, but he said he could afford it. So funny! And it was quite large for only ninety-nine-cents. "And quite delicious," Brad added.

Chapter Twenty-Two

After all the love and laughter we had crammed into Kurt's seven-day visit, I now found myself alone. I'd just dropped Kurt off at the airport and drove back home, my head popping with thoughts of him and of our romantic days and nights together.

Moxie greeted me, and I gathered him in my arms. He purred while we settled on the sofa together. "I'm missing Kurt already," I said to him.

I ruffled up his fur and drew him close. I knew Moxie was going to miss the sparring matches he and Kurt had, with Moxie standing up on his hind legs, throwing his paw at Kurt every time Kurt threw a soft punch at him.

I watched a movie on television and had a snack of crackers and cheese before the phone rang. Kurt said his truck was cold from sitting at the airport parking lot in Pittsburgh, and it took a while to heat up. "February in Ohio is much different than February in California," he said.

"There was no traffic on the way home," Kurt said, "so I made it in an hour. I thought about you all the way home, my darling. I feel even closer to you now that we're engaged."

"My exact feelings," I replied. "I'm holding Moxie now and admiring my ring."

"I'm glad you like it, Eva. It's been a long day, and I'm really beat. But I wanted you to know I got home okay, and I wanted to thank you for a wonderful time. I don't know when I've laughed so much. It was great spending time with Brad and Nancy, too."

"We did a lot of fun things, and I'm going to miss you," I said.

"I miss you and love you, sweetheart, and I'll email you in the morning."

"I love you back, and get some rest. Bye now."

The next morning, I ate my breakfast and checked my email, but nothing from Kurt. He's probably sleeping in, I surmised.

I dressed and then drove to the nursing home to visit Wanda. I was only there a few minutes when her doctor walked in. We discussed her move to the Madison Assisted Living facility. After hearing about the activities and amenities it provided, he gave his approval. "I have to stress, however, that although your femur is healed, you don't want to cause any further damage to it."

"When can I be released?" Wanda asked.

"As soon as there's a room available or you have a caregiver to take care of you at home. Does that work for you?"

Wanda nodded.

"In the meantime, I'll write a couple of prescriptions that I want you to take for your asthma and anxiety. I'll just refill your other prescriptions as necessary."

Wanda and I hugged, and I told her I'd get her prescriptions filled and then contact a caregiver friend to help out until all the arrangements could be made for her move.

After getting the prescriptions, I headed home and checked out my emails. One was from Kurt.

"Dear Miss Consummate,

"You please me no end. As I shaved this morning, I noticed my moustache on the bathroom vanity. I wonder how many women would do this for their lover?

I marvel at the endless ways you have in keeping your man satisfied from afar. I must tell you that I really like your cat. When I was growing up, I never had pets, and when I had my boys, I got them a dog, who ended up being **my** dog. But I was never around a cat until Moxie. He's a handsome cat, and I think I've finally won him over with our boxing matches. Now I have two pussies.

"As tired as I was last night, I couldn't fall asleep, so I wrote a little poem for you. It's titled 'Eva's Demur.'

"At last I've found the guy I need,
He is my favorite crony,
If tho I could make a change,
A much larger pepperoni.

He's nice enough to be with,
He's the world's greatest necker,
If tho I could make a change,
Just a slightly bigger pecker.

But alas, I think I wish too much,
In feathering my little nest.
Lord, don't change the way he is,
I will do the rest."

"All my love and then some more. Kurt."

I hurriedly responded that I love the poem about his pepperoni, but I really think it's a salami. I said that Wanda would be discharged as soon as I could find a caregiver, and then we'd work on arrangements for her move to Madison. I said this email would be short because I have to find a caregiver. "However, you can expect a responsive poem later tonight. ILUAUP. Eva."

Getting out my phonebook, I checked for Joy's number and called her. She was glad to hear from me and said she was semi-retired but would be happy to take care of Wanda for the short time it entailed. I thanked Joy and hung up. What a relief to get that taken care of.

After dinner, I sent an email to Kurt with a poem I'd written.

"Dear Major Kurt,
    "I'm overwhelmed by your poem about your pepperoni and feel it needs a response."

"WHO WOULD'VE THOUGHT

Who would've thought an unused twit
guarded by a genteel lassie
could have caused such a tizzy fit
to a pecker's classy chassis.

Pepperoni's not my choice of meat,
the calories are not a treat,
I prefer your fat-free pecker
and an ice cream double-decker.

Age has a way of changing bods.
We accept them as they are.
But love never changes when it's true-
It simply moves up the bar."

"An ardent admirer."

The next morning when I got to the nursing home, Wanda was eating breakfast. I told her about Joy, and she's eager to meet her. I called Wanda's doctor who said he'd write a release for tomorrow morning. I packed Wanda's clothes and paid her bills in the office. "I plan to change your bedclothes and dust the furniture tonight, and I'll be back for you in the morning."

As I drove home, I was happy that Wanda was moving forward with her life, but I felt overwhelmed by all the work I face with putting her home up for sale, disposing of her furniture, and packing up her artwork and personal possessions with my own pending move and club obligations. But the *Good Lord* only gives us as much as we can handle, and I guess he sees me with broad shoulders rather than big tits.

When Wanda and I pulled into the driveway the next morning, Joy was sitting in her car. I handed Wanda her walker and introduced her to Joy. Walking into the kitchen, we discussed Joy's duties. I left as Wanda was making a grocery list of items she wants Joy to pick up. It was only twelve noon, and I felt exhausted, so I drove home and took a long nap. When I awoke there was a voicemail from Lexie. I hadn't even heard the phone ring. She said the repairs on the inspection report had been completed and that the escrow was ready to close. I called her back and she said Shelly had gotten the price of the home down another five hundred dollars, complaining about the old furnace. "And the sellers took care of all the repairs, Mom."

We discussed the State Farm loan I'd obtained, and I said I'd make sure that loan money and my savings account money are wired to escrow.

That's great, Mom. And I have the Power of Attorney, signed and notarized. So as soon as the money arrives, I'll meet with Shelly at the escrow company."

I then told her about Kurt giving me an engagement ring for Valentine's Day.

"You had an inkling, and you were right. Describe it to me."

I told her it was a two-carat diamond solitaire set in white gold.

"It really sounds pretty. And did you give him the toe ring?"

I said I had, and she laughed as I told her about painting Kurt's toenails.

We then talked about Aunt Wilma's health. "She has the sniffles, but otherwise, she's doing great for one hundred," Lexie said. "She complains about being cold, so I bought her a couple of jogging outfits, and she likes them."

"For the two years she lived in a nursing home out here, I had to buy her dresses."

"She sees all the other women wearing slacks, so I guess she feels it's okay."

"I thank God that she's gotten so sweet during her old age. I remember when she used to fight with everyone, me included. But now she seems to appreciate what everyone does for her."

"Mom, she's a smart woman. She knows we're taking care of her. Why would she take a chance on alienating us?"

"You're right. I'm so glad she's happy there. I'll buy her a couple of jogging outfits and send them to you. As for the escrow closing, I'll make sure the money is there for the closing. I love you and look forward to starting a new life in Georgia in my new home."

"Stephen and I are eager to work on your house. Love you and I'll call tomorrow."

Before going to bed, I checked my emails again, and one was there from Kurt.

"Dearest Fiancee,

"I love the poem about my pepperoni. It's rarely out of my pants, except for a shower or to pee. I'm already looking forward to next month's visit. There is now only the slightest remnant of the love bite you put on my neck. The love mark must be renewed when we next meet. You are so damned exciting, my love, and don't forget that I'm the boss between-the-sheets.

"During that long period when I was caring for Pam, I had concluded that my libido went south, never to be felt again. You brought it back for me, and I am pleased no end.

My age has exerted a negative effect on the quality of my erection, but near the end of my last visit, I noticed that I was erecting easier and the credit goes to you. Our love-making is so energetic and dynamic, what healthy man wouldn't respond? Oh, yes, thanks for the wonderful times in the shower and tub.

"I made it to church this morning, but the weather was looking bad and the attendance was cut pretty badly. My good friend Al Curtis assumed that I would return a married man. He wanted to learn of the visit high points, and I told him we had a great time. Must go now. Sleep well, baby. NMI, Major Kurt."

"P.S. 'Cats are smarter than dogs. You can't get eight cats to pull a sled through snow.' Jeff Valdez."

"P.P.S. 'Dogs come when they are called; cats take a message and get back to you.' Missy Dizick."

Chapter Twenty-Three

As I sauntered into the kitchen for my morning coffee, my cell phone rang. Lexie said the escrow had closed and the home in Smyrna is mine. "I have the keys, and Stephen and I plan to make a list of things that should be done before you move in."

"That's so exciting!" I exclaimed. "I have a few more projects to finish around here, and then I'll put this home up for sale."

I brought Lexie up-to-date about Wanda's plans to move to Madison, and Lexie got concerned about the workload I'd be undertaking. "I'm going to farm out what I can – maybe to the realtor," I said. "I know my energy limitations."

Lexie reiterated that she and Stephen are happy I'll be moving closer to them.

Since it's a little early for lunch, I decided to visit Wanda and Joy. Wanda lay on the couch, her legs stretched out, with a blanket covering her. Wanda was telling Joy about widowed women in the Village making casseroles for the men who had recently lost their wives.

"We call it the casserole club," I said, laughing.

Wanda said she's glad to be back home and looking forward to her move to Madison. She said Joy has gotten a couple of lovely women to tend to her needs in the afternoons and evenings. Wanda said she's talked to Sally and told her she's watching the birds feed from her kitchen window. She said Sally told her about the snow geese that gather on her front lawn.

"Wisconsin sounds lovely," Wanda said, a dreamy look in her eyes.

Since Wanda and Joy were enjoying one another's company, I walked back home.

Kurt's email was fresh on my mind about him being boss between-the-sheets, so I wrote a poem for him.

"MY FIRST LOVE

To me, you are my first love,
and I'll do my best to spark your heart.
I expect returns on my investment,
fine-tuning and improvs are your part, Mozart.

"I concede you're master of the bedroom
and you take me to unknown heights.
But don't think you're CEO in other places.
Your sophisticated lady insists on equal rights."

"I love you, and yes, you make me happy.
Your gal."

I also wrote that Joy and Wanda really hit it off, and that Wanda talks with Sally regularly. She's assured Wanda she'll be included in all holidays and family gatherings.

I said that Lexie called, and we discussed repairs that should be done before I move.

"Nothing new here. I hope you like the poem. I think it's time I get one back from you—a real tear-jerker this time; okay? I love you. Your sophisticated pussycat. Eva."

Walking from room to room, I focused on the packing of my books. One box would hold all of my office books about writing, one box would hold my literary books, and one box would contain the anthologies published with my essays in them. Sitting on the floor with the open boxes, I marked them and filled them. By the time I finished, the afternoon was gone, and I was exhausted. Turning my computer on, an email from Kurt appeared.

"Dear Little Miss Sandor,

"I love your poem and am so happy you're my fiancée. I'm glad you're pleased with me, and I don't look to change. To me, you will always be my little Miss Sandor. I can't wait to kiss your lips again and watch you smile. Stay well because we have a lot of ground to cover in the next few years.

"I went to the gym today but didn't stay long. While I walked the track, I started coughing and my eyes started watering. When I got home my knees started to buckle as I walked the stairs. I made myself some Cream of Wheat and hot tea and lay down for a while. I think I caught another cold, but I think I'll survive with more sleep.

"I received a hint of spring today. Clear skies and snow rapidly melting away. Soon as we get around to it, I will whisk you off to the beach. We need to play in the sun, my dear. Keep me posted on your house and Wanda's affairs.

"I'm sending a tissue soaked in after-shave for my favorite cat. Your devoted Kurt."

I decided to respond immediately because I wanted to take a long, hot bath and get ready for bed early. I, too, had started sniffling, and my throat felt scratchy.

"Dear Lover,

"I don't know what happened, but I've also caught a cold. My head feels big and stuffy, and it's not ego. After I finish this note, I'll use nose drops and suck cough drops. As for your cold, if you were here, I'd give you some of my pee to gargle with.

"Lexie called earlier today and read me the list of repairs she and Stephen came up with. Remove wallpaper in the entryway and both bathrooms; then paint the bathrooms; and refinish hardwood floors throughout the house."

"I don't know whether I told you, but Lexie says I'll be entitled to a rebate for buying a home in Georgia. She says it's not just for first-time buyers. You'll have to check this out to see whether it applies to the home you recently purchased in Ohio.

"It won't be long before I'll get another freebie ticket from the airlines. Maybe you and I can meet again in Smyrna and sleep on an air mattress and figure out what actually needs to be done before I move. I love you and can't wait to see you again. YXYZ. Eva."

* * * * *

After an evening snack, two Tylenol, and a hot bath, I fell off to dreamland. I slept until ten in the morning, awakening with gook in my eyes and a runny nose. I washed my face and brushed my teeth and shuffled to the kitchen with Moxie at my side, meowing for his kibble.

Instead of my usual cup of decaf, I had two cups of hot tea and my oats, two Tylenol, and two Echinacea & Golden Seal tablets. I hope it works this time as packing sucks out a lot of energy.

I lounged in my robe, read the paper, and then went into my email. One had arrived from Kurt a few minutes earlier.

"Dear High Sugar,

"I went to bed last night at eleven o'clock and awoke for the first time at four-thirty.

After being up an hour, I again fell asleep and woke up at eight. I threw down some cereal, shaved, then drove to the mall for some coffee and a goodie. Back home and finished yesterday's paper. Quit yawning. You knew from the start I was a boring guy.

"My dick is so long, it has its own zip code. My dick is so long, it goes out and in with the tide. My cousin is so ugly, when she goes to the beach, the tide goes out and never comes back. What do you mean, my dear, that I'm running out of things to say? Well, sometimes I feel like I have to meet a deadline or suffer a severe brow-beating from you. Good thing about this daily routine is that my typing speed has greatly improved.

"Yeah, you are younger than me by eleven months, five days. By the time you were born, I was already jacking off. I matured early. But, what the heck, you are now in my sand box. I love the suggestion that I might lose all my illnesses if I gargle with your pee.

"As far as meeting in Smyrna for a fling on the pretext of working, that would be great. Just pick the dates. Until tomorrow. Master of Your Heart. Your man, Kurt."

"P.S. Can't seem to figure out what 'YXYZ' stands for. Are you sure you know?"

I giggled as I read the P.S. Of course, I didn't know what those letters stood for.

It had been a while since I'd written a chapter on my new novel, *Vengeful Heart*. Since I felt too listless to do anything physical, I read the last chapter and started a new chapter, wondering whether my heroine was too savvy for my targeted audience to like her. Leaning back in my chair, I wondered whether I even liked her. What a rotten turn of events. I'm now half-way through the novel. Rather than proceed forward, I typed up a character analysis. I knew what my heroine wanted and what she had to do to get there, but the problem is with the heroine herself. If the readers don't like her, why would they want to read a book about her?

After typing for about three hours, I gave up and called Ray to discuss the problem I had with the heroine. He totally agreed with me that she needs to be more sympathetic; and we kicked around scenarios in which I could make that happen without redoing many pages. We then discussed the songs he's written. I told him how much Kurt and I like 'I Want to be the One,' and I encouraged him to sell the album to a song publisher, but he isn't interested.

Ray wanted to know how Kurt and I are getting along, and I filled him in—said we're having fun emailing one another and finding out more about each other. He said Kurt seems like a nice guy from talking with him at several writer's club meetings, but he still cautioned me to go slow. "You still haven't met his family, and you have yet to experience how you'll fit in with them. And yes, it does matter to one's relationship. What would you have done if Kurt hadn't fit in with your family? Would you have gotten engaged anyway?"

"You present some good arguments," I said. "I can't help wondering whether his sons and their wives will like me and accept me. I have no clue from what Kurt tells me. It's as though they're not at all curious about me. Very strange."

Ray told me that he and his wife Sharron met on a cruise ship where he was one of the entertainers. He said they really hit it off, but he wasn't ready for a relationship at the time with his many entertainment gigs and traveling so much. It was seventeen years later that they met again on a cruise ship and Sharron proposed to him, and he accepted."

"Timing has a lot to do with a relationship," I said. "I don't feel that Kurt and my relationship would have survived had we married right out of high school. But with both of us having gotten our educations and work experience behind us, I feel that we're now at the same place in life and on the same intellectual level."

"Those things do matter," Ray said. "And I'm glad we had this talk. I just want to know you're happy and this is what you want."

"I really appreciate you, Ray."

"I know."

After hanging up, I answered Kurt's email:

"Dear Mr. Universe,

"Your last email was soooo funny. You have a knack for writing humor, did you know that? I've been busy today packing up books and writing on my novel, *Vengeful Heart.* I seem to have written myself in a corner—not realizing that my heroine is a bitch who knows it all. Who in the world would be interested in reading about her? I talked to Ray today and he's given me some good ideas about how to rework the issue. I don't know what I'd do without his sage advice. I also told Ray that you've been enjoying his music album and have said that 'All of the songs are beautiful, and he should get a music publisher to see what his options are.'

"I don't have anything else to say, so I'll close with a cute joke someone sent me."

"NEW NATIONAL SYMBOL

The government announced today that it is changing its national symbol to a condom because it more accurately reflects the government's political stance.

A condom allows for inflation, halts production, destroys the next generation, protects a bunch of wieners and gives you a sense of security while you're actually being screwed."

"It just doesn't get more accurate than that."

"YXYZ. You figure it out. I love you, Eva."

Chapter Twenty-Four

Wanda has been back in her home for over a week and getting used to being spoiled by caregivers but worried about depleting her savings. Since the doctor's report and first-month's rent had been sent to the Madison facility, Wanda is just waiting for a private room to open up.

When I walked over to see Wanda, I found her and Joy packing up Wanda's unwanted clothes and kitchen ware for the Battered Women's organization. Wanda has also been gifting her original paintings to friends and relatives, and she let Kurt and me choose two each when he visited. She's won many awards for her paintings, and we're thrilled to have them.

"Hang onto the power of attorney I gave you so you can sell my condo and furniture," she said. "I hate to bog you down with my chores, but I don't know what to do," she fretted.

"It's okay," I said, putting my arms around her. "Things have a way of working out."

Wanda told me that Sally will arrange the move, including plane reservations for her husband and Wanda. I offered to drive them to the airport.

When I got back home, I found an email from Kurt:

"Dear Dark Eyes,
     "I think perhaps my unusual head cold finally went south. I hit the sack last night at eleven and slept until nine-fifteen in the morning. I had to

tap a kidney a couple of times during the night, but I guess I really needed that sleep.

"I met Joe and Marla for lunch, and you and I were the topic of conversation. My friends want to know all about us. I tell them most everything. Yes, even about the toe ring and you painting my toenails. Joe doubled over with laughter.

"I returned home thinking I would hit the gym, but when I got upstairs, I changed my mind and lay down and slept soundly for two hours.

"No, I haven't looked into the house rebate yet. I understand it's for first-time home buyers only, but I'll check since you're not a first-time home buyer.

"Our snow is all gone, but it gave up with daunting reluctance. I got sick of hearing the snowman next door bitching about his snowballs. We all have problems, but I must concede that balls are very important. I think my balls were made in China…one hung hi, and one hung lo.

"You probably have forgotten how mellow spring can be at this latitude. Do you still want to meet in Georgia, or do you want to come north to my home in April? I can't wait to show you off to my friends.

"I liked the New National Symbol.

"I'm working on YASRFM and WTDP. I sure can't figure out YXYZ. LUM. Kurt."

Reading Kurt's emails made me laugh, and I appreciate that, having written over forty humorous essays for *The*

Ventura County Star as a stringer. Early in my writing career, I wrote about living with my abusive husband and sold them to *Womans World* for five hundred dollars each. But I soon tired of re-living those depressing experiences and started writing humor.

As I'm musing about my past, Susan called wanting to know how my cold is. I told her I've been taking Echinacea & Golden Seal, along with sleeping in every morning, and I feel that knocked the bug out of me. She wants to know what's happening with Kurt and me, and I told her some of the jokes he sends in his emails. "He has a great personality, and we have a lot in common." I then relayed Wanda's decision about moving to Madison, and she feels relieved for me. Every time I talk with Susan, I get choked up, causing me to vacillate about moving so far from her and my grandkids. I have to tell myself that Susan is happy in her marriage, and the grandkids are now adults, and that the airlines have planes in the sky every day.

I ran errands and picked up some Vitamin D and eyeliner at Rite Aid. Since Kentucky Fried Chicken is across the street. I ordered the three-piece combo and hurried home.

After eating, I emailed Kurt to tell him I'd visited Wanda, and she said Sally has things under control for her move. She's just waiting for a private room to become available. I said I'm rethinking my idea of meeting him in Georgia or Ohio because Wanda may be moving then.

"It probably will be best if you fly out in March and help me finish packing so I can move the first of May. I still have over one hundred pig knick-knacks to pack, plus some touch-up painting to do before I put my home on the market. I've got to start checking on what my Capri model is selling for, and I need to find a realtor. I'm getting excited about my move. I gave Lexie the go-ahead to hire someone to refinish the hardwood floors in a reddish oak color.

"I'm eagerly awaiting your visit, my darling. I'm gonna be all over you like a maggot. And how are you doing with composing my poem? If I really like your poem, I may give you a lap dance. ILU and INU. Your Hungarian Gypsy."

In Kurt's reply email, he conceded that he should fly out in March so we can finish packing and then I could put my condo up for sale in April.

"I've been looking forward to your Ohio visit, but it's more important to stay on schedule and get you moved. About the lap dance, I'm ready. I'll even put a pole in the living room of your Smyrna home for you to perform.

"It sounds like Wanda could be moving before you do. Wouldn't that be a goal to shoot for? I hope it happens when I'm visiting so I can help out. I'm glad she made the decision to move close to her family. By the way, the rebate doesn't apply to me. I bought my home before the rebate was offered.

"I finally got over my cold. I think I slept it away. Is yours gone yet?

"Nothing new on this end. Give me some dates to visit in March. It won't be long until we hold hands again. I love meeting you at those baggage claim stations, and the ride home with you; and I long to kiss your sweet lips again. My poem follows. YOS. Kurt."

THE SECOND TIME AROUND

"Twas not the marriage bed
Old friends sought to cover.
Precious little was even said,
Emerging soon as lovers.

Hovering then between her hips,
Pondering, was sex so just?
All doubt removed, when on their lips,
Faint smiles did signal lust.

Had decades concealed a simmering truth?
Both never conscious knowing.
Till the gulf of time snared their souls,
Now God will keep love flowing.

Few beautiful days together spent,
Still, anxious hearts abound.
Little doubt, clear message sent,
The second time around … The Major."

Kurt opened himself up with this poem, and it made me tear up. Since there was nothing on television that interested me, I grabbed a yellow pad and pen and sat on my sofa with pillows behind my back, while titles of poems drifted in and out of my thoughts. Finally, one title stood out from the rest, and my fingers fairly flew composing my poem. When I'd finished, I sent a short email to Kurt, along with my poem.

"Dear Sexy Major,

"I like your poem a lot. I love this creative side of you, plus your tender side, plus your sexy side. It seems like ages since I've seen you, and I so want to feel your arms around me and your lips on mine. And I'm glad you're finally over your cold. But if it comes back while you're here, I'll make you a pot of hot pee. I slept my cold away.

"You'll find my poem at the end of this email. Once I get hold of a title, the poem writes itself. It's always difficult to know when to end it; however, I remember you saying the same thing.

"Our club meeting is Saturday, and I plan to bake two cakes. The speaker has photographed many famous writers including Norman Mailer and Gore Vidal, and he'll be sharing those pictures with us. Duke, the writer who helps set up the chairs and speaker's podium with Ray is a personal friend of the speaker and recommended him. It will be a nice change to have a photographer speak.

"I'll be busy tomorrow getting my column ready for 'The Scribe.' I plan to write about 'Point of View.' You pick the dates for your visit. Other than this Saturday, I'm free to make love any day.

"Much love and then some. Your sex kitten."

"WHAT IF?

What if you had been my first love
And wedded we'd become?
Would I have treasured every day with you?
Would our union have been as one?

Would holding hands have held such bliss?
Would we have laughed and loved as now?
Would our souls be there in every kiss?
Would our love endured our vow?

Making babies with you? A perfect dream.
The thought of it melts my heart.
Would they have looked like you? Smiled like
      me?
Be mischievous and smart?
Showering together, breaking bread,
Ordinary things, that's true,
Become extraordinary things when you're
      around
Because fate has destined me for you.

I'll never know what might have been,
I can only guess, somehow—

What I do know is this. I'm in love with Kurt.
He's my yesterday, my tomorrow, and my now.

"OTKYLA. Forever yours. Eva."

Chapter Twenty-Five

After my morning cup of decaf, I scraped off wallpaper border from both bathrooms. But like everything else, they'd become dated. When I finished up, I found an email from Kurt.

"Lovely Eva,

"I received your poem, and it brings tears to my eyes each time I read it. The what-might-have-been always evokes the bitter/sweet side of life. Fun to contemplate, but sad in knowing that it could have been. The part about making babies really gets to me. Children are the kickstands of our lives. I'll always wonder how it would have felt giving you my strong semen and watching my baby grow inside you. Yes, strong language that I enjoy fantasizing about. Thank you for the poem. I am sure more heart-felt poems will follow. I think I've broken your code for OTKYLA. Is it 'Oh, to kiss your little ass?' Although, that doesn't sound like it would come from you.

"I'll close now as I want to hit the road and get some breakfast. I'll make my flight reservations and let you know what they are. I can't wait to see you and make love with you again. Our last lovefest was truly fantastic. We finally got to mix our DNA.

"Cats are intended to teach us that not everything in nature has a function." Garrison Keilor. "I'm the only man you'll ever need. ATKU. Kurt."

After reading Kurt's email, I leaned back in my chair and froze. He'd misinterpreted two words in OTKYLA. They were 'Oh, to kiss your LIPS AGAIN <u>and not</u> LITTLE ASS.

I poured myself another cup of coffee and answered Kurt's email.

"I'm glad you liked the poem. Assuming you and I had gotten together in our younger years, I have no doubt we'd have pumped out a brood of kids, and we both would have kept in shape chasing after them and breaking up fights if half had my liberal views and half had your conservative views. I'm sure some would have gone into politics. Who knows? One might have been poet laureate.

"I stare at your pic in uniform every day while I'm working at the computer, and I sift through our naughty pics weekly—so fun. Yes. We must do this again—same lovers, different poses. You were pretty kinky for not having done this before.

"You mentioned that beating a woman is a kind of sex drive, like Ned did with me; and I agree. When I'd fight back, he wanted me more; so I acted passive and disinterested to just get it over with, and that usually worked.

"It's all in the past, and I survived. I still have to pinch myself to realize what a special love we have. ILU and INU for the rest of my life. Lucky Eva.

"P.S. LA means LIPS AGAIN."

Saturday's meeting drew a full house with the famous photographer; and my cakes were a hit. I doctored up cake mixes—using lots of lemon in one of them with a light lemon glaze. For the other one, I buttered a cake pan and put in melted butter, brown sugar, and pineapple slices and I poured the yellow cake mix over the top, making it into a pineapple upside down cake. Ray had arrived early and made a large pot of decaf that we all enjoyed with slices of the cakes. I often wonder whether our desserts aren't a bigger draw than the speakers.

* * * * *

Kurt was arriving the following week. And at his suggestion, I would just ride by the United Airways arrival terminal about fifteen minutes after his projected arrival time, which would give him ample time to grab his bag off the carousel and be waiting at curbside.

So, that's what we did, and on my first drive-by, Kurt was at the curb with his luggage. After pushing the trunk opener, I hopped out of the car and kissed the white-haired stud.

"Perfect timing, and you look beautiful." His voice was deep and husky as he settled in the passenger seat. "Can't wait to kiss you more thoroughly."

"And I can't wait to get your clothes off you. Are you as excited as I am?"

"Haven't you noticed this bulge in my pants? Every time I think of you, it gets bigger."

"Let me check it out." I reached for him while trying to edge my car away from the curb.

"Please concentrate on driving. This bulge will still be here when we reach your condo."

And he was right. After greeting Moxie, we both headed for the bedroom. We lay on the bed gazing at one another and sharing sweet, ardent kisses. My man was the best kisser in the world, and I was happy in his arms.

"I can't believe the tingling feelings racing through me," I said, blowing in Kurt's ear.

"Isn't it great!" he responded. "I thank my lucky stars we met up again and fell in love."

"It's hard to believe how your pecker responds. You **are** eighty-one."

"You're the right person for me, that's why." He paused a moment. "A pilot friend of mine, in his late forties, told me a story about his and his wife's sex life. He said he couldn't get his dick up when engaging in sex with her and thought that part of his life was over."

"Over in his forties?"

"Yeh, and he said he accepted it. Then when he was out of town on an assignment, he'd gone to the USO, and a gal there asked him to dance; and while they danced, his cock started pressing against his pants. He knew it wasn't the right thing to do, but as the evening wore on, they checked into a motel. The gal was reluctant to have sex, and he said it was okay because he was married and didn't want to cheat on his wife. But after a few steamy kisses, logic fell to the wayside, and they tore each other's clothes off, and he said he pounded the hell out of her."

"After that illicit episode, did he end up wanting to have sex with his wife again?"

"No, he started seeing May whenever he could; and he and his wife divorced, and he ended up marrying May."

"Wow! What a story. I feel rather sad for his ex-wife. What happened to her?"

"She moved back to her hometown and connected with a fellow she used to know."

"Life sure is weird at times, isn't it?" I asked.

"Yeh, and it sure is horny at times. Like now."

I wondered briefly if I should seduce a promise from Kurt to eat at an Indian restaurant, but I decided to bring the matter up at another time. It had been a month since we'd seen one another. So, we tore each other's clothes off, and Kurt pounded the hell out of me. Sigh.

The next morning, we drove to Coco's for breakfast, had bacon and eggs, decaf coffee, and overdosed on their honey-bran muffins. "Almost as sweet as your kisses," I said.

Kurt's chest puffed out.

* * * * *

During Kurt's visit, we wrapped and packed about one hundred miniature display pigs, and I finished cleaning out my file cabinets; and Kurt shredded the last of the unwanted papers.

One day we drove to the Ventura Pier and walked the beach. We sat in beach chairs we'd brought with us, and we stared at the waves and each other in awe. A fellow in his mid-twenties stopped by. He said he's visiting from Canada and stops at various beaches for introspection.

Another day Kurt and I drove to mid-Wilshire to the La Brea Tar Pits. No excavation was in process that day, but we strolled the grounds, stopping at various sites to view some of the discoveries. We stopped at Pit 91 right in the heart of Los Angeles. It was hard to believe these tar pits are in a section of town surrounded by shops and activity.

As we drove home, Kurt looked over the brochures he'd picked up and asked, "Can you believe all the extinct creatures who roamed Ice Age Los Angeles over ten thousand years ago?"

"It's a fascinating place. I bring my out-of-town guests to the pits." I laughed.

"I take my guests to the Moundsville State Penitentiary. Have you ever been there?"

"Our Civics class took a field trip to the penitentiary, and we saw the room where prisoners on death row were hung. A very sobering experience."

"Yeh, it is. But they stopped hanging prisoners years ago and now use lethal injections."

"Let me tell you something I bet you don't know," I interjected. "At the time our class went to the Moundsville Penitentiary, the warden's name was U. Ketchum. Isn't that hilarious?"

"That is funny, and I didn't know that."

"There are lots of places I'd like you to see in Los Angeles, but time is running out."

"It's okay. Every state has its own unique flavor. Georgia is filled with Civil War museums that I'd like to check out. I've read a lot of books about the Civil War, and I'm now reading 'Grant' by Ron Chernow."

"Did you know that in the Civil War days shoemakers didn't make a left shoe and a right shoe? They only made one shoe? And that shoe, when worn on the same foot day-after-day, molded to that particular foot?"

Kurt laughed. "Are you making this up?"

"That's the same reaction I got from my brother when I told him. At the time we were visiting Lexie in Georgia and had gone to a Civil War museum in Andersonville. Since my brother didn't believe me, I asked the curator there, and he said, "Your companion is right.""

Chapter Twenty-Six

I interviewed Sharron Black, a go-getter realtor, to see whether she could set appointments to view similar condos as mine, with add-ons, so I could assess my competition. She said she'd get on it immediately.

I then called Wanda, and she said she'd heard from Sally, who told her a private room is now available at the assisted living facility in Madison.

"Wow! The timing couldn't be better."

"Sally said she drove to the facility to see the room and said it's very nice and has a large window overlooking a rose garden. How perfect is this? I told Sally I'd have you call her to make arrangements for my flight to Madison."

"I think I hear excitement in your voice; am I right?"

"Yes. Sally has sent me pictures of her son with Mike and his son with his deceased wife. The kids look a lot like my husband, and that puts an ache in my heart—an ache because Larry can't enjoy this time with me."

"He's in your heart. You'll still enjoy meeting the family together."

"What a lovely thought, Eva."

"Let me share more good news. I interviewed a realtor earlier today who will show me similar properties as mine; afterwards, we can stop by to see whether you'd like to list with her."

"If you feel she'll do a good job, just hire her. You have my power of attorney." Tears slid down Wanda's cheeks as she said, "You've been closer to me than family."

When I got home, I called Sally to coordinate flight reservations, saying I'll be free all next week. The plan is for her husband to fly into Los Angeles on Monday evening, stay over-night, and he and Wanda would depart for Madison on a seven o'clock flight the next morning.

* * * * *

On Tuesday morning as I pulled into the Holiday Inn, Mike walked towards us. His only bag was a backpack in order to accommodate Wanda's four suitcases. Traffic was light on the way to the airport, and when we arrived, Mike removed Wanda's luggage while Wanda and I hugged. As I pulled away, I turned and saw Wanda throwing me kisses. I was shaken, wondering whether she is doing the right thing entrusting herself to 'relative strangers.' While I pondered the significance of those words, I prayed Wanda will be glad she moved to be near them.

* * * * *

Later that day, I met Sharron at one of the condos with an add-on; but it wasn't as cheery as mine. We viewed three more similar condos, but they also weren't as appealing. Sharron said, "When you walk into your condo, you're met with a bright, warm feeling, and the renovations are first-class. I think we should list it for five thousand dollars more than the other models."

I nodded my approval and said, "When I'm ready to list."

Next, we toured Wanda's condo, and after reviewing comps of her condo, Sharron arrived at a listing price and said, "This place is a mess, but nothing a coat of paint can't cure."

Pulling the handyman's repair list from my purse, I handed it to Sharron. After reviewing it, she said she'd urge potential buyers to buy the condo 'as is' and then upgrade it whenever they could afford to do so. I said I wanted to speak to Wanda first, and Sharron agreed.

I was eager to phone Kurt about the day's events but decided to wait for Wanda's call. The phone rang as I finished a bland TV dinner. Wanda said she'd arrived tired but in one piece and was settled in her private room. "The room has a large window overlooking a rose garden. The staff is friendly and helpful; and Sally said she's glad I joined her family."

"That's sweet," I said. I told Wanda about the listing price Sharron came up with, and Wanda offered no argument. "I just want it to sell quickly, and whatever you get for my furniture is okay with me. I love you and appreciate you," she said.

"I love you, also, and get a lot of rest."

I poured myself a glass of Rose. I was exhausted but too wound-up to sleep. It was time I called Kurt to let him know what all had transpired in one day.

"That's great about listing Wanda's condo! But quite a burden on you to empty it and sell it when you still have lots to do before you list your condo for sale."

"I'll get it done."

"I'm glad I saw Wanda during my last visit because she'll probably be in Madison when I visit in March. I hung her paintings, and I especially like the one of the two birds perched on a limb. It has a First-Place Award tucked in a pocket on the back, and I can see why. She's a pro."

I told Kurt what Sharron said about listing my condo higher than the competition, and he agreed. "I'm sure it will sell fast because of all the work you put into it."

"Say, have you spoken to your sons recently? You haven't mentioned them in ages."

"I speak to them every Sunday morning, and if anything important occurs, we talk sooner. Doug drives seventy-four miles to work every day from Maryland to Washington. I think it's starting to get to him, but he loves his job."

"Sometimes it would take me an hour to drive fourteen miles on the 405 Freeway from my home in Van Nuys to my job in Westwood. But that's what people do in California. They live where houses are cheaper and drive hours to work where the money is good. I'm glad those days are over. I didn't retire until I was seventy-two and burned out."

"I was fifty-five when I retired from the State Employment Office. Before that, remember, I was in the air force for twenty years."

"You're retired for twenty-five years? You could've had a third job and three more kids." "No, thanks, to both of your fantasies."

"Well, I better get off here and hit the sack."

"Bye, sweetheart. Know you're loved."

As I was preparing for bed, Lexie called. "I hope it's not too late for a call, but we haven't talked for a while."

I told her about Wanda's move and listing her condo. "I'm going to list mine in April." "As I recall, all of your homes have sold fast because you're a good decorator."

I asked what progress is being made on my Smyrna home. Lexie said a neighbor is helping her wash woodwork and clean the house. "We found mold on the front door and on the bathroom vanities. But I bought disinfectant and bleach, and we're wearing rubber gloves; so it's not a worry. Remember, the house has been vacant for over three years."

"Didn't you tell me a widow who lived there died of MRSA? I'll worry about you!"

"We're being careful, Mom. There's not a home in the south that doesn't have mold."

I asked about Aunt Wilma and she said Aunt Wilma has a boyfriend, the fellow with the missing leg, who sits by her at the dinner table and makes sure she gets whatever she wants.

Lexie wanted to know if Wanda was excited about moving, and I said, "She likes the facility and her room and she said Sally is glad Wanda joined her family. Isn't that neat? Wanda is also excited to have her sister-in-law as a companion again. They used to be good friends."

"Moving closer to family is a no-brainer," Lexie said. She asked if I'd be hiring a moving company or whether Kurt and I plan to rent a truck and move the furniture ourselves.

"Listen to you. Did you forget my guy is eighty-one, and I want to preserve his energy for love-making instead of lying in a hospital bed with a sprained back?"

"You're so funny, Mom. I don't care how you get here, just so you get here safely."

"We will. And tell Stephen it's okay to remove the gas stove and cut off the gas, but I'd like him to leave the refrigerator so we can enjoy cold water and sodas. Kisses to Stephen."

"Will do. Love you, Mom."

Kurt called first thing in the morning while I was relaxing in my robe.

"Well, my dear, what have you planned for my next visit? Are we done shredding?"

"I believe we are, and other than reworking the by-laws to comport to the wishes of the club members and the law, my schedule is clear."

"When are you planning to list your condo?" Kurt asked.

"I'm thinking April 1st. I'd like to move in May."

"Sharron thinks that the upgrades I made by refinishing the cabinets and installing new floor tile in the kitchen and bathrooms are all pluses."

"You did all of that yourself?" Kurt asked, amazement in his voice.

"I'm a very handy person to have around."

"So why do you need me?" Kurt joked.

"You'll be my boy-toy."

"I can handle that," he said smugly, "with flourish."

"I like that 'with flourish.' Can you tell me what that entitles me to receive?"

"No, but I'll show you the next time I see you."

"I can hardly wait. Before I forget, would you like to attend our next club meeting in April? Gene Perret will be speaking. He's written for some of the greatest comedians and television shows, such as *The Beautiful Phyllis Diller Show*, *Welcome Back, Kotter,* and *Three's Company*. He was also Bob Hope's head writer for the last twelve years of Hope's career."

"I bet he has some funny tales to tell about being Hope's head writer. Let me know when he'll be speaking, and I'll make my reservations to include that date."

"I already know the date. It's April 15th, so come a few days earlier, okay?"

"I sure will. I know you're under a lot of pressure, so I'll wait in the wings until you need me. You, of course, realize that Moxie is the only one you can sleep with, besides me."

"You must also realize he's the only one, other than me, that you can sleep with."

Kurt's guttural laugh thrilled me.

"Oh, yes, Moxie got the hanky soaked in your cologne, and I find it all over the house."

"I'm glad he's enjoying it. ... Well, sweetheart, I'll close now. I'm crazy in love with you and can't wait to see you."

The next morning I awoke with an email awaiting me from Kurt.

"Dear Chocolate Eyes,

"My old friend Stumpy will give me a lift to the airport and pick me up on my return trip. The long-term parking and shuttle routine is for the birds.

"Got my tooth fixed today, so I can bite you. Got my ears cleaned so I can hear you.

My eyes are o.k. and I expect to see all sorts of things. Yeah, time is growing short.

I'm already packing. Both cameras are loaded with fresh batteries. I want to take a lot of good pictures and the other kind, as well. Can you smell a good week on the horizon?

"Now that I'm in weight training, perhaps I can pick you up. Remember when we both fell to the floor when I tried to lift you? Viva Las Vegas. Time to hit the road for coffee and a goodie. Know that my arms will be wrapped around you soon. Your excited lover."

Chapter Twenty-Seven

I got up early and cleaned the house from top to bottom while the handyman washed the windows inside and out. When finished, I called Sharron to say I'm ready to list my condo. She told me again to plan on my home selling quickly because of its move-in-ready condition.

"Kurt wants to be here when I say my last goodbyes to my friends." Sharron thought that was very thoughtful of him and hoped she could meet him while he's here.

I'd placed an ad in the local newspaper to sell Wanda's miscellaneous items and small appliances, and they sold quickly. One scroungy but pleasant guy paid two dollars for each of the forty music albums he bought. One lady paid one hundred fifty dollars for Wanda's etagere with unusual seashells.

A few days later as I was cleaning out Wanda's garage, a young lady stopped by and wanted to view Wanda's condo. I tried calling Sharron, but she didn't answer. Not wanting to pass up a sale, I walked through Wanda's condo with the young lady Karen.

"I really like the layout and can see myself living here, but it's a complete mess." That's when I whipped out the handyman's estimate of renovations from my purse and handed it to Karen. Her eyes lit up like lightbulbs. "Can I take this home while I check out my finances?"

I handed her Sharron's realtor card and told her to negotiate with Sharron. As she walked to her car, I swear I saw a zip in her step that wasn't there earlier.

Within a couple of days after my listing, an elderly couple walked through my condo with Sharron. Moxie and I sat on the patio, and I heard the wife say she liked the front door with the stained cut-glass insert of a large red rose, and she commented on the skylight in the living room containing a smattering of stars. They didn't make an offer that day, but I was hopeful.

Later in the week, several other interested people came through. Sharron said one couple tried to negotiate the price down, but she felt it was too soon for that, however. By the end of the week, we had an offer from the first couple that had looked at my condo. The offer was more in the ballpark, but still a little low. After thinking things over, the first couple withdrew their offer and accepted my original listing. They would pay cash and wanted a twenty-day escrow. I agreed if I could rent-back my condo for a few days. They agreed, and we signed the papers.

I called Kurt to share the good news. He was ecstatic that my condo sold so quickly.

"Because the price was right," I added.

"Because you worked your ass off putting it in the best light possible."

"When are you planning your move to Georgia?" he asked.

"As soon as the escrow closes, and I have a check in my hands."

"Since I'm flying into Los Angeles in April, I think I should stay until we get you packed and have sent the furniture movers on their way; and then we can start our drive to Georgia."

"That sounds super, Kurt! I can't believe things are working out for us."

* * * * *

I immediately started selling things. My spare bedroom furniture went to a couple who wanted it for their father. They also bought my treadmill. I already knew how expensive it is to move a heavy treadmill. I sold my old bedroom set to a young couple who agreed to wait until the movers emptied my home before returning to get it. They were very happy to get a queen bedroom set, and I was happy for someone to take it off my hands, let alone pay for it.

* * * * *

On April thirteenth I picked Kurt up at curbside at United Airlines about eight in the evening. Traffic was heavy, so I just popped the trunk, and Kurt put his luggage in. We kissed warmly as he seated himself in the passenger seat, and we talked non-stop to Camarillo.

As I pulled my car into the garage, Kurt got his bag out and followed me into the kitchen.

"Wow! Look at all you've accomplished since my last visit."

He picked me up and swung me around while Moxie watched. "I think you lost weight."

"Probably due to running over to Wanda's condo to sell things, and back here to clean."

While I gathered Moxie in my arms and kissed him, Kurt petted his furry head.

"I can see a light at the end of the tunnel," I said brightly.

"I hope the tunnel stays lit for the twenty-day escrow. That's an awfully short escrow, but since you can rent-back, I guess it's no problem. Any bites on Wanda's condo?"

I told Kurt about cleaning Wanda's garage when a young lady pulls into the driveway and asks to see the condo. She liked the layout, saying it was perfect for her, but she didn't like the disrepair of the condo. That's when I whipped out the handyman's renovation list, and a smile crossed her face. I gave her Sharron's number and told her to negotiate with Sharron."

"Wasn't that a stroke of luck?" Kurt said.

That night in bed, Kurt showed me what 'with flourish' meant: a sexual act that drove me crazy. I felt glutted, replete, and sated all at once. Now my man will get the 'flourish,' and I gave him an 'around-the-world adventure' that he'd never experienced before, or so he said.

Kurt and I are still in the 'lover's high' stage of romantic love, explained by experts as having elevated levels of dopamine in our systems, much like a cocaine hit that you want to feel again and again. No doubt about it, we're attracted to one another physically and chemically. Whatever the chemical is, we're happy to enjoy it at the ages of eighty and eighty-one. This should reassure seniors that romantic love can happen at any age. It's beautiful, and it's healthy.

* * * * *

As the sun broke through the windows, I opened my eyes and nudged Kurt. "Gosh, it feels good to just lazy in bed," he said.

"It's nine o'clock and I'm eager to get hustling. I want to call moving companies for estimates, and I want to put a note on the bulletin board at the association office about pictures and miscellaneous items for-sale. Then I'm free for the day."

"I'd like to have breakfast at IHOP and then drive to the Camarillo Airport for one last time. I enjoy viewing the planes stored there and hanging out with the guys. Would you mind?"

"Not at all. I'll brew a pot of coffee while I call Mayflower and Alliance Movers."

Over breakfast, Kurt said he'd pay for the gas and food for our trip to Georgia.

"I appreciate that," I said, "but I'm just glad to have a traveling companion."

He won the argument; and I offered to pay for the motels.

Kurt's animation at the Camarillo airport while viewing the aircraft, and discoursing with the guys attending them, was contagious. We spent over two hours there. I'm sure Kurt was thinking he'd rather live in Camarillo than Georgia. But the matter is moot.

We grabbed a sandwich at the café next door and then drove back to my condo so I could get the by-laws emailed to Ray for distribution. Ray and I then engaged in an exchange of emails concerning the meeting Saturday. We work together on the newsletter, and we always agree on content. I confide in Ray regularly, and I'll miss this true friend very much when I move.

Kurt and I spent the rest of the day visiting my Camarillo friends for last goodbyes, although many were meeting Kurt for the first time. We stopped to say goodbye to Vince and Patty. Vince was in charge of ordering supplies for the homeowner association when I served on the board of directors. He said he used to live in Smyrna and had liked living there; but he wanted to retire in a warmer climate.

We then walked next door to visit Ed and Ilene. When I was on the board, Ed was insurance committee chairman; and he and Ilene and I shared many home-cooked dinners.

Visiting Natasha was emotional. Her husband and I connected because of our writing ventures, in which I'd been critiquing Gerry's memoirs about living in England and working for the queen's elite cavalry of horsemen. Gerry, smart man, taped his memoirs before passing.

We made one last stop to say goodbye to my neighbors across the street. He's had a series of heart attacks, and his wife's dementia is worsening. "She may not recognize me," I said. She did, however, and gave me a huge smile. Kurt shook hands with her and Charles and accepted a cup of decaf from Charles. Charles told about the day he'd had his first heart attack. "I didn't know what to do with my wife, and I saw that Eva was at home; so I started to wheel Carla across the street. I didn't have much time as the ambulance was on its way. Eva met us in the street and told me to go home and lie on the couch. She assured me she'd care for Carla."

We didn't stay long because Teresa was arriving to make dinner and to help them bathe. I hugged Carla and Charles, and I made a point to wish Teresa well. One day when I was ill, Teresa brought me some delicious chicken soup.

"I can see why you're going to miss your friends," Kurt said as we left. "You've all bonded. But you'll make new friends. I know it's hard to believe that now, but you're the kind of person that will always have a lot of friends."

I teared up when Kurt said that, but it reassured me that I should look forward to this move as a new adventure with my beloved fiancé and my Georgia family.

* * * * *

The writer's club meeting was held the next day, and I took a crockpot of meatballs. Another member brought a Texas sheet cake.

Nancy and Brad arrived at the hall the same time as Kurt and I did, and after greetings, the guys sat next to one another. Gene Perret appeared as I was concluding the monthly meeting, and members helped stack his most recent books on a table by the podium.

Perret told of traveling with Bob Hope as his Head Writer during Hope's last twelve years of his career. Perrett said many of his funniest one-liners came to him as he soaked in the tub after Hope's gigs. He received three Emmy Awards and one Writer's Guild Award, although he'd been nominated for seven Emmy nominations, including one for original music. He authored over forty books, and members lined up to buy his books and to talk with him.

After cleaning up the hall, Nancy, Brad, Kurt and I ate at a Chinese restaurant nearby.

"The guy could be a comedian himself," Brad said. "He had some funny material."

Kurt said he always liked Bob Hope's humor.

It was fun getting caught up on things going on in our lives. I thought about how I'd miss Nancy, and I wondered whether I'd have another friend I would enjoy and trust as much.

It was great having Kurt here for the final days of my life in Camarillo. Fourteen years, to be exact, although I'd lived in California for forty-one years—over half of my life.

Sharron called when we got home and said the woman I'd shown Wanda's condo to a week earlier had decided to buy it and use the handyman's guide to make renovations.

"Whoopee!" I shouted as I hung up the phone.

Kurt wanted to know what all the hullaballoo was about, and I told him Wanda's condo had sold. He popped a bottle of Burgundy, and we toasted the sale.

Kurt seemed very talkative, telling me about setting at a table at the Mall with Joe and Marla just before flying out here, and relating our intentions to drive to Smyrna when the escrow closes. Although my fiancé has a very good command of the English language, he consistently uses the word 'setting' for the word 'sitting,' and that drives me nuts.

"It's sitting, not setting," I said, standing in front of the recliner he's relaxing in. "And every time you use the word 'setting,' I'm going to pinch your balls."

Kurt starts yelling, "Setting, setting, setting," and I sat on his lap and pinched his balls. "Dear Diary," he said.

"Are you still writing in your diary?" I asked, getting cozy in his lap.

"It's been about six months since I wrote in it, and it's a journal, not a diary."

"You've been writing in it since President Kennedy's assassination; right?"

"Yeah, I thought my sons might enjoy reading it after my demise. I've been including bits of history with bits about my own life."

I asked if I'm in it, and Kurt said the first entry of me is when we meet in Vegas.

"I've been wanting to get away like that again, and guess what. I have tickets for two nights' stay at the Aquarius Casino & Hotel in Laughlin, and two tickets to see Tony Orlando."

"How did you manage that?" Kurt asked.

"Donna and I would go there quite frequently, and we'd build up points from gambling. These are enticements to keep us going back."

Kurt asked how far Laughlin is from Camarillo, and I told him about a four-hour drive.

"It sounds like fun. But who would watch Moxie?"

"I'll ask Rebecca, Carole's daughter, to watch him this time."

"What about Donna. I thought you said Moxie loves Donna."

"That's another story I'll tell you about later."

"Then let's do it. But let's run some bath water and set in the tub first."

"Do you want me to pinch your balls again?"

"What do you think?"

Chapter Twenty-Eight

The trip to Laughlin was uneventful, and I pulled into the parking structure at the Aquarius Casino about three o'clock in the afternoon. Kurt and I checked into our room on the third floor and immediately lay down for a nap. The next thing I felt was hot breath on my neck.

"Hey, sleepyhead," Kurt said. "Do you want to stay in bed or get some food and do some gambling? I'm feeling faint."

"I was just feeling amorous," I said, but I got up, put the lust button on pause, and called Moxie. I said I love him and hope he's having fun with Rebecca.

After a lovely dinner and two hours of losing on the quarter poker machines, we headed back to our room. On the way, we stopped to get tickets for the boat ride down the Colorado River tomorrow afternoon; we also confirmed our tickets for the Tony Orlando show tomorrow night. The tickets were in the fourth row, right section. Kurt and I were impressed with such good seats that cost me no up-front cash—just a year's worth of losing on the quarter machines.

After imbibing large margaritas with dinner and playing the slots for several hours, we were ready for a tussle between the sheets.

"I love how passionate you are," Kurt said, as I undressed in front of him. "And I love your big boobs."

"And didn't I hit the jackpot with your pecker that grows with every kiss? You remind me of Pinocchio. Yes, you have a Pinocchio pecker."

"Then kiss me and watch it grow," Kurt said; and I obliged.

I'll let you imagine what happens when two naked bodies slip into bed next to one another—two hot, naked bodies. And let me repeat: Love in your Golden Years can be hot!!!!!

It was a blistering hot day as we cruised up the Colorado River, drinking cold beer. An overhead fan circulated the air somewhat while a warm breeze slowly swept the deck. Kurt had started up a conversation with the couple sitting next to us, telling them about our reconnecting sixty-two years after having graduated high school together.

Dorothy, the wife, said, "What a sweet story." Her husband had a glassy look in his eyes as Kurt continued. "My fiancée tells me every day how happy I am, and I agree with her because she knows about those things. And she is the most unjealous person I know. For my birthday last year she bought tickets for the Hollywood Bowl, including the bus ride to the Bowl. The thing is, it was a trip celebrating the Women's Club of the Catholic Church, and the bus driver and myself were the only two men on a busload of fifty women."

"Didn't you sit next to a woman who spoke German to you before the show and during intermission?" I asked.

"You're right. I did enjoy myself."

Kurt had an enthralled audience in Dorothy and her husband, so he continued. "Eva and I are happy in love after sixty-two years. Sometimes I have to pinch myself to believe it's real."

"Darling, pinching you is my job; remember?"

I drank a third beer, which I never do, but the heat was unbearable.

Dorothy's husband spoke. "You best rethink a move to Georgia if you think today is hot. Our son lives in Georgia and wants us to move there, but Dorothy doesn't like the humidity."

"If it's only in the summer months, I'll learn to deal with it," I said.

* * * * *

When we got back to the Casino, Kurt wanted to go to the room to nap; but I wanted to gamble, so I took a seat at the quarter poker machines and played for another hour. After winning two hundred dollars, I went up to the room. Kurt was asleep, and I lay down beside him. I love this man. He's good-looking, generous, and fun to be with, but I don't like the part of him that always feels the need to entertain people. *Who else has that same trait?* I thought. It's right at the tip of my tongue, waiting to slip out. Well, Ned Kanecki, of course, my first Leo husband. He'd get mad if I told jokes and got any attention. In fact, many an abusive attack took place when the evening's attention was focused on me. Will I have that to look forward to, or will my stopping to tell jokes cure things before they got out of hand? I can't even remember how long it's been since I told a joke to anyone. Something to think about and to discuss with Kurt.

* * * * *

After a delicious dinner of steak and lobster, we entered the ballroom where Tony Orlando would be performing for the nine o'clock show and were ushered to the fourth row. Very good seats, I mused. Soon the house lights dimmed, and Tony Orlando ran onto the stage to wild applause. The first thing he did was acknowledge his wife and mom, who were sitting in the row in front of us. His mom looked like a typical Italian mom, with thick dark hair and laughing eyes, slightly heavy through the midsection. Tony's wife, also a brunette, had lovely, smooth skin, delicate features, and a shapely but full figure. It was fun seeing them react to Tony's wit. We all sang along to "Tie a Yellow Ribbon Round an Old Oak Tree." From then on, the audience was his. His voice was still deep and throaty; he was still handsome, but now with greying hair. Although someone's Italian cooking had added a few pounds to his midriff, he still cavorted on the stage like a young bull, and his skill as an entertainer had not diminished one iota. He was one hot *daddy,* and the audience loved him.

A highlight I remember was when Tony introduced the lady who made the song, "Meow, Meow, Meow" popular, singing it on commercials while advertising cat food. She sang it tonight point perfect, and the audience gave her a resounding applause.

* * * * *

That night in bed, wrapped in Kurt's arms, we did a little reminiscing. I asked if he remembers the musical entertainment television show, *Tony Orlando and Dawn,* and he said he and Pam watched it faithfully.

"I loved it, and I think Tony still has his deep, rich voice," I said.

"That's one of the best shows I've ever seen," Kurt responded. "Thank you for bringing me across state lines to see it."

"You're welcome, but that's not the only reason I brought you across state lines," I said, placing my hand on his pecker. "Now tell me a lie, Pinocchio."

Not missing a beat, Kurt said, "I just found out my dick is a Democrat."

I asked him how he knows that, and he said his dick enjoys screwing people. He then said he's switching back to a Republican and wants to know what political persuasion my twickie is.

I said it's a Democrat and that I'm allergic to Republican dicks.

"You sure know how to hurt a guy."

"You fell into that one. But just kidding. I think your pecker is a perfect size for me."

"It does fit you perfectly," he said, mounting me and slowly urging it into my play zone.

"I love you, Kurt," I said and felt Kurt's pushes get stronger and faster.

"I love you more, Eva."

"That's probably why our love-making is so great. Don't you think?" I asked.

"Everything is better when you're in love," he responded.

"Did I ever tell you about my friend Grace never having an orgasm?"

"Please, Eva, I don't want to hear about Grace when we're making love."

"Oh, okay. I'll nibble on your ear instead."

"If you need to nibble on something, I have the perfect item for you to nibble on…but I'll have to withdraw Dickie for a minute."

"Oh, no you don't. I'll just keep my mouth shut, okay?"

The next morning we had an early breakfast, played a few slots, and headed back to Camarillo. It took about five hours of shared driving. Moxie came running into the kitchen to greet us. I picked him up and loved on him while Kurt brought our suitcases in.

The escrow on my home is set to close on Friday morning, four days away, and there's a lot to do before then; and of course, the May writer's club meeting is Saturday. The speaker, Louise Cabral, is speaking for the second time before our club. She's written a book, *Islands of Recall*, in which she gives guidelines for writing one's life story, and I'd bought it the first time she spoke. It helps jog one's memory about childhood and teenage experiences, and adulthood. Louise is a very effective speaker, and members are excited about her return engagement.

The hospitality chair is bringing cold cuts, and another member is baking a white coconut cake. All I have to do is to show up and conduct the meeting and present the Nominating Committee's slate of officers. A vote for officers would then take place at the June meeting, at which time I would fly back from Georgia to conduct that meeting, the last one of my term.

Although the buyer had agreed to let me rent back my condo after the escrow closed, Kurt and I decided to hole up in a local motel for Friday and Saturday night instead. My bedroom set was picked up on Friday morning by the young couple who bought it a few weeks earlier, and the rest of my furniture would be picked up by Mayflower Movers Friday afternoon; so there was no incentive to rent an empty condo for two days.

Saturday's meeting went very well. After announcing the slate of officers, I said that if any member wanted to nominate another member for an office, they were free to do so, as long as they asked for and received that person's consent before our June meeting.

Before adjourning, I stated that not only the election of officers would take place at the June meeting, but members would also be voting on the amended by-laws.

Nancy, Brad, Kurt and I had dinner together after the meeting. I wondered whether I would ever share a special friendship with someone in Georgia as I have with Nancy. We're both Catholic; we're both writers; we share many of the same values. Her husband and Kurt have begun a kindred relationship that won't be easy to duplicate, either. We would miss them. We didn't linger at the restaurant because I felt sorry for Moxie spending the day alone; and I had phone calls to make before hitting the sack. Nancy and I both had tears in our eyes as we hugged.

The first call was to Lexie. I wanted her to know we'd be on our way in the morning. She said she and Stephen took an air mattress and bed linens over to my home just in case we arrived before my furniture did. I thanked her and said we are looking forward to my move.

"Don't push it," she said. "Take your time and enjoy the trip."

We talked about Aunt Wilma, and Lexie said Aunt Wilma is excitedly looking forward to seeing me and meeting Kurt, although she'd met him twice before.

I then called Susan to say we're all packed and would stop by in the morning around eight o'clock. She offered to make breakfast, but I told her we planned to eat on the road later.

Hanging up, I heard bath water running. Stepping into the bathroom, Kurt looked up at me intently and said: "I knew you'd like a leisurely bath, and so would I."

He then wiped away my tears.

Chapter Twenty-Nine

Kurt had set his I-Phone alarm for seven o'clock, and when it rang, we both jumped up and got dressed. I put fresh food and water in Moxie's dishes, and Kurt and I finished packing.

How lucky we were that Moxie liked to travel. Although his bed sat on top of a suitcase in the backseat, he chose to lay across my lap. He was tired, having stayed up all night smelling the animals that had left their scents in the motel room before we'd arrived. So he was ready for a snooze as Kurt slid into the driver's seat and started us on our journey.

It was a little past eight when we pulled in front of Susan and Rob's condo. Picking Moxie up, I walked to the front door with Kurt following. Susan ushered us in, and we all hugged. Susan then served hot coffee and donuts.

Moxie sat on the couch next to me, befuddled by the roomful of people, and I felt him draw close. After downing a donut, Brian knelt in front of Moxie and started petting him. Moxie isn't the most social cat in the world, but he loves Brian and remembers him from previous pats.

When Brian's interest waned, Marie sat next to Moxie and me. As she petted Moxie, she said she'd miss me and would like to fly out to visit when we got settled.

Susan and Rob talked about driving to Georgia to see us, and I suggested we could all drive to Savannah where *Gone with the Wind* had been filmed. We were making wonderful plans to see one another, and that made me feel good.

I vowed not to cry when we left, but I couldn't keep that vow. Kurt said later that I said I was probably making a big mistake by moving, although I don't remember saying that.

Kurt drove while Moxie and I returned to our previous positions. I told Kurt about the time my daughters and I drove cross-country from Ohio to California after my divorce from Ned.

"That was in June 1965 right after school let out. I wanted to allow enough time to get settled in a home before enrolling the girls in school. Susan was eight and Lexie was twelve."

"Didn't Ned try to stop you from moving the kids across the country?"

"My divorce was granted on the ground of *extreme cruelty,* and I was awarded full custody of Susan and Lexie. I don't remember whether Ned asked for joint custody or whether the court made that determination on its own. Since I didn't have family or a job in California, I had thought Ned might try to stop me from moving our daughters out of the state, but he didn't."

"That's interesting," Kurt said.

"Anyway, I bought myself a new, black, Chevrolet Impala ragtop, and we drove to California in it. Susan and Lexie took turns sitting in the front passenger seat. We'd stop at nice motels for the night, usually ones that had pools, and the girls would swim either before or after dinner. I wanted to build good memories rather than dwell on the past."

"That sounds like a positive plan. And how long did it take you to get to California?"

"Four and a half days."

"You made good time."

"We drove around five hundred miles a day, sometimes more. I'd decided to have Mayflower move my daughters' bedroom set with their twin beds so they'd have familiar belongings in California. I also had my living room and bedroom furniture sent. Since my furniture wasn't considered a full load, I was told it would probably take three or four weeks before it would arrive; but it actually took six weeks."

"Where did you stay while waiting for your furniture to arrive?"

"We stayed with Julie, her husband and four kids until the furniture arrived. I'd rented an apartment close to the grade school, and when the furniture arrived, we moved into it."

"That's a long time to stay with someone. When Pam and I moved back to Ohio, we stayed with her sister Deena and husband Ed for two weeks and couldn't handle the regimented schedule Ed imposed, and we moved out within a week. Deena was easy to get along with, but Ed was difficult, always upset over something and changing plans. When we weren't living with them, we all got along fine."

"It was tough having six kids under one roof, but we managed. Julie and I were like sisters, having been friends since we were five and seven, and we stayed in close touch through the years. Her husband Bob was a great guy, and we all spent a lot of time together, always enjoying holidays together. Now Julie and Bob are gone; and I miss them very much. Julie's daughter Carole still stays in touch. Strange how life goes on with its many twists and turns."

"I'll buy that. Look how you and I got together."

"I think it's because of the high school class reunions we attended."

"Definitely. After Pam died is when I contacted you and everyone in the class I could think of. Crazy how we started emailing one another after that. And look at us now."

"Your emails were so funny. I'd find myself laughing later in the day."

"I must confess I got a lot of my material out of joke books and a small book of favorite sayings of famous people."

"Now I wonder who the real Kurt Miller is," I said, opening a bottle of water and taking a couple of chugs, then passing it to Kurt, who emptied it.

"I'm sure you'll find out more than I'd like for you to find out during this trip," he said.

"I hope so," I retorted. "We'll soon be entering San Bernardino County, still in California. I think we can find a restaurant there."

And we did.

Kurt and I stopped short of reaching our goal of five hundred miles the first day, but it wasn't set in concrete, and we were so darned tired. Not too tired to forego a bounce between the sheets, however. We made love in seven different states before reaching Georgia: California, Arizona, New Mexico, Texas, Louisiana, Mississippi, and Alabama. By the time we reached Georgia, we were too tired to think about sex. It was the evening of our fifth day on the road that we arrived in Smyrna, and as Lexie had said, we found an air mattress in the main bedroom, all made up and ready to sleep on. After Kurt had brought in our suitcases, he announced that we'd traveled two thousand three hundred and twenty-four miles.

We quickly peeked in the different rooms. The hardwood floors looked awesome with their fresh coat of stain and varnish, but the rest of the house looked dismal. The kitchen stove and wall above it were covered with soot, which made one suspect a fire had erupted there; the kitchen floor was worn and cracked; and dirty wallpaper covered both bathrooms and the foyer.

"Maybe it looks so bad because we're tired," I said.

"No, this house is a real mess," Kurt replied.

"I'll call Lexie to tell her we've arrived."

"And I'll bring in Moxie's water and food. For some reason he doesn't seem to be interested in checking out the house."

"Probably because it smells moldy, although Lexie and a neighbor washed the woodwork with bleach water."

"It could use airing out," Kurt said, as I fished my phone from my purse and called Lexie.

She said it was a relief to hear we'd arrived safely. She then said she and Stephen would come over in the morning, probably around ten, so Kurt and I could sleep in.

Kurt and Moxie were already sleeping when I hung up.

In the morning when we walked into the kitchen, I noticed a Mr. Coffee with a bag of Maxwell House Coffee and four cups sitting on the counter that we hadn't seen last night. When I opened the refrigerator, there sat a gallon of milk and a package of cinnamon rolls.

"Honey, do you want me to bring in the two large boxes sitting on the back seat? What are they, besides heavy?"

"Dishes and pots and pans so I can cook before my furniture arrives."

* * * * *

Lexie and Stephen arrived with a card table and four chairs. After hugs, I brewed another pot of coffee, and we discussed plans to renovate the house.

"Gutting the kitchen should come first," I said.

"You read my thoughts," Stephen said. "I also suggest ripping out the kitchen flooring and installing a heavier sub-flooring. Kurt and I can start ripping as soon as we finish our coffee. Is that okay with you, Kurt?"

Kurt gulped and nodded.

"Once the flooring is down," Stephen said, "you can have kitchen cabinets and granite countertops of your choice installed."

"We could drive to Builder's Surplus to order those things," Lexie said, "while the guys work on the flooring." So that's what we did.

When we got to Builder's Surplus, Lexie worked with Hilda, the lady in charge of ordering cabinets and countertops. She handed Hilda a draft sheet of the dimensions of my kitchen with the appliances and cabinets drawn in.

"Where did you learn how to do that?" I asked, amazed.

"While working with Stephen. Is there anything you'd like to add?"

I described the eating Island I envisioned with a black granite top and fancy black legs. "Perhaps Stephen could build the frame and I could spray paint it and the legs black."

"See how fast you catch on?" Lexie said. "This is your home, and it should be renovated exactly as you would like it to be."

No sooner had we gotten home than the doorbell rang, and two Mayflower employees stood there, asking where we wanted the furniture placed.

* * * * *

Lexie and Stephen declined my dinner offer, so Kurt and I went to Charley O's for dinner and then stopped by to visit Aunt Wilma. She'd just finished dinner and was in a wheelchair watching television. She saw Kurt and me as soon as we walked in, and she acted almost giddy. I leaned down to kiss her, and she grabbed my hands and held them. Then she looked at Kurt. I said, "This is my fiance, Kurt." He hugged her and she stared at him and then looked up at me.

"Your fiance is a big man," she said, rolling her eyes. "Oh, my, you're so little…" Kurt roared.

He pushed her wheelchair to the back of the room where we could have a quiet visit. While talking, a resident I'd met while visiting my aunt when house-hunting, maneuvered his wheelchair next to Aunt Wilma's and joined our conversation. He said he'd been in the military; and he and Kurt talked about their service years. My aunt and I chatted about my move to Smyrna. She gave me the most beautiful smile.

* * * * *

For the next few weeks, Stephen and Kurt worked in the kitchen: installing heavier sub-flooring, gutting the kitchen of the cabinets and readying it for the new, cherry cabinets and beige and black-flecked granite countertops to be installed by Builder's Surplus. Stephen also installed a tankless water tank in the closet that houses the washer and dryer, and he hung cabinets for laundry supplies - all of which are hidden behind shuttered doors in the kitchen.

While the men worked, Lexie and I drove back to Builder's Surplus to pick out a dark red front door with an oval panel of cut glass in the center. It was expensive, but worth every penny because it was elegant. I also set aside double French doors that would lead to an outside deck.

On the way home, we stopped for burgers and fries. As we ate, I pointed to the large window in the kitchen where the wall cabinets ended and asked if Stephen knew of someone who could remove the window and make it into a double door leading to an outside deck. As luck would have it, Stephen has a bricklayer friend he'll put me in touch with. He didn't know of a tile man to install large marble kitchen floor tile, but I'd find one.

The guys finished what they were working on and called it a day. I could see the relief cross Kurt's face. My out-of-shape fiance isn't a worker, he's a lover.

Although we were both tired after showering, I turned off the lights and yelled, "Find Me!"

"If I find you, what's my prize?" Kurt shot back.

"Duh, we're both naked." I slid under the bed.

"Well, say something. How else am I going to find you?" Kurt pleaded.

I sensed he was walking by, so I grabbed his legs, and he screamed and fell to the carpet.

I tried to hold my breath, as he was lying next to me, but I had to exhale.

"Aha, my prize lies before me," and Kurt pulls me out, but not before we both got bruised up from banging into the bedframe.

"Remind me not to take you up on this game again."

Chapter Thirty

While sitting in the reception room at a Kaiser facility in Atlanta, awaiting my first visit with a new cardiologist, I struck up a conversation with a woman also waiting to see her doctor. She said she'd just finished renovating her kitchen; and I said my husband and I were in the process of renovating our kitchen and asked if she knew of a tile installer.

"No," she responded, "but I have a wonderful handyman who can do anything."

I asked her for his name and number, and she handed me his card.

"Be sure to tell Julio that Faith recommended him."

As soon as I got home, I called Julio to set an appointment for a quote.

* * * * *

When Julio arrived, he smiled engagingly with straight-set white teeth. He was thin, in his late twenties, and neatly dressed. "I've never done tile work before, but I know I can do it."

After surveying the room, he said he could tile the kitchen for three thousand dollars, "if you furnish the supplies."

Before firming up the deal, I took Julio into the master bedroom where my fiance and my son-in-law were working, and I introduced him.

After chatting with Julio, Stephen gave his approval.

Julio thanked us and said to let him know where I'd be buying the tile, and he'd pick them up and bring them with him when he started the job.

I told Kurt and Stephen that Julio suggested a tile store in Vinings that had recently opened up and was offering specials.

"That sounds great," Stephen said. "By the way, I really like the bathroom vanity, cupboard, and mirror you bought for the master bathroom."

"Yes, I got the set for one hundred fifty, and it came with a decent sink. I think they were on sale because of the cinnamon color, but I love that color and want to tile my bathroom floor with beige and brown tile. Just let me tile the room before you set the vanity in place."

"I plan to remove the wallpaper in here tomorrow and then you can take over. So now would be a good time for you and Kurt to go shopping for tile."

Kurt put the address of 'Floor and Décor' in his GPS, and we arrived in fifteen minutes.

The store was having an opening day sale, and Kurt and I selected a yellow marble tile with white streaks. After paying for it, we had it set aside for Julio to pick up.

On Monday morning, Julio started tiling the floor. He was meticulous in cutting and pasting the tile and setting it in place, finishing the rows off by pounding them with a mallet.

While working, he told us he was part of a combo that played at various bars and nightclubs throughout Cobb County. I was surprised to find out he played the accordian. I had always felt in my later years that the accordian was a lost art. Two of my high school classmates played the accordians. Although Carl Bullock was proficient on the instrument and even played at school assemblies, my cousin Dorothy was always taking lessons.

I trotted back in the bathroom to tell the guys about Julio playing an accordian in a combo and that he'd like for us to attend one of his gigs. Kurt nodded, and as expected, he repeated his favorite accordian joke for Stephen.

"Two musicians – a clarinet player and an accordian player – had just finished a set at the Bandar and took a break. The accordian player put his instrument in the car while the musicians went back in the nightclub for a drink. The clarinet player warned him not to leave it in the car as someone could come along and steal it, but the accordian player left it in the car anyway.

"When they came back from their break to get the clarinet and accordian, sure enough, the windows were smashed in and glass was everywhere. When they looked in the back seat of the car, two more accordians sat there." Stephen doubled over with laughter.

The guys finished removing the wallpaper and were cleaning up the room. In the morning, I would lay the small squares of floor tile.

Since it was only three-thirty and still light outside, Stephen and Kurt decided to remove the old front door and hang the new, red front door with the large oval cut-glass in the center. As they worked, I had to stop myself from drooling – it looked so beautiful.

Nick, Stephen's bricklayer friend, was coming over Saturday to remove the den window and cut into the outside brick to transform it into a door that would lead to my soon-to-be deck.

I liked Nick instantly. He was friendly, and his face had a kindly look.

The second day Nick worked, he told me he was bipolar and took meds to control his mood swings. "I really like laying bricks. It roots me in reality." He told how he'd use the bricks he'd removed to face the doorway. "Believe me, it will look like it's always been a doorway."

* * * * *

Kurt and I went out for an early dinner and stopped by to see Aunt Wilma first. The administrator, Caroline, came over to speak with us. Evidently, Aunt Wilma had lost one of her front teeth earlier in the day and nobody could find it.

"Perhaps she swallowed it?" I asked.

"It's possible," Caroline replied. She then added, "Did you know it was a false tooth?"

I was floored. I'd never seen a false tooth that looked so real and matched the other front tooth so well.

As we left the facility, I asked, "What am I going to do about getting her another tooth?"

Kurt asked if she has dental insurance.

My face must have dropped because Kurt said, "When my son Doug started to date Barb, his now wife, she needed dental work, and I paid for it. So, I guess I can pay for Aunt Wilma's dental work, as well."

"Would you do that, Kurt?" I asked, my voice trembling.

"Of course," he said.

"I'll make it up to you in sexual favors," I whispered in his ear.

"Of my choice?" he muttered, his eyes rolling back in his head, probably fantasizing.

"Why don't you stop while you're ahead," I shot back.

That night in bed, I gave Kurt a down payment on my aunt's dental work. He squealed in delight as I fondled his balls. "Do you know your balls smell like babies' feet?"

"How would I know? I never smelled them."

"Well, they do." I felt him shiver, so I guess he liked the way I toyed with them. "Do you know one ball is lower than the other ball?"

"All guys' balls are made that way so they don't rub against one another."

"I didn't know that, and I've known a few balls in my lifetime."

"That's not something I particularly want to hear – about the balls in your lifetime."

"I'm sorry, I didn't mean to hurt your feelings, but I am eighty, remember? But what I can't understand is all the glory bestowed on men's balls, even calling them the family jewels? They aren't ugly like women's pussies are, but they're not show stopper, either."

"I can't believe you're saying that. I think your pussy is pretty."

"I think you need an eye exam. You know, one day I got out my magnifying mirror and put one leg on my vanity stool and positioned the mirror under my pussy and tried to get a good look at it. I wish I hadn't done that because it's even uglier when magnified."

Kurt laughed uproariously.

"Did I tell you the joke about the husband who was hurrying to get to work and forgot his briefcase? When he returned, his wife was exercising naked, with her legs around her neck.

"Her husband sees her and says, 'For Pete's sake, Myrtle, put your teeth in and comb your hair. You're getting to look more like your mother every day.'"

I started giggling even before I got to the punch line, and Kurt was laughing so loudly and trying to get his breath that I worried he was going to pass out.

What a mess we were, laughing so hard and trying to make love during a laugh attack. Finally, Kurt rolled off me, and we called it a night.

The next morning, a Sunday, Kurt called his son, Doug, and they talked quite a while. Kurt had Doug on the speaker, and I heard Doug say he and Barb are planning a family barbeque in a couple of weeks and hoped we can make it.

I said, loudly, for Doug to hear: "We have nothing going on, except for next week, when I'll be flying back to Los Angeles for my last writer's club meeting."

Doug said it wouldn't be next week.

Kurt handed me the phone, and Doug and I spoke, mostly about the weather. I told him I am looking forward to meeting him and Barb and handed the phone back to Kurt.

When Kurt hung up, we talked about the drive to Ohio. "It's about an eleven-hour drive," Kurt said. "We probably should drive half-way and stay overnight and continue the next day."

"Since both of us will be driving, we may decide to drive all the way in."

Kurt asked if I'd mind staying a month. "I've been away for several weeks, and I have things to do back there."

"Depends if Stephen needs us. I'm okay leaving this quagmire of dirt we're living in, and I'm also eager to meet Doug and Barb. I'm surprised she hasn't wanted to talk to me on the phone."

"Maybe she'd rather meet you in person," Kurt said.

"Maybe," I replied.

Kurt said Doug's cabin at Piedmont Lake is about forty-five minutes from where he lives. He said Doug is building a new cabin in front of the old cabin because there's a lot of open land there. "He's been working on it for several years when he has time off work. A classmate from Texas and his wife own the cabin next door, and Lee often takes vacations when Doug does to help him out. Lee is a construction superintendent."

"It must be fun having a home away from home to crash in."

"It will be when the new cabin is completed, but now it's like another job for Doug."

"I'm really eager to meet your family. Do you think they'll like me?"

"Of course."

"Didn't you tell me Barb was married before?"

"Yes, she has a daughter, Laura, who was three years old when Doug and Barb got married. She's now in her twenties and attending college. Laura's father rarely saw her, so Doug became the substitute father."

I asked if Barb is the one who needed dental work that Kurt paid for, and he nodded.

"I'm also willing to pay your aunt's dental bill. How much work can she need done at one hundred? She probably doesn't have many teeth left."

"She's always taken care of her teeth. I'd say she has a mouthful that need pulled."

"Oh, crap."

"A promise is a promise," I iterated.

The next day Stephen came over later than usual because he had errands to run. He joined us at the eating Island and smiled. "This kitchen turned out really nice. You deserve a lot of credit, Eva, for designing the Island. I just built the frame."

"I appreciate everything you've done to turn this house into a home," I said.

Stephen's face turned beet red. He always had a difficult time accepting compliments.

As Stephen worked, Kurt and I talked about setting an appointment for Aunt Wilma's dental work. "Lexie gave me the phone number of her dentist, but I'd like to wait until I return from California to schedule the work. She acts like she doesn't even know her tooth is missing."

"It can wait," Kurt said. "Say, do you think we can shower together tonight and work ourselves up into a sexual frenzy? This will be our last romp for a week."

"Why don't we try out the extra-large bathtub in the hallway bathroom? I'll drop some lavender bath salts in the water."

"And I'll uncork that bottle of Grey Riesling I just bought," Kurt said.

"And you can wash my boobs and pussy, and I'll wash your pecker and lop-sided balls."

Chapter Thirty-One

How do you feel about conducting your last meeting of the writer's club?" Kurt asked, as he drove me to the Atlanta-Hartsfield Airport for my flight to California.

"I'm sad because Saturday may be the last time I see these writer friends. A good many had joined the club fifteen years ago when I did, and we've shared rejection slips and successes through the years. Ray has only been a member for five years but he's one of my best friends."

"He seems like a really nice guy," Kurt said. "Anyway, enjoy yourself in California, and don't worry about Moxie. We'll just chill out and spend some guy-time together eating tuna and watching the 'Animal Planet.'"

* * * * *

Kurt navigated his car into the Departure lane and pulled into the Southwest Terminal. Grabbing my suitcase from the trunk, he set it in front of me. "I love you, baby, and I'll miss you, but enjoy your friends."

"I love you, too," I said, turning and walking into the terminal.

* * * * *

I usually engage in conversation with the passenger seated next to me, but I wanted to focus on Saturday's meeting. So, I smiled, and the lady in the black suit smiled back, opened her laptop, and started typing. We stayed silent, in our own heads the entire flight until the pilot announced we were approaching Burbank and would be on the ground in fifteen minutes.

After retrieving my suitcase from the baggage carousel, I called my daughter, who was waiting in a nearby parking lot. When she spied me, she edged her Mazda to the curb. We hugged, and she tossed my suitcase in the back of her SUV, and we headed to the I-5.

As we sped along the freeway, she said Rob would drive me to Enterprise Rental in the morning so I can rent a car for the weekend. She confided that although she and Rob are separated, they remain good friends and still see one another.

I told her how surprised I was when she told me about their break-up.

"We've been having problems, and I thought we could work them out; but we couldn't. I'm just not ready to talk about it. Please understand, Mom."

"It's okay." I told her about all the work we're doing on my Smyrna home. "Although it's structurally sound, it's been vacant for three years. Kurt is working right along with Stephen, although Kurt is twenty years older." I wet my parched lips and said, "I'm having a kitchen window transformed into a double door leading to a projected outside deck."

Susan said that would probably add value to my home. "And in the meantime, you'll enjoy it. I'm always sitting on my front patio."

I confided to her that I hadn't met Kurt's adult sons nor their wives yet, but that we plan to drive to Kurt's home in Ohio for a get-together after I get back to Georgia.

"I'm sure it will work out when they meet you," Susan said.

It took over an hour to get from the Los Angeles Airport to Susan's condo in Valencia. Approaching her front door, my senses filled with the aroma of spices. "What smells so good?"

"Stew simmering in a crock pot. I didn't invite the kids because I knew you'd be tired; and we'll see them tomorrow."

While eating, Susan asked about my relationship with Kurt, and I told her we're still hot for one another and that it's nice knowing the same people and sharing things about them.

She asked about Wanda, and I told her that Wanda likes Wisconsin and has bonded with her nephew's wife. She said she's glad to hear that.

I told her how excited Aunt Wilma was in seeing me again. I said I'm living in Smyrna and will see her more often. Her eyes turned to Kurt; and I said, 'This is my fiance, Kurt. You met him when he visited you in Oxnard.'

"He hugged her, and she said he's a big man and I'm a little woman, and she rolled her eyes to the back of her head. Kurt had a hard time suppressing his laughter."

"Aunt Wilma can be so funny. She's one hundred and still reads in Hungarian and English to the other residents. When we visit, we sit by the window and watch the geese glide by on the pond. Aunt Wilma's roommate joins us and tells us how much she likes Aunt Wilma."

Susan poured fresh coffee and said, "I remember the time she came to visit us for a weekend when Lexie and I were in high school. On Monday morning when we tried to get in the bathroom, Aunt Wilma announced she was taking a bath. So Lexie and I washed up in the half bath. That was very thoughtless of her."

"Yes, she used to be self-absorbed and even nasty at times. But thank heavens, she's mellowed out and is very considerate and loving now."

"Nasty people usually just get nastier when they get older," Susan said.

"That didn't happen with Aunt Wilma. From what I can see, and from what Lexie tells me, she's very appreciative of what everyone at the nursing home does for her, and they all love her. In fact, all the old men there have a crush on her."

"Lexie and Stephen visit her weekly, and she flirts outrageously with Stephen. You know, she's always liked men."

Susan laughed. "Does she even know who Lexie and Stephen are?"

"She does, and look at how she recognized me after four months? She's still quite lucid for her age, and she still has twenty-twenty vision with her glasses on."

Our conversation shifted to her and Rob, and she confided the reason for their split. "It ultimately came down to a choice between Rob and Brian, and I chose my son," she said.

I sympathized, but I didn't say anything. She'd made her decision.

* * * * *

After renting a Mazda medium-size vehicle and having coffee at Starbucks with Rob, I drove to Leisure Village to visit friends. Natasha was waiting on the patio as I pulled in the driveway, and after hugs, we drove to 'Saffron Indian Cuisine' for lunch. Natasha told me she took a job as a Russian interpreter working from her home to supplement her income.

She talked about how she misses Gerry and said she's not ready for a new relationship. "I remember when Gerry first got ill, and you drove him to the hospital and then back home when he was discharged. But his last heart attack came so fast that I had to call an ambulance; and he never made it back home. I didn't have time to prepare myself for his loss," she cried.

We both dabbed at our eyes reliving those incidents; and we vowed to keep in touch.

I then drove to Donna's condo. We'd become estranged just before I moved to Georgia. I didn't feel good about our breakup. We'd been friends for fourteen years, ever since I'd moved to Leisure Village. When Donna went on vacation is when I learned she used to live on Wheeling Island, and Donna learned I used to live across the Ohio River in Tiltonsville, Ohio. We both were born at the Martins Ferry Hospital, one year apart.

I remember riding the streetcar to the Wheeling Island Roller Rink several times a week. Donna and I figured we skated at that rink at the same times. It's hard for me to pin-down our breakup except to blame Marlene who lied about what I'd said behind Donna's back and what Donna had said behind my back. Marlene was devious that way, we found out after the fact.

I was on a mission as I parked my car in Donna's driveway and ran up to the patio and rang the doorbell. Donna opened the door and opened her arms. We hugged and cried while drinking cups of coffee. She said after I'd moved to Georgia, she found out the truth and never spoke to Marlene again. "Would you believe she even talked me into putting her in my Will?"

As I slid into my car, ready to pull away, I heard Donna shouting from her doorway. "You call me, you hear?" Tears streamed down her face and my face; and my heart rejoiced.

* * * * *

Susan had just started dinner and said she didn't need any help. "Just sit on the patio until the family shows up." The patio overlooks a public golf course that's filled with stately trees and luscious greenery. Enveloping myself in the natural beauty of the landscape made me feel alive and significant. And I felt very lucky to have my best friend back in my life.

Rob showed up first, looking dapper in a short-sleeved, red-checkered shirt and jeans. After a hi and hug, he slid the screen door aside and asked if Susan needed help. He got the same response I did, so he sat down and put his elbows on the picnic table where I could see the tattoo on his arm: "Susan, my wife for life." That made me sad.

Brian and Marie showed up within minutes. Nobody seemed uncomfortable as we chatted about the warm April weather and what we were doing. Rob had been laid off a few months ago when the real estate market dropped. He seems optimistic now, however.

Marie told us how excited she is about earning a psychology degree and said two of her professors had left indelible impressions on her because of the different ways they had encouraged her to look at ordinary things.

Brian is a guy who doesn't recognize his many attributes: he'd been born with good looks, an engaging personality with a witty demeanor, and smarts greater than the ordinary person. Although he's tried college, he feels it isn't for him. He said he's reworking his resume and feels good about his future.

When it came time for me to talk about what I'm doing, I said I'm writing a book about falling in love at eighty. Although everyone laughed, they all had positive comments.

Susan called us in for dinner, which was delicious. She wouldn't let anyone help with clean-up because she wanted everyone to continue sharing more of their lives, which we all did.

* * * * *

The writer's club meeting the next day went very well. The by-laws were passed by acclamation, the slate of officers presented by the Nominating Committee was approved, and the new president took over the rest of the meeting. The members spent considerable time networking, exchanging email addresses, and eating pizza.

I flitted around talking to Nancy, the new officers, Ray, and other friends. Nancy gifted me with a booklet titled 'Memories' that contained personal notes and pictures of members.

My last goodbye to Nancy and Ray brought tears to my eyes and an empty feeling in my stomach. Although Nancy and Ray barely tolerate one another, they are both my treasured friends whom I will miss more than anyone.

Chapter Thirty-Two

When the plane landed in Atlanta, I headed to baggage claim. Kurt, parked at the curb, spied me through the glass sliding doors, and hurried in to retrieve my luggage. "Hi, lovely," he said, kissing me deeply and leading me to the car. "It's wonderful to see you, and I want you to know that I changed the bed sheets. Can you dig out my favorite nightie to wear tonight?"

"Did I hear you correctly? You're going to wear **your** favorite nightie tonight?"

"Smart ass. You'll be wearing **my** favorite nightie tonight."

"Have I ever seen you wear your favorite nightie?" By now I was laughing so hard that my tears blinded me.

"What's so funny? You know what I mean. Get in the car."

* * * * *

As Kurt drove to Angla Drive, I told him about my week in California. "It was bittersweet seeing my family and friends again. I stopped to see Donna, and we had a long talk and we're best friends again."

"I'm glad to hear that," Kurt said, patting my hand.

I told him about Susan and Rob separating, and he was shocked, saying they seemed fine when we moved a month ago.

"Susan said a fight occurred between Rob and Brian, and she sided with her son. Rob is still invited to family functions; and I told him about our dinner with Rob and the grandkids. "He's still very tight with Marie; but you could feel a certain tension between him and Brian."

"There's nothing we can do except be friends with your entire family." Kurt reached for my hands and squeezed them.

Kurt talked about the jobs he and Stephen got done this past week. "Stephen got the living room chandelier and the foyer light hung, and I helped him install a new fuse box. I think he's ready for you to hire a handyman to finish up."

"Before I left for California, I cut out an ad from the church bulletin about a handyman-parishioner looking for jobs. I'll give him a call."

Moxie heard the door open and came running out to greet me. I bent down to pet him, and he licked my face and hands and followed me into the bedroom; and he sat in my lap while I called Dr. Zachary's office. His receptionist said there's a cancellation tomorrow at three, so I called Caroline and arranged to pick up my aunt at two-thirty.

I phoned Lexie to let her know I'm home and to tell her about my aunt's appointment.

"You'll like Dr. Zachary," she said. "He's very gentle and caring."

Stephen came by later, and Kurt reminded him about our plans to spend time in Ohio.

"No problem. Nick is supposed to frame the new den doorway with bricks tomorrow, and I'll hang the French double doors and lock the place up so you can feel secure."

* * * * *

As the receptionist ushered Aunt Wilma into the dental office, she seemed a bit nervous.

Dr. Zachary suggested replacing the front, false tooth; but after a more extensive examination and finding pyorrhea in her gum sockets, his assessment was to pull eight teeth, leaving four bottom teeth."

When Dr. Zachary found out my aunt doesn't have dental insurance, he discounted his fee to twenty-three hundred dollars.

I appreciated the discount but still felt bad for Kurt having to pay that amount for my aunt's teeth. And I stepped out in the reception room to tell Kurt the news.

"Don't worry, honey, I'll take care of it."

"You already have the down payment," I whispered, turning and stepping back into the dental office to resume holding Aunt Wilma's hands while the dentist numbed her gums. She screamed and fidgeted but finally calmed down. I, however, was a complete wreck.

While waiting for the numbing to kick in, I assured her the worst was over.

As Dr. Zachary worked, he said he thinks we should forget about the false tooth and just pull all of her teeth. I can pull half today and pull the other half the next time I see her. I'll give her a mild anesthetic first. At her age, I don't think she needs a Pepsodent smile. And I don't think she'll accept a set of false teeth. That will reduce your bill another three hundred dollars."

"Sounds great! But how will she chew?"

"She'll eat soft foods or pureed foods. She may be on that diet now," Dr. Zachary said.

"I think that's a good plan, if I can get her back in here."

* * * * *

The dental assistant said my aunt had very little bleeding. "However, Dr. Zachary wants to wait a couple of weeks before pulling the rest of her teeth."

I told her about our trip to Ohio and asked if I could make an appointment when we got back. Mina said that would be fine. So Kurt paid the bill with his charge card, and we led a tired and weary Aunt Wilma to the car with pain pills for when the numbing wore off.

* * * * *

The day before our Ohio trip, we packed our bags, put our utilities on vacation status, and went to bed early. In the morning, I awoke with Kurt standing over me. "What's wrong?"

Kurt acted agitated, and that's when I noticed him dabbing at his nose with a blood-stained towel. I jumped out of bed, inspected the blood still dripping from his nose, and called 9-1-1. The phone medic gave instructions for Kurt to pinch his nose and lean his head forward so as not to swallow the blood. The nosebleed stopped about the same time the paramedics arrived. They recommended that Kurt go to the E.R., and they helped him get on the stretcher.

After changing into street clothes, I drove to the E.R. to pick up Kurt. He said a small Oriental woman doctor examined him and released him, but not before advising him to see his doctor for a more extensive exam. Kurt is on blood thinners, so his blood could be too thin, or his high blood pressure (179/120 that morning) could have caused the nosebleed.

"I'll see my doctor in Ohio," he said, as we headed back home. "But let's relax today and leave tomorrow, if no more incidents occur."

So that's what we did. The next morning, we got up at seven, after an uneventful night, drove four hundred miles, checking into a Super 8. After dinner and showers, we both came back to life. Moxie was busy checking out smells from previous tenants. I looked at my handsome husband with his just-washed, rumpled hair, and he gave me a sexy smile. Pulling off my nightie, I danced in front of him with my boobs bouncing.

"Get in bed," he ordered, "and I'll give you a loving that will make you scream for more. I want you here, at the end of the bed."

It took me a second to follow his command. As he stroked me and nibbled on my boobs, I could feel his penis pulsating against my thigh. His hands and fingers were everywhere, teasing me, while my desire mounted. Then I felt his penis inside of me; but after a few seconds, Kurt stopped to wipe his nose. He then continued until we both climaxed. I sat up and noticed Kurt holding a blood-stained towel on his nose. "Oh, no, not again. Should I call 9-1-1?"

"No, I stopped it," Kurt said, "by pinching the end of my nose."

My eyes flew to the bloody sheets. Stripping the bed, we threw the blood-stained sheets on the floor. The only item not covered in blood was the gross bedspread I threw on the floor earlier. So, we picked up the bedspread, covered ourselves up with it, and promptly fell asleep.

The next morning, we got up early and viewed the bloody mess, which looked like a shoot-out at Room 119.

My fiancé was generous with the maid's tip, and as we left, he told the office clerk about the bloody sheets, and he said she never stopped reading her paperback.

* * * * *

We took turns driving and made it to Kurt's home around four o'clock. The home looked like a split level, but once we got up the stairs from the garage, all rooms were on one floor. I carried Moxie up the stairs, following Kurt into the bedroom.

Lying on the bed, I watched Moxie smell his way around the room. Looking out the windows, I saw lush greenery everywhere. I grew up in a small town, about ten miles north, and I looked forward to walking the streets and seeing the house I'd called home until I married Ned.

I called Lexie to say we arrived safely, and Kurt called Doug, who would be driving to Piedmont with his wife on Friday to prepare for the barbeque on Saturday. Although I was looking forward to meeting Doug and Barb, I was feeling nervous. I'd heard tales of children not accepting the father's girlfriend, and I had hoped I wouldn't fall into that group.

Kurt had been making his phone calls from the den in the basement, and I heard his footsteps on the stairs. "Honey," I called, "would you bring Moxie's stand with you?"

"I already have it," he said, entering the bedroom and placing the stand near the window.

Moxie immediately jumped on it and stared out the window. Kurt and I smiled.

"Did you have a chance to look around?" he asked.

"Very nice. But don't you miss not having the dining room furniture?"

He said he never used it and that Doug and Barb are enjoying it. "By the way, I called Joe and Marla, and we'll be having lunch with them tomorrow. They are anxious to meet you, and I'm anxious for you to meet them, as well. They're my best friends."

I asked if they're the friends Kurt told about my painting his toenails, and he said he tells them everything.

The next day at twelve noon, Kurt and I met Joe and Marla at the Hometown Pizza and we jabbered away. Kurt told about Joe's Mom waking Joe up one night for him to play the piano for friends that had stopped by after a night on the town.

Learning that Joe was a talented piano player, I told him and Marla about my brother's endeavor in putting together a combo of musicians, while in high school, to play at different functions around the Ohio Valley. I also said when I was practicing the piano, my brother would sit on the front porch, saying he didn't want anyone to think that was him playing the piano.

As we were getting ready to leave, Joe said he and Marla had been eager to meet me to see what kind of a person Kurt had fallen in love with. "To be honest," Joe said, "we liked Pam. She was very quiet but very pleasant. And I want you to know that we like you an awful lot."

Marla said, "Pam was not at all outgoing."

Joe said he thinks we get along good is because Kurt is an introvert and I'm an extrovert.

"Really? I think Kurt is an extrovert," I said.

Joe and Marla shook their heads.

"Before we leave," I said, "I have one more story to tell." So, I told them about our recent motel escapade when Kurt had a nosebleed during our love-making session. "Blood was all over the bedclothes. I don't think we'll be welcome back at that motel."

Joe pursed his lips, smiling. "You're my hero, you know. Finished the job again; right?" Kurt sheepishly nodded his head, and Marla laughed robustly.

Chapter Thirty-Three

Kurt and I drove to Tiltonsville and parked in front of St. Joseph's Catholic Church. Standing on the sidewalk, I gazed at the church. My emotions ran high as I remembered all that had occurred in this church: my baptism, first holy communion, and confirmation. I remembered singing in the choir at the eight o'clock Mass, studying the Catechism, receiving the communion wafer, and marrying my first boyfriend in this church.

What had been happy memories had turned into very sad memories when I applied for, and was granted, an annulment from my husband of thirteen years on the ground of *psychological immaturity.* I had never heard that term before, but it fit Ned perfectly.

"You look like you're deep in thought," Kurt said. "What are you thinking?"

"About the many years I attended this church, and of the many lessons I learned here."

"Let's talk about it while we walk around to see if someone we know will show up."

"Sure, and I'd like to see my old home and the home you lived in."

Nobody was on the streets as we walked; and the town looked like it was sleeping. When we rounded the corner to Grandview Avenue, a young gal about eighteen to twenty, started to walk towards us. Kurt asked if she knew the Sandor family who used to live on this street, or the Hittenberger or Miller families. She shook her head.

"We probably won't see anyone we know, Eva. We've been gone for over fifty years."

"This is the corner I was standing on when Pretty Boy Floyd and his gang robbed the bank. I was five years old, but I still remember standing on this corner and watching two men run in the bank; and I remember the guy in the get-away car staring at me, although he didn't move or say a word. I watched as the bandits ran back out of the bank, jump in the car, and race away."

"That's the damnest story," Kurt said. "Wasn't Pretty Boy Floyd shot and killed by the police later that day in East Liverpool, Ohio?"

I nodded as we walked up Grandview Avenue to the one-hundred-year-old home I was born and raised in. A mid-wife delivered me, but my parents took me to the Martins Ferry Hospital for a check-up.

My heart raced with happy memories as we viewed my old home. It was now yellow. Mom's favorite color was a dusky pink, the color it remained during my growing-up years. The house was small, and I slept in an attic bedroom. So did grandpap. I told Kurt about the hot summer nights. "I could have boiled an egg on the windowsill. In fact, I spent many a summer night sacked out on the back-porch glider."

"I wish I'd known that," Kurt joked. "I lived with my grandma and grandpa in Sharpesville when growing up. During the summers and my last two years of high school, I lived with my Aunt Thelma and Uncle Pete in Tiltonsville. The summer nights didn't bother me as much as the cold, winter nights. I really enjoyed living in Tiltonsville," Kurt said, as we walked up the avenue, stopping at the First Methodist Church, which now wore a modern facade.

"I attended this church when I spent the summers in Tiltonsville, and later when I moved in with my aunt and uncle. I think I told you that Pam and I got married in this church."

"Yes, you did. Isn't it lovely walking around and reminiscing?" I asked.

We passed Dr. Lee's medical office. He was the only doctor in town back then. "I can still recall him laughing and saying szszszszsz at the end of his laughter," Kurt said.

"Me, too," I said, a bit amazed that Kurt remembered that.

Kurt stopped and said, "It's fun walking around our home-town, holding hands, and recalling the past." He kissed me warmly and said, "Let's go around the corner where I used to live and where I'd watch you pass by on your way to church."

Before heading back to St. Clairsville, we stopped at the Vine Cliff Inn for a sandwich and a coke. Nobody there knew us, either. If it weren't for our own memories, nobody in Tiltonsville, so far as we could tell, had known Kurt or me, although we had lived our formative and high school years in Tiltonsville. What a weird feeling—like a twilight zone movie.

When we got back to Kurt's home, I lay on the bed with Moxie, petting him. I don't know why, but I cannot get used to Kurt's bed. When I sit near the edge, I get the feeling I might fall off the bed. I think it's because the mattress is too soft. Later that night, when Kurt and I were getting amorous, I saw Kurt catapult over the foot of the bed. I propped myself up to look at him, and I, too, was propelled out of bed. Neither of us got hurt, except for a rugburn to Kurt's face. Climbing back in bed, we picked up where we'd left off, in each other's arms.

The next day, I called my childhood friend Grace to set a meeting place, which I always do when visiting in Ohio. Her first husband died several years ago, and she'd recently remarried. I remember how she hated to cook, and she and her family ate at Don's Drive-In regularly.

After two rings, Al answered; and I introduced myself. He said Grace is looking forward to seeing me, and so is he. "She's not home from work yet. Do you mind if I have her call you after we eat? I'm cooking stew, and she likes to eat as soon as she gets home."

"That's fine," I answered. "Looking forward to meeting you, Al."

I hung up and giggled. Grace sure hit the jackpot. Her husband is cooking.

Within an hour, Grace called, and we made plans to meet at the Wheeling Island Casino at noon tomorrow since that was her day off.

* * * * *

After hugs, we ordered a pizza and talked over one another. She told me about falling in love with Al. "We met at his bowling alley, which he's since sold. We love to dance, and once a week we go out to eat and then dance at the Eagles Home. Al is special, and I love him dearly."

"And he cooks," I added. We both had a good laugh.

She asked how Kurt and I are getting along, and I said we're crazy about one another and learning new things about each other every day.

"Remember the good times we had playing cards with our husbands until Ned started cheating on me? And to think it was with your sister."

"When I told you, I thought you wouldn't believe me, and I'd lose your friendship."

"I had my suspicions about Ned, but I never knew for sure until you confirmed it."

"It really hurt me that my sister was a part of that."

"And to think I gave her my clothes after I'd lost weight."

"Did I ever tell you that Ned said I'd never have sex as good as what we had?"

"That was an odd thing to say, especially since he cheated on you."

"The first guy I had sex with after Ned was my second husband Phil who was a gentle lover, nothing like the selfish Ned, and he had a much larger pecker; and he made sure he always pleased me." I sipped my water. "Maybe the sex was better with Phil because he and I loved and respected one another. I believe a woman has to be in love with a guy to really enjoy sex, and a guy just needs a place to put his pecker. That may be crass but it's closer to the truth."

"Did I ever tell you that when Andy and I were married, I never had an orgasm?"

"Yeh. Andy joked that when you two made love, you'd ask if so-and-so had paid their rent, and he'd say: 'For

Pete's sake, Grace, if you can't enjoy sex, shut up and let me enjoy it.'"

Since we were discussing sexual experiences, I asked if Grace ever had an orgasm.

"Yes, I did. One night when Al and I were having sex, it just happened. Wow! What an experience! I really love Al. We've been married for a year, and it's been a really good marriage. Al has two daughters, like me, but I never got close to his daughters, and Al never got close to mine. But we really enjoy and appreciate one another, and the sex is terrific!"

I told Grace about Kurt's two sons and their wives. "I'll be meeting his youngest son and his wife on Saturday." I explained that they live in Maryland but have a cabin at Piedmont.

"Hope for the best but plan for the worst," Grace said, standing and stretching. As we walked to the slots, she whispered in my ear, "I never got close to Al's daughters because they won't accept me. But that will have to wait for another time. Let's hit the slots."

While driving back to Kurt's home, I thought about my conversations with Grace. I can't believe Al's daughters won't accept Grace. She's very compassionate and has scads of friends. She chauffeurs people here and there and visits patients in nursing homes she hardly knows.

When I got back to St. Clairsville, Moxie and Kurt met me at the door. I kissed them both and told them about the wonderful time Grace and I had gossiping, but a lousy time at the slots. I got Kurt current about our classmates, and I told him about Grace and Al's loving relationship.

"Did you tell her about our relationship?" Kurt asked, dropping his frame on the sofa.

"Yes, and I told her what a wonderful kisser you are."

I noticed Kurt's chest puff out, almost bumping Moxie off his lap.

* * * * *

D-Day had finally arrived. I don't even remember what the D represents now. I dressed down in jeans, a long-sleeved white blouse, and a jeans' jacket. I brushed a dab of toothpaste over my engagement ring and ran water over it to make it sparkle.

It was nine in the morning. Kurt and I opted to have coffee and pecan rolls at Panera's before driving to Piedmont. Kurt looked fit in a long-sleeved red pullover and dark jeans.

As we drove to Piedmont, lush greenery sprouted up on both sides of the highway. When Kurt turned off the highway, the road narrowed and was mostly dirt and pot-holed for the couple of miles that led to the cabin. When we pulled up to the cabin, Doug came down to meet us and shook my hand. "Glad to finally meet you," he said warmly. He put his arm around his father; and we three walked up to a patio where a couple were seated. They stood and introduced themselves: Jean, a former classmate of Barb's, and her husband, Lee, a friend of Doug's when Kurt and family had lived in Texas and who owns the cabin next-door. Doug said Barb was making a salad to go with a large grill piled with meat that sat about five feet away.

Jean and Lee were very friendly. She congratulated Kurt and me on our engagement and asked to see my engagement ring. I held out my right hand, and she said, "That is absolutely gorgeous." She asked if we'd made wedding plans yet.

I told her we were renovating my home in Georgia and were in no hurry to marry.

Kurt and Lee talked about the new cabin Doug is building with Lee's help. Barb came out and placed the salad on the patio table and turned to greet me, which was a pat on the hands.

"Don't get up," she said. So I didn't. But I was confused about the curt greeting.

Doug walked over with the platter of meat and held it while each of us selected from the sausages, steak, and ribs. "Dig in," he said. Jean passed around a bowl of potato salad she'd made, and the rest of the side dishes made their rounds.

"After we eat, I'd like to show dad the progress I've made on the new cabin," Doug said.

Barb seemed a little distant, and the conversation was stilted. If Jean and Lee hadn't been there, bringing Kurt and me into the conversation, I would have felt irrelevant. Doug joked with his dad, and I think he actually was oblivious of the cold-shoulder I was getting from his wife. Barb never mentioned Kurt's and my engagement nor asked to see my ring.

After cake and coffee, we all walked down to see the new cabin. The outside frame was up, the windows were in, the roof was on, and some plasterboard was up. Kurt said he was impressed, and so was I.

"I can't wait to move," Barb said. Where did the enthusiasm come from? I wondered. She'd been in lockdown all day.

Since it was getting dark, Kurt and I said our goodbyes. I hugged Jean and tried to put my arms around Barb, but she was as responsive as a board. Doug shook my hand and said he and Barb would meet us at the Cracker Barrel in the morning on their way back to Maryland.

On the drive to Kurt's home, we talked about the barbeque. Kurt praised Doug for the delicious meat he'd prepared. I told him that I like Doug, and that Jean and Lee are great; but I felt Barb was rather distant. Kurt said he hadn't noticed that, although she had seemed a bit quiet.

"She didn't even ask to see my ring, and that's something Jean did immediately. And Barb never congratulated me on our engagement. Did she congratulate you?"

"I don't think so, but I'm not sure."

"Well, I think that's very odd. And when I tried to hug Barb as we were leaving, she didn't respond." Of course, Kurt said he didn't notice that, either.

"Maybe you're just over-reacting. Let's see what happens at breakfast tomorrow."

Chapter Thirty-Four

When Kurt and I arrived at the Cracker Barrel, Barb and Doug were standing at the entrance, and they greeted us with "Good Mornings." No handshakes or hugs; and Barb entered first, giving our names to the hostess.

"Come along with me," the hostess said, grabbing menus from the dais.

Everyone appeared solemn while selecting items from the menu. Kurt started the conversation by complimenting Doug on the array of meats he'd barbequed to perfection; and I mentioned how much I enjoyed meeting Jean and Lee.

Doug said that Lee helps with cabin projects whenever he gets a long weekend.

The conversation was strained, and Barb did nothing to keep it flowing. She asked no questions about Kurt's and my relationship or how we met. I gathered from her cold attitude that she didn't approve of me. Then I got to thinking about what Grace said about her husband's daughters not accepting her. However, they were daughters—not a daughter-in-law like Barb.

As we ate, Kurt started to tease me. "Eva loves to install tile. She earned her apprenticeship in Camarillo when she installed tile in the kitchen and on both bathroom floors. In Smyrna she laid tile in the master bathroom and in the kitchen over the sink and countertops. By now, she's advanced to professional status, and I'm hoping she'll help me renovate my kitchen."

"After we're done with my home, we can start on yours," I said.

Barb said she was not looking forward to the six-hour drive back to Maryland; and I said I enjoyed our trip to Ohio with our cat.

Kurt and Doug talked non-stop; and I believe they were totally oblivious of the tense relationship Barb and I floundered about in. But this was only the second time she and I had met. After she thought about the happiness Kurt and I brought to one another, she might have a change of heart. In any case, I decided not to make a big deal out of it to Kurt. Doug was friendly, and he'd made an effort to make me feel comfortable.

The next couple of weeks in St. Clairsville went by quickly. For two Sundays in a row we attended St. Joseph's Catholic Church where we visited with Jim, a high school friend of Kurt's, and his wife, Joan, on the church steps after Mass. I told Jim that I was surprised to see him at Mass, and he explained that when the kids started to arrive, he decided it would be best to have them all embrace one religion; and that would have to be Joan's because she'd been raised Catholic and stayed active in the religion. He said he's never been sorry.

My friend, Jordan, a school teacher, who was a year younger than I, had been talking to friends nearby, and after Jim and Joan left, he walked over and hugged me and introduced himself to Kurt. Jordan had moved to California to teach fourth grade at a school in Oxnard where we lived. And one very pleasant coincidence was when he taught my daughter Susan in the fourth grade. He also gave her a Key Lympet in a jar. She treasured that sea creature and then decided to take it with her when she visited her father in Ohio. She asked if he'd like to keep it on his Bar in the basement, and he nodded; so she left it with him. When she flew back the following year, she was heartbroken when she learned he'd thrown it away.

Jordan said that after living and teaching in California for five years, he moved back to Tiltonsville. He said although he liked California, and the teacher's pay was better than in Ohio, he had a son in Ohio that lives with his ex-wife and he misses seeing Larry on a regular basis.

"I'm still single," he added, "and I'm so set in my ways, I'll probably stay single." He asked if Kurt and I planned to start a family, and I said it depends on how active my eighty-year-old egg is. Jordan roared.

While in Ohio, I walked next door to visit with Deena, Pam's older sister, who has a lovely brick home next-door to Kurt's home. She embraced me warmly, and I was sorry for even thinking, in my early relationship with Kurt, that she might be interested in him. We had a good time reminiscing about school friends. Deena reached for my hands, wanting to see my ring. "Kurt did a good job picking it out," she said, smiling, "and I'm happy for the both of you."

Deena's husband Ed had died several years before Pam had, and although she said she didn't mind living alone as long as she was healthy, she said she misses her husband daily.

Kurt and I also dropped by McDonald's where our classmate Vince and his wife meet daily with a group of friends for breakfast. They appeared to be a jolly group, laughing and telling jokes. Not to be outdone, Kurt told a few of his one-liners. "Doctor, doctor," the nurse called nervously, "there's a man in the waiting room that says he's invisible." The doctor replied: "Tell him I can't see him now."

A man shows up at his dentist's office, very disturbed. "What can I do about my yellow teeth?" he asks. "Dentist's reply: 'Wear a brown tie.'"

The last one was stolen from Rodney Dangerfield. "My cousin couldn't pass her driver's test after five attempts. She couldn't get used to the front seat."

Everyone cracked up.

When we got up to leave, Vince stood and shook hands with Kurt and hugged me. While walking away, Vince said, "Don't wait so long before showing up again."

* * * * *

Our stay at Kurt's home was very fulfilling in that we visited with four classmates that we'd been close with in high school. Our graduating class was small, only sixty-two in the entire class, and we'd all known one another from first grade.

I regularly fly to Ohio to attend class reunions, only missing one, and I consider myself a reunion junkie. Although Kurt missed several reunions due to his military service, he also calls himself a reunion junkie. We both treasure the times we spend with our classmates.

"Remember the last reunion Pam and I attended, and you were there?" Kurt asked.

"Yes, and you asked me to dance and Pam whispered to me, 'He doesn't know how to dance.'"

"I can't understand why she'd say that since I've been dancing for years."

I just smiled as I remembered how we hopped all over the dance floor.

"That must have been ten years ago," Kurt said. "I never went to one after that because Pam took ill, and I couldn't leave her."

"I recall when Julie and I rode our bikes out to visit Pam when we were in high school. The ride must have been four miles or longer. Pam was so glad to see us, and her mom made us sandwiches and put Lima beans on our plates. I'll never forget that because I love Lima beans. We played hopscotch and jumped rope and had the best time. Julie and I sure were tired after pedaling all the way back home."

"Pam came to my home a half dozen times for lunch. Mary Bender often joined us."

"I may have said this to you before, but I feel good that you and Pam were friends." "Me, too."

Although Kurt and I had a pleasant time while in Ohio, visiting classmates, time had run out before we had an opportunity to meet Grace's husband and to visit with them. However, I'd called Grace several times after our casino venture. She wanted to know how the family barbeque turned out. I mentioned the cold treatment I got from Barb, and the fact that Deena and her family had been excluded from the barbeque, as well as Kurt's oldest son, Ron, and his wife. "Yet, it was called a family barbeque with Kurt and me and two cabin neighbors we'd just met."

"Didn't I warn you?" Grace asked. "I think they're worried you'll get their inheritance." We prepared prenuptial agreements," I responded. "And I know Kurt told his sons about them because his youngest son wanted to read them, but Kurt nixed that request."

"Beats me why they won't accept you. You and Kurt have known one another for years."

I told Grace I was sorry we didn't get to meet Al and have time to visit with them, but our visit was too short. "Take care of one another, and give our love to Al."

* * * * *

Kurt and I were enjoying a glass of red wine, waiting for the Channel 4 News to come on. "Let's toast our love," Kurt said.

I clinked my glass against his and told him that I love him and I've been enjoying our visit with friends and attending St. Joseph's Catholic Church. "I guess we can no longer wonder whether people from Tiltonsville will remember us and know that we attended school there."

"Yeah, I remember thinking that when walking around the town. But some of our classmates got married and stayed in Tiltonsville, raising their kids there, and they will remember us," Kurt said.

"When I talked with Jim, he told me he has an autistic son who's thirty and he and Joan have two other sons and a daughter. He said his oldest son lives in a small town near Smyrna."

"Maybe we can all get together when they visit their son in Georgia."

"Wouldn't that be great?" Kurt said. "Strange how we lose touch. Jim and I were best friends when I lived in Tiltonsville."

I said we meet so many people while raising our kids and in our jobs that it's difficult to keep up with all our classmates, too, but that I thought Kurt and I did a pretty good job of it.

"Especially you, Eva. You're always telling me this person and that person contacted you, and I love you for the attention you shower on people. And look at the friendship you've had with Julie for over seventy years. Amazing."

"I'm so glad you're interested in keeping in touch with our friends because I sure am."

"After the news is over, I'd like to take a couple of pictures of you in that red dress. I don't see you in a dress very often, and you look very sexy."

So, after the news, Kurt asked that I sit on the bathroom vanity, sans my panties; and he pushed my dress up ever so slightly. "Now spread your legs and let a little bit of curly hair show. Also, drop the top of your dress to show those luscious breasts."

"I can do that if you promise not to show Jon Ryan the picture as you did when you showed him that pic of you in your robe with your pecker hanging out."

"I promise," he said. "I don't know how I missed that. My pecker isn't that small, is it?"

"Take it out and let me look at it."

Kurt quickly unzipped his pants, revealing a rigid pecker you could hang a dishrag on. "Put your mouth on it," he coaxed.

"No."

"Why not?" he pouted. "Aren't we committed to one another?"

"How about for your eighty-second birthday?"

"You promise?" he said, brightening up.

"Yes, I promise." Leaning forward, I licked his earlobes.

"Why can't you do that to my pecker?" he asked, urging it into my vagina and watching it slowly disappear in front of the vanity mirror.

Chapter Thirty-Five

"I can't believe how fast that four weeks sped by," Kurt said, backing out of the driveway of his Ohio home. He was taking the first shift of the drive back to Smyrna.

"Me, either. I really enjoyed getting to know Joe and Marla, and I was glad we could meet at the mall for lunch. It was so funny when Joe noticed the carpet burn on your forehead; and I thought he was going to laugh his head off when I told him that we fell out of bed."

"That was funny," Kurt said. "We've been meeting at the mall for years. It's convenient and private and we can sit there and talk as long as we like. While some people itch to get away from small-town living, Joe and Marla love it. After Joe served his stint in Japan during WWII, he and Marla moved back to St. Clairsville and raised their kids there."

"How many children do they have?"

"A son, Joey, who's married and lives in St. Clairsville and works for the power company. His wife also works, and they have no children. Joe and Marla's daughter, an engineer, lives in Columbus near her ex-husband who shares custody of their four-year-old son with her."

"Are you glad you came in for a visit?" Kurt asked.

"Visiting with our classmates was a hoot and visiting our old stomping grounds was very nostalgic. I'm just sorry we didn't have time to meet Grace's husband."

"You spent time with her at the casino and by phone, and hopefully, we'll be back soon." "I was looking forward to meeting your son, Ron, and his wife at the barbeque."

Kurt said he doesn't know why Ron couldn't get time off since he's been with the same moving company for fifteen years. He'll definitely work it out the next time we visit in Ohio."

"Joe and Marla really approve of you, Eva, and that makes me very happy."

"They're my kind of people. And I could see how much they think of you."

"What I can't understand is why Deena wasn't invited to the barbeque. She's family, and she could have driven to the lake with us. …there was plenty of food."

"Gosh, I never thought of that. Doug and Barb usually invite her."

"What did you think of Doug?" Kurt asked.

"He has an outgoing personality and tried to include me. I can't say the same for Barb. She avoided me like the plague. If it weren't for Jean and Lee, I would have felt abandoned."

"Barb was busy setting the table and making side dishes."

"She never asked to see my ring, although that was one of the first things that came out of Jean's mouth. Even the next day at Cracker Barrel, Barb didn't greet me but instead walked ahead of us. Surely you noticed how quiet she was at breakfast."

"She didn't have much to say," Kurt responded, "but I didn't see that as excluding you."

"She never asked me anything—how we met, if I had children—nothing."

"Jean and I had a long conversation. She told me she's a nurse, and I told her about my novel-writing. She asked about my children; and she told me about her son."

"Now that you mention it, it is odd that Barb wasn't curious to find out about you." "Time will tell why," I said. "By the way, what did Doug have to say about me?"

"He didn't say anything about you." Kurt looked like he was delving deep into his brain to come up with something that wasn't there.

"You asked me what I thought of Doug. Why didn't you ask him what he thought of me."

"I don't know. We hadn't seen one another for a while and had a lot to talk about."

"I find it odd that I wasn't the topic of your conversation or Doug's or Barb's. She was very distant and hardly spoke to me. But let's drop it. I just want you to know how hurt I am."

"I can understand your feelings," Kurt said, "and now that I'm aware of this, I'll pay more attention. I promise."

"Thanks, honey. I'd like nothing better than to have a relationship with your family."

I decided to stop talking about the barbeque because it only upset me. However, I couldn't help recalling the warm welcome Kurt got from my family when Susan and Rob hosted us to a family dinner. My family plied Kurt with questions about us and hung on his every word. When Lexie and Stephen met Kurt, they also readily accepted him, most likely because I said this is the real thing. I'm thinking Kurt didn't impress on his family just how strong our bond is, and therefore his daughter-in-law thought she could break us up, or perhaps as Grace had said—she thinks I'm a threat to her and Doug's inheritance. Time will reveal which one it is.

"Moxie sure scared us," I said, breaking the silence. "After walking up and down the block screaming for him, and even enlisting a neighbor to help out, we find him under the sofa."

"I know I looked there," Kurt said, shaking his head.

"I felt like smacking him for putting us through that trauma. But when I saw his pushed-in nose and huge amber eyes staring at me from under the sofa, I could breathe again," I said.

"I just felt relief," Kurt said.

I stroked Moxie as he lay in my lap, and I drifted off to sleep during Kurt's allotted time at the wheel, and he did the same during my driving time.

We stopped at a Knight's Inn at Grayson and got Moxie settled in the room before walking across the street to Sonny's Barbeque for dinner. While sipping my tea, I asked my fiance if he'd like hanky panky tonight.

"You must be kidding. After driving seven hours, I don't think I can find my pecker."

However, after a nice, hot meal, and a nice, hot shower, Kurt found his pecker. And I'll leave the hot details to your imagination.

I took the wheel in the morning and stayed the course until we drove across the Smyrna city line around one in the afternoon. "Why don't we stop at a Waffle House for lunch?"

"Good idea," Kurt said. "And afterwards, I'll run into Kroger's for milk and bread."

"And ground sirloin for hamburgers," I added. "I'm too pooped to cook."

"No hanky panky?" Kurt asked, a familiar gleam in his eyes.

"It depends on whether you can find your pecker," I said, smiling.

"Remember the old saying: 'use it or lose it?' At eighty-one, I'm too young to lose it."

* * * * *

As soon as we got the suitcases and cat in the house, I planned to call Lexie; but then I noticed the framed French doors.

Kurt sucked in his breath. "Is that a wow factor in this kitchen or what?"

"I thought you said the black granite Island with the fancy legs was the wow factor."

Kurt just shook his head. "They both are."

"I'm going to call Lexie to tell her we're home."

"Mention the doors," Kurt said, putting the groceries away.

"Kurt and I love the French doors. They make the kitchen lighter," I said to Lexie.

"You'd never know that had been a window before, would you?" Lexie replied.

She asked how the barbeque went, and if I felt like I was welcomed into the family.

"Soso to both questions," I said. "I'll talk to you about it tomorrow as I'm completely drained. Be sure to tell Stephen we're crazy about how the doors turned out."

After a quick meal of hamburgers and chips, Kurt, Moxie, and I took a nap and woke up at ten o'clock. Just in time to take a quick shower and go back to bed. Moxie, however, came to life, munching on his kibble and throwing his toys around. He was obviously happy to be home. The next day I called for an appointment to have the rest of my aunt's teeth pulled. Due to emergencies, she couldn't be seen until next week. Since she was in no pain, it was okay.

I sat in the recliner while I called Lexie and told her about the cold treatment I got from Barb. "All I can say is to hang in there. Surely she and Doug will see how happy you and Kurt are and be glad that their dad has someone to care for him and share things with."

I told Lexie about my discourse with Grace and her telling me that Al's daughters never formed a relationship with her, and that Al never formed a relationship with her daughters.

"So, what if it's like that? It is what they make it, and if they won't embrace you, so be it. Just be your own pleasant self for Kurt's sake. I just wonder what's behind their behavior."

After I hung up, I found Kurt watching television and asked whether we should go buy paint for the kitchen and bathrooms. He agreed, so we drove to Home Depot and afterwards we visited Aunt Wilma. I wondered if she knew how long it had been since we'd last seen her, or if time was just a four-letter word to her.

We found Aunt Wilma sitting in front of the window, watching the geese. She saw us as we walked in and seemed excited to see us. I leaned down to kiss her, and she tilted her head to kiss me back. Kurt kissed her, as well, and she beamed. We pulled chairs over to the window, next to her. She grabbed my hands as I asked how she is. She said she's fine and answered my questions, but she didn't initiate any conversation. She held my hands tightly as I spoke to her. I asked if her gums hurt, and she shook her head. I then told her that on Monday we'd be taking her to see Dr. Zachary again for him to complete her dental work. She made a grotesque face, so I knew she understood what I said. "Don't you worry. He told me he's going to put you to sleep so you won't feel any pain at all. Her eyes lit up and she said it was okay.

She told us about a male singer that entertained the patients at the nursing home a few days ago. "He sang 'Danny Boy,' she said. "I didn't hear that song for years and years, and it made me cry. It was my brother's favorite song."

"Your brother Joe was my dad. Do you remember that?"

"Of course I remember," she said.

"When I was a very little girl and my brother was a couple years older, he started crying and couldn't stop. My father picked him up from his bed and threw him on the floor."

I couldn't breathe for a moment. "Are you sure?"

"Of course I'm sure. My mother ran into the bedroom and picked my brother up and rocked him in the rocking chair and made him feel good again."

I was horrified. I remember my mother telling me that she and my dad never lived alone, that grandpap moved in with them after his wife died at the age of forty-two. I never knew my paternal grandma, but I always remember my paternal grandpap as loving and caring. While growing up, he was my best friend. Aunt Wilma's revelation shocked me.

My aunt continued. "My father made me go to work when I was sixteen because he couldn't feed all of us. We lived in Collier, West Virginia. I loved going to school and got good grades. No matter how much I cried and mother pleaded with him, nothing made a difference. I thought my life was over. But a friend got me a job as a maid for a wealthy family in Elm Grove, and I moved in with them. I tried to see my mother once a week because we missed each other so much. It was hard for her to get away, as she had to care for my brother and sister and father."

"How long did you work for that couple in Elm Grove?" I asked.

"For about a year. Then I married Bill Rigo from Martins Ferry. I was friends with his sister, and she introduced us. Then my precious mother died of pneumonia. So, when Bill wanted to move to California, I was ready for a new life."

"I'm awfully tired," my aunt said. "I usually take a nap."

I called one of the aides over, and she said Miss Wilma could take a nap before dinner.

I hugged my aunt and told her I love her, and I'd come back soon to see her.

Kurt and I didn't speak until we reached his car.

"What a story," he said.

"I've never heard her talk so much. I guess the song 'Danny Boy' brought up all those repressed memories that needed to come out."

"I found her to be very believable," Kurt said.

"I did, too, and I was amazed at how articulate she related that incident. Although I knew my grandpap as a different person than she did, I'm not discrediting the way he treated her and my dad. As I recall, my dad and grandpap never seemed to be close. When we'd chat at the dinner table, my grandpap and my dad rarely spoke to one another. Maybe I just got my answer. And to find out that it was my quiet, non-demonstrative mother, grandpap's daughter-in-law, who gave him a home and knitted us all into a family. Incredible, and a lot to digest. I hope I'm as lucid as Aunt Wilma when I'm one hundred, and that I will be as humble and kind as my mother."

"I hope we live that long," Kurt said.

Chapter Thirty-Six

We're not even half done painting the interior of this house, and we've used up six gallons of paint," I wailed. "My legs and arms are so sore from climbing up the ladder to cut in a paint line and then down the ladder to paint next to the baseboard. We're too old to be painting."

"We're pushing ourselves too hard. We should take a break and go sight-seeing."

"I think that's a great idea," I said. "Let's talk about it after we get back from taking Aunt Wilma to Dr. Zachary's office to have the rest of her teeth pulled."

* * * * *

Aunt Wilma was ready when we picked her up, looking lovely in a red-flowered blouse and a navy skirt. She loves an occasion to dress up, even a trip to the dentist's office.

As we got her out of her wheelchair and into the front seat of the car, I asked if she knew where we were going.

"Yes, Caroline told me it's back to the dentist's office, and I remember you telling me that the dentist would put me to sleep so I won't hurt."

I could see Kurt smiling as he started the engine.

I noticed that early in the day, my aunt's memory is quite keen. Later on, when she gets tired, is when she gets confused.

When we arrived at Dr. Zachary's office, his assistant came out and greeted my aunt with a big smile and told her how pretty she looks. I pushed my aunt's wheelchair into the dentist's office and helped Mina get her in the dental chair. My aunt held my hands tightly.

Dr. Zachary soon came in and said, "My, look at you. You look like you're going on a date." That won her over completely. She opened her mouth when asked, and the dentist rubbed a numbing compound over her gums and then administered an anesthesia that made her sleepy.

"You can wait in the reception room," he said to me. "She'll be fine. And I'll call you when she's ready to leave."

Sitting in the reception room and hearing no screams, we assumed my aunt was sound asleep. After an hour, the dentist stepped out and said my aunt was awake and ready to leave.

Aunt Wilma was groggy, but she was fine. Kurt took the pain pills from the dentist; and we both thanked him.

Aunt Wilma dozed on the way back to the nursing home, and when we got her to her room, an aide put her to bed. "I'll save her dinner for her, which will probably be soup," she said.

Her roommate wanted to know how things went, and I told her Aunt Wilma was put to sleep and didn't know the remainder of her teeth had been pulled.

"I'll watch her and make sure she doesn't need anything," she said.

As we walked out, I said to Kurt: "That was worse than painting."

"I agree, but your aunt handled herself very well. Probably better than I would have."

"It's because we were honest with her and prepared her for what was going to happen. By the way, I'm going to need some dental work done. I think I need a root canal."

"Why tell me?"

"Didn't you pay for Barb's dental work and for my Aunt Wilma's dental work? Why wouldn't you pay for my dental work, especially since you'll be getting paid in sexual activity?"

"Who said I won't pay for your dental work? Duh!"

The next couple of weeks Kurt and I painted and painted. Although we put two coats of paint on the living room ceiling, it still looked spotty. Lexie said it was because we'd applied water-based paint over oil-based paint.

"Do you realize we used up eighteen gallons of paint on the interior of my home, and it's only fifteen hundred square feet?" I asked.

"I thought we might have used more than that considering all the doors and windows in this house. Do you think we might wait a while before having the deck built?"

"There's no hurry. I've got an appointment to see my Kaiser doctor again tomorrow, and I need to find a cardiologist for the both of us."

"Maybe you can ask someone in the waiting room if they can recommend a cardiologist. You found the tile installer that way."

"Good idea. I should have thought of that."

"I also have to find a Vet for Moxie, and also a pet sitter, so we can take some trips. I'd love to drive to Warm Springs, Georgia to view FDR's summer home. It's not far from here."

"I'd like to drive to Savannah where *Gone with the Wind* was filmed," Kurt said.

"And what about the animal park where the animals run free and come up to one's car?"

"We'll do all those things," Kurt said, "but for now, come sit on my lap."

I did, which led to some heavy petting, starting with deep, warm kisses that still thrilled me after being with my guy for a year. I then thought about what one of my married friends had said about the thrill only lasting two years.

"Did any of your married friends ever tell you that this thrilling feeling we have for each other only lasts two years?"

"Not true," Kurt said. "Ours will last forever."

The next day I saw Dr. Nuygen, and I told him that my husband and I had been painting and had used up eighteen gallons of paint.

"What have you been painting?" he asked.

"All the rooms in our house."

"Have you ever taken a dementia test?" he asked.

"No, I haven't." I wondered what brought this on.

"Do you mind taking one?" he asked.

"Not at all."

His nurse Karen came in, and she said she was going to tell me three words and said for me to remember them as she would ask me to repeat them later: brown, sunburst, chair. When she asked me a few minutes later, I remembered all three. But about ten minutes later while the doctor was giving me a breast examination, all I could think of was brown and chair. The doctor asked me to think real hard what the last word was, but I couldn't remember it. I imagined losing my driver's license and going home in a taxi.

Then the doctor handed me a sheet of paper and asked me to draw a clock, showing ten minutes after eleven. I drew a circle and put the numbers in and put a star where the eleven ten should be. He looked at me strangely and asked, "Where are the hands?" I nervously drew in hands on the clock, and I even drew in the minute hand.

"That's fine," he said, taking notes. "I won't have to see you for three months, unless you need to see me sooner."

I left in such a hurry I forgot to pick up the appointment card from the receptionist. Instead of driving straight home, I stopped at Taco Bell and pigged out. All the way home I thought whether I should change doctors. Is this crazy? What if I fail the dementia test next year? I decided not to tell Kurt about this unsettling experience. Not today, anyway.

That night when getting ready for bed, I noticed beige paint splashes on my toes. Why didn't I see this paint when I was in the doctor's office so I could have shown it to him?

A couple of days later while we were eating breakfast, Kurt asked, "How was your checkup with the new doctor? You didn't tell me about it."

I broke down and told him about the dementia test. "Why would he give me one?" I wailed. "That really disturbs me."

"Look, if I were the doctor and an eighty-year-old lady said she used up eighteen gallons of paint painting her house, I might have given her a dementia test, also. He doesn't know you. Give him time to find out you're much more active and healthy than most sixty-year-olds. In fact, next time you see him, make sure you tell him we're screwing five times a week."

"I'll do that."

Lexie told me recently about a senior center that's only about two miles from our home, so I told Kurt about it. "Seniors can relax there, play cards, or shoot pool, and since we're missing a social life, I think we should check it out."

Kurt agreed, so off we went.

The activities director greeted us and showed us the library, kitchen, and conference room. "If you join our center, you'll be able to use all the senior centers in Cobb County."

So, we joined on the spot, and that day Kurt taught me how to shoot pool, which I enjoyed very much. Then we had a coke and spoke to a few seniors there. But before heading back home, we signed up for dancing lessons scheduled for Tuesday and Thursday afternoons.

"Gosh, I'm glad we did that," I said enthusiastically.

"Me, too," Kurt said. "Although I already know how to dance."

"That's the funniest thing I've heard all day. Remember our first dance at the class reunion, which consisted of jumping in place and then hopping all over the dance floor?"

"You'll see who can dance when we start our dancing lessons," Kurt said confidently.

I kept my laughter to myself.

Our first dance lesson was Tuesday at three o'clock. Seven women, including myself; and four men, including Kurt, showed up. They all looked to be in their fifties and sixties, but that made sense since this was a senior center. The women were all nice looking. Only one woman was on the plump side but had a pretty face and a winsome smile.

Two of the men were quite attractive, and one was bald and had a belly.

Our instructor, Lita Loma, told us she's been a dancing instructor all of her adult life and has her own dance studio in Marietta. Her dark hair and huge, hazel eyes made me think she's of Spanish descent. She had lovely teeth and wore black tight pants that showed off her trim figure.

Lita had everyone line up in one row and asked us to introduce ourselves by name and the city where we live. She then stated we'd be learning three dances in the six-week class: the Two-Step, the Waltz, and the ChaCha. In this first class, she said we'd be learning the Two-Step.

She explained her moves as she performed them, and we followed her, repeating the steps. She then asked one of the attractive men, Romano, to join her. She put a record on, and they danced the Two-Step. She and Romano had evidently danced together before as their bodies were in perfect sync. She then had us partner up and follow their lead. I was amazed at how well Kurt had paid attention to Lita's instructions, because his feet moved in rhythm—no jumping.

Lita asked another gentleman to dance and put on another record. I felt bad for the women who had no partners, and I asked Kurt to dance with one of them. He did, and Romano asked me to dance. Kurt was shocked to see Romano and me dance past him. I felt a bit guilty as we danced by a woman dancing at the side of the stage by herself and asked Kurt to dance with her when the record changed. He did, and the gentleman with the belly asked me to dance and plied me with questions. This time when we danced by Kurt and his partner, Kurt gave me a dirty look. I crossed my eyes at him. How could I refuse to dance with him? How would Kurt feel if one of the women refused him? We were a small group and needed to get along.

As we danced, Lita came by to give us tips on what we were doing wrong and to enforce what we were doing right.

While taking a break, Lita showed us ways to stretch and breathe deeply to reinvigorate ourselves. When she put on another record, Kurt announced that we came together, and we would be dancing together.

"But there's another gentleman I haven't danced with."

"And you won't be, either," he said.

That night while showering, Kurt said he got jealous seeing me dance with other guys.

"That's okay, as long as you don't try to punish me for something that was innocent."

"I don't know how innocent it was when you twice asked me to dance with other women while you danced with other men."

"How did I know they'd ask me to dance?"

"Honey, I know you're eighty, but you were the cutest woman there."

"Kurt, darling, not only were you the most handsome man on the dance floor, but I was very impressed with your moves."

"You ain't seen nothin' yet, baby. Now lie on the bed, on your back, and put your legs around my neck." I giggled, but I did it. However, I think I'll keep those moves to myself.

Chapter Thirty-Seven

On Sundays, Kurt always called his sons, and this Sunday was no different. After talking with them, he sat beside me on the couch and told me how they're doing. "Doug and Barb are okay, working five days a week. Ron and Clara would like to visit us in Ohio for a long weekend the latter part of July, if that's okay with us. I said I'd call them back after checking with you."

"That's fine with me"

"It's difficult for Ron and Clara to coordinate their times off work since he works for a moving company, and she works at Walmart. That's why they didn't make the barbeque."

I nodded.

"We'll have to pick them up at the airport on Friday evening and deliver them back on Monday afternoon."

"I look forward to meeting them and hope things go better than the meet-up with Barb."

"Ron is very layback and easy going. I'm sure you two will like one another. Clara was married before and has two adult children and two teenage grandchildren who live in Utah."

"Ron said he hopes Doug and Barb can drive in at the same time so we can all visit."

"That would be nice. I was just thinking, however, that we may miss the Cha Cha dancing lessons since we'll be spending a few weeks in Ohio."

"I'm really enjoying those classes," Kurt said. "I think we've mastered the Two-Step."

"I'm impressed that you can remember the steps and follow-through." I caught Kurt smiling, probably because I rarely give him compliments. Kurt's body never seems to move from the waist up, but he moves his feet in rhythm to the music from the waist down. Aloud, I said, "No doubt about it, after a few more lessons, we'll be showing off at the senior center dances."

Kurt's eyes got bright. "You really think so?"

"Absolutely. And please call Ron to make flight reservations for July."

On Tuesday at our third dancing class, Lita introduced us to the Waltz, which Kurt seemed to excel in. Lita even singled him out to dance with her in front of the class. Kurt lit up like a glow worm and performed very well. I told him how proud I was of him.

We only had a few sessions of the ChaCha before we left for Ohio. Kurt wanted some time at his home before picking up Ron and Clara.

* * * * *

Ron and Clara arrived on a Friday night in July, and Kurt and I drove to the Pittsburgh Airport to pick them up. They were waiting at curbside, and Kurt opened the back of his SUV and Ron threw in two duffle bags and climbed in behind Clara, and off we went.

I turned around to greet them, and they seemed happy to meet me. Although it was six in the evening, traffic was fairly light as we pulled into the lane marked "Weirton," and drove along the West Virginia side until we got to the Steubenville, Ohio bridge. Then we followed Route 7 all the way to Martins Ferry, Ohio, where we stopped at a

Robert Evans restaurant for dinner. We talked about our families, and yes, Clara wanted a close-up look at my engagement ring. Both Ron and Clara congratulated us on our engagement.

Another half hour of driving, and we were at Kurt's home. Moxie didn't come out of our bedroom, so I went in and loved on him while Ron and Clara got settled in the guest bedroom. It wasn't long before Ron headed for the shower – he was used to going to bed early as he had to get up at four in order to drive to work and punch in at six o'clock.

I'm not sure how it happened, but only Clara and I ended up at the kitchen table, talking and drinking herbal tea. She told me that when she was in high school, she got in with a bad crowd and got pregnant. She said she and her boyfriend got married and had a son; and a year later they had a daughter. She said her husband resented the responsibilities he was faced with and started blaming her for everything, and it wasn't long before they got a divorce.

"My mom babysat a lot while I worked part-time in a grocery store. I also had to hire sitters as it was just too much for her watching two small kids."

I told her how my husband and I divorced when our daughters were seven and eleven and that I then moved to California to live near a close friend and her husband. "She had four kids and we helped one another out in many ways. We were as close as sisters."

I told Clara I enjoyed getting to know her, and that we'd better hit the sack as we'll have a busy day tomorrow. She reached out to hug me. and I hugged her back. I was very happy as I climbed into bed next to Kurt. At least Ron and Clara like me.

The next morning, Moxie sauntered out of our bedroom and met Clara and Ron. He particularly liked Ron because Ron spent time talking to him and petting him.

* * * * *

The trip to Piedmont was pleasant, and we arrived a half hour before the barbeque was to take place. Clara and Barb hugged, but I just greeted Barb and Doug with a happy hi. Unless Barb initiated a warmer reception, I wouldn't be putting myself out there to be slighted.

Doug had baby back ribs and steaks on the grill; and a rich, meaty smell permeated the air. Ron and I sat next to one another and talked about his dad and how he respected him for being in the service and following his dream of becoming a pilot very early in his life. "I think he was only ten years old when he decided he wanted to be a pilot, and then he followed through. I never knew what I wanted to do, even after I graduated from high school."

I told him I'd always wanted to go to college but that my parents couldn't afford to pay the tuition. After my daughters were raised, I did attend college and graduated magna cum laude from Cal State Northridge with a degree in English Literature.

Ron said it was great that I'd followed my dream.

We chatted about his job that he'd held for thirteen years. "I'm going to check about switching jobs when I get back home because I'm getting too old to be moving heavy furniture."

Ron and I were getting to know one another, and it was all good. Soon Barb and Clara came out with macaroni salad and baked beans. That evidently was the cue for Doug and Kurt to load a couple of platters with the barbequed meat, and we dug in.

Kurt and Doug did most of the talking while we ate. Kurt mentioned the great cook-outs they had with Deena and her family. "Why weren't they invited today?" he asked.

"I don't know," Barb said. "We haven't seen Clara and Ron for a while and I just thought we'd get caught up on what's going on in our lives."

I mentioned that I'd visited Deena several days ago, and we had a nice time talking about the status of our high school classmates." I then added, "I sat across from Deena at study hall."

"I didn't know you knew her," Barb muttered.

"You have to realize how small our school was," Kurt said. "There weren't three hundred students in our entire high school. Our graduating class only had sixty-two students."

After a couple of hours, and running short on conversation," Kurt said we'd be leaving. Ron said he'd like to take a nap, which he did when we got back to Kurt's home. So did Clara.

Kurt petted Moxie a few times and also fell asleep. I watched a game show and pulled the window up for Moxie to breathe in some fresh air. He immediately jumped on his stand.

While having sandwiches that evening, Clara's cellphone rang. She'd had it on speaker phone, so we heard Barb ask her and Ron to drive back out to the cabin and spend the night.

"I don't want to do that," Kurt said.

"I don't believe we were invited," I replied.

Kurt handed Ron the truck keys, and Ron and Clara drove off. I was happy that the brothers could spend time together, and I hoped Clara would tell Barb how we were starting to bond; and I hoped Ron would tell Doug and Barb about our sharing bits of our lives.

When Clara and Ron returned the next morning, Ron was his usual, friendly self. Clara, however, was very cool to me and remained that way until she and Ron returned to Utah. She never attempted to hug me at the airport, although Ron hugged Kurt and me. "Thank you for your hospitality" was all she said as they left. It felt as if someone had stepped on my heart.

Kurt and I were silent on our drive back from the airport. Then Kurt said how he enjoyed watching his sons interact with one another.

"Did I ever tell you that Ron had a unicycle and was quite good at maneuvering it? The local press even took pictures of him doing tricks on it. It was hilarious."

"It takes a considerable amount of balance to operate a unicycle," I said, clearly impressed with Ron's agility.

I decided to wait until later in the day to discuss the cold shoulder I was now getting from Clara, as well as Barb.

While eating dinner that night, Kurt mentioned how nice it was to enjoy the barbeque with his sons and their wives. "The opportunity rarely arises when we can all get together at the same time. And I noticed how you and Ron seemed to hit it off. What were you talking about?"

"He's so easy to talk to. He was telling me that he's going to talk to his manager to possibly change jobs because he's too old to be handling heavy furniture."

"He didn't mention that to me, but he's right. And I hope he follows through."

"Remember when I told you of staying up late one night drinking herbal tea with Clara and her telling me about getting in with a bad crowd and getting pregnant?"

"Yes, and I remember how good you felt about starting a relationship with her."

"Well, did you notice when she and Ron came back from spending the night with Doug and Barb that Clara's attitude towards me took an about-face, and it was obvious someone had turned her against me. Then at the airport, she didn't even shake my hand."

"I did notice a coldness about her, but I didn't think more about it because you said you two spent Friday night getting to know one another. What would have changed her feelings?"

"Who did she see in the meantime? She and Ron spent the night with Doug and Barb, and now, all of a sudden, Clara doesn't like me. I know what happened. Now Barb has Clara in on an attempt to break us up. What other explanation can there be?"

"It's hard for me to believe that's what's going on. Doug and Ron included you in their conversation and seem to like you."

"They're probably not even aware of what's going on. The next time you talk to Doug, can you tell him that I feel like I'm being shunned by his wife, and just listen to what he says."

"Yes, I can do that."

"How much longer do you want to spend in Ohio?" I asked.

"I thought you wanted to visit some friends," Kurt said.

"Yes, I want to visit Grace and Al. I feel bad we didn't meet Al during our last visit." "Then let's do it."

Grace and I made plans to have dinner the next evening at "The Outback," not far from where Kurt lives.

Kurt and I slept in and spent a leisurely day. In the evening we arrived at the restaurant first and sat in the foyer until Grace and Al arrived. It was great seeing Grace again and meeting her husband. Kurt and Al seemed to click, and we spent an enjoyable evening exchanging stories about our relationships. Grace and I stayed away from any mention of her deceased husband or of my cheating husband. We laughed when Al told us of his culinary inclinations. "I've always loved to cook and thought that might be a problem. But I soon found out that Grace was quite happy giving up that function."

After treating Kurt's next-door-neighbors to dinner and having several more lunches with Marla and Joe, Kurt said he's ready to head back to Smyrna. We had one problem, however: how to get Kurt's SUV to Georgia. Kurt said he'd have it shipped after we drove back.

"That's crazy! I'll drive my car with Moxie, and you can drive your SUV. You can either follow me, or I'll follow you."

"That's great of you, honey, but are you sure you'll be okay doing all that driving?"

"No problem."

"Well, how about you follow me? We have our cell phones in case we get separated."

So, that's what we did. I followed Kurt until we stopped for lunch at a Cracker Barrel and Kurt put gas in our cars. Then I followed him until we reached Grayson, where we stopped for the night. It wasn't easy following him as cars kept coming between us, but we took our time and arrived in Smyrna tired, but safe, and with another vehicle.

Chapter Thirty-Eight

The first thing Kurt and I did upon returning from Ohio was to hire Mark Acosta, a handyman who'd been advertising in the church bulletin. He's five-feet-three and strong as an ox. He installed a new vanity in the guest bathroom and replaced the window above the tub with glass blocks. I can stand in front of the window again without cars screeching to a stop.

Mark is very congenial and can do all things construction. I'd guess he's in his sixties, but he won't tell.

Kurt and I have finished all the work we plan to do around the house and are now ready for our trip to Warm Springs. Lexie's friend, who has three cats of her own, will be pet-sitting Moxie. Since Moxie let her pet him, we hired her on-the-spot.

"Why don't you check the map to see how far Warm Springs is from Smyrna?"

"I can do that," Kurt replied, pulling out an Atlas. "I can't believe it's only eighty miles from Smyrna. Is there another place in the area you'd like to see?"

"How about the wild animal zoo that lets the animals roam the grounds?"

He nodded, so I looked up animal zoos in the Warm Springs area and found the Wild Animal Safari in Pine Mountain, not far from FDR's home.

"Let's go the day after tomorrow, and I'll firm up with the petsitter."

I called Lexie about our plans, and she said Calloway Gardens is also in that general area. She said she'd check on Aunt Wilma. "Yesterday when we were at the home, she was eating what looked like three piles of green mush. She said each pile was different and quite delicious."

"She constantly amazes me," I said.

"You know, Mom, that was awfully nice of Kurt to pay her dental bills."

"He has a big heart," I said, "and I'm thankful I have him in my life."

After arising early, having a quick breakfast, and tending to Moxie, we left for Warm Springs. We drove on I-85 most of the way, with lush greenery abounding on both sides of the freeway. We stopped for lunch at a small café on the outskirts of Warm Springs.

"The drive was under two hours," Kurt said, pulling a chair out and seating me.

As we ate, we planned our visit in Warm Springs. We'd check in at a nearby Marriot Hotel and spend the afternoon viewing Franklin Delano Roosevelt's Little White House.

Kurt said he remembers the fireside chats FDR held over the radio. "Do you remember how he started his chats?"

"My Fellow Americans," I replied.

"My grandma and I never missed any of his fireside chats. She liked to keep up on world events, and so do I."

"My parents and I huddled around the radio to listen to him because my brother was stationed in Europe; so I devised a plan by which we'd know exactly where he was. In his next letter, he would start each paragraph with a letter of the town, and when I'd hook them together – voila – we'd know. My brother did that, and we found out he was in Aachen, Germany. But let's get going. I'm eager to see The Little White House."

Parking was plentiful on this weekday in August, 2010, as Kurt pulled his SUV into a parking space. We gathered brochures that told the story about FDR's first visit to Warm Springs in 1924 hoping to find a cure for the infantile paralysis that had stricken him three years earlier.

After FDR's visit in 1924, he came regularly to swim in the warm springs; but it wasn't until 1932 while governor of New York that he had the little pine house built. Not until 1933, when he was President of the United States. that it was named "The Little White House."

Kurt and I walked through the small rooms with awe at their simplicity yet functionality due to FDR's crippled legs. We also viewed the garage that housed his black 1926 Ford Roadster. We walked the grounds and viewed the pools, now closed, that he'd swum in for relief from the polio; and I bought a small bottle of the spring water that I still have to this day. I can't decide which body part to rub it on.

We were tired when we parked at the Marriot; so we ordered in. We both had the top sirloin plate. We'd brought a bottle of wine with us that we enjoyed with dinner.

"I was moved when we saw the living room where FDR died while conversing with a friend," Kurt said. "In fact, the whole experience brought back memories of World War II and of the rationing of gasoline and even sugar," he said.

"And of the Works Progress Administration (WPA), the Civilian Conservative Corps. (CCC Camps), and the many other programs FDR started to keep the economy rolling," I said.

"It's nice we're the same age and have experienced many of the same things," I said.

"Absolutely," Kurt said. "But what are we doing sitting here in hard chairs? Let's get a shower and talk in bed."

"That'll be a first," I snickered.

* * * * *

While lying in bed, naked, Kurt grabbed his phone camera and took pictures of our feet.

"Can you tell my feet are tired?" I asked.

"No, but I can see a bunion on each big toe."

"Isn't that crazy? I don't know why they grew there. I've never worn small shoes, except maybe a couple of times when I fell in love with shoes that didn't come in my size."

"The old-wives tale is that bunions grow on the feet of nymphomaniacs," Kurt said.

"That fits me since I've met you. So, what's the sign that shows a guy is a sex addict?"

"I guess a guy who walks around with a hard-on."

"That fits you," I said, laughing.

"Since I've met you, it does." Pulling me on top of him, he showered me with kisses. When stopping for air, I said it's exciting to stay in a hotel and we should do this more often.

Kurt agreed. "It's been a wonderful day viewing FDR's summer home with you, and then ending the day in a sizzling embrace with you on top."

I raised my head slightly and asked, "I wonder if Eleanor shared this closeness with her husband? Do you think Franklin ever pulled her on top?"

"I'd say that was their favorite position due to his paralyzed legs."

"That's not nice to say. Maybe they didn't have sex."

"They had six children, and they all looked like him."

"Let's pretend I'm Eleanor and you're Frankie."

"Sounds good to me, Eleanor. And by the way, I'm interested in having another child. So, do your thing."

"Okay, Frankie. How's this?" I asked, while slowly moving up and down on his appendage. "And how's this?" I asked, moving more quickly.

"Can you keep up that pace for another hour? I think we may have twins this time."

The next day, after breakfast, we checked out of the hotel and drove to the Wild Animal Safari. Opting to drive through the 560-acre park in the comfort of our car, we encountered scads of exotic animals from around the world roaming freely in their natural habitat. A baby giraffe had poked his head through the passenger-side window. Petting him gently, I urged his head out of the car. We saw buffalo, gazelle, rhinos, hippos, zebra, and ostrich. Peacocks were strutting their stuff, Llamas were spitting on everything, and squealing pigs rolled in the mud. Actually, I can't remember when I've had so much fun.

* * * * *

"I'm glad we checked out of the Marriot before visiting the safari," I said, climbing in our dirty car, "because now we can go to Callaway Gardens or head home."

"What do you want to do?" Kurt asked.

"I want to head back home. We can cover Calloway Gardens in a day trip."

"I need to find a gas station to clean the car windows," he said, starting the engine. "Those animals were sure curious about us."

"Sharing history with you was special," I said.

"It was a hoot. Say, have I told you today that I love you?" Kurt leaned over to kiss me.

"I love you, too, and just the other day I told Lexie that I'm thankful you're in my life. I keep forgetting to ask, but have you mentioned to Doug that I feel shunned by Barb?"

"Yes, I asked Doug, and he thinks it's a girl thing."

"What does that mean? That Barb just doesn't like me and therefore won't accept me?"

Kurt said, "It's no big deal."

"To me it is. I've never been purposely ignored like this before in my life."

Kurt shook his head. He then spied a gas station and stopped for gas and cleaned the snot and saliva from the windows. When he got back in, I decided not to pressure him about Barb. I'm sure he isn't happy with the situation but doesn't know how to handle it.

"I know you want to spend time in Ohio, and you probably should go before the cold weather arrives."

"I was thinking the same thing. Why don't you go with me?"

"Not this time, honey. I want to make valances to hang over the windows, and I have some writing projects to finish."

"Why don't I go in October. Then I'll be back to spend the winter with you in Georgia."

I nodded.

"In case you need me, I'll come back sooner. Is that okay?"

"That's perfect. And if I need help, Lexie and Stephen are only two miles away."

"I'll sure miss you," Kurt said. "But I have to keep up my home in Ohio."

"Remember when I lived in California? We saw one another one week a month."

"Compared to that, this arrangement is heaven," Kurt said.

"I think it's great to have time apart to do our own thing. I plan to get a lot of writing done and to see Aunt Wilma more often. I'm so happy to have her nearby."

"That took some planning, but it worked out."

"I'll be visiting her, and I'll attend Mass more often. I love St. Thomas' Catholic Church and the weekly sermons. In fact, they apply to real-life situations that seem to relate to me."

"I really like the First Methodist Church that I attend. It has a smaller membership, and I've already made many friends there."

"I know. The last time I went with you, the last couple of pews were filled with women in their forties and fifties, and you, my dear, were the only male sitting there."

Kurt's laugh came from his gut. "That's just how things worked out."

That didn't make me jealous because the women were glad to see me when I attended, and I saw no flirty-flirty with my fiancé, although I know he would have loved it.

"Do you remember what day tomorrow is?" I asked.

"Yes, it's my eighty-second birthday. What do you have planned for me?"

"I want to surprise you."

Kurt smiled the rest of our drive home.

It felt great to be back home. As soon as Kurt opened the door, Moxie was all over me. Listening to him purr, I petted him and pulled him close. I love this cat so much, it's as though I birthed him. Kurt then trotted in with my suitcase and lay on the bed with us.

"This is your family," I said.

"Yes, and I love you both." He petted Moxie and wrapped me in his arms.

The next night, I treated Kurt and my daughter and son-in-law to dinner at Copeland's in Atlanta while a piano player pounded out oldie's tunes. We ordered from the buffet that consisted of crab and shrimp, along with an extravagant array of meats and salads. Another table was covered with desserts. We had a great conversation talking about our trip, Calloway Gardens, and other historical sites. I said we would have stopped at the gardens but I wanted to celebrate Kurt's birthday with her and Stephen.

That night in bed, Kurt thanked me for the wonderful birthday dinner and said he washed his pecker three times.

"So?"

"You made me a promise for my birthday. Do you remember?"

"I didn't say which birthday, did I? Why can't you dream up another kinky position?"

"I guess," he pouted.

"You sound like Debbie Downer. How many eighty-year-old ladies would indulge you like I do?"

"You're absolutely right. Now climb on top, Eleanor, and go at it."

Chapter Thirty-Nine

Kurt left for Ohio the first week of October, 2010, and he called every night around eight o'clock. We said how we miss each other and swore our love and commitment to each other.

He said he's trying to get his lawn in shape. "Although I have a gardener to cut the lawns, I take charge of trimming the bushes and shaping them."

"What shape are you giving them?" I giggled.

"I make everything round. When I doodle, it's also in circles. I wonder what that means?"

"I think it means you can't make up your mind."

"That makes sense."

"I hope you're not going in circles regarding the way you feel about me?"

"No, that's on solid ground."

Kurt said he's been bagging mountains of leaves that land on the patios, and he plans to paint the downstairs bathroom and clean out the garage, and nap twice a day.

"That's a lot of work to do in a month's time," I said.

"Fall is the time to work on the landscape, so that comes first. And what have you been doing, my love?"

"I did a little grocery shopping today and bought some upholstery material for valances from Jo Ann's, I played with the cat, and I answered several emails."

"How do you get so much done in a day? I trimmed three bushes and went to lunch with Joe and Marla, then my usual naps, then dinner, and here it is eight o'clock."

"Moxie misses you."

"How do you know?"

"I caught him smelling your tennis shoes today."

"He did that when I was in Smyrna. Doug said he's driving down to spend the weekend with me."

I asked him what they plan to do, and he said they'll drive to the lake and shoot at bottles.

"And shoot the bull."

"That, too." Kurt's voice turned tender. "Know that you're loved, Sweetheart, and I'll call you tomorrow night."

"Love you back."

It sounds like boring conversation; but not to lovers. We read between the lines and get sweaty over nothing. It has to do with hormones, and what our voices sound like to one another, and not particularly what we're saying. If you've ever been in love, I'm sure you get it.

The second week, our apart conversations started getting racy, like remembering what we used to do when making love, and the third week was what we planned to do to one another when we saw one another again. And the fourth week was more sex talk and telling each other what we wanted our partner to do to us. The fifth week, Kurt headed back to Smyrna. He called when he was at Grayson spending the night. "I'll be in Smyrna tomorrow early afternoon," he said. "Clear the hallways so my protruding pecker doesn't break anything when I walk through."

Can you believe this sex talk coming from the mouths of eighty-one and eighty-two-year-old seniors in love? I probably wouldn't believe it, either, if I weren't one of the participants.

When Kurt arrived, we both turned to mush. It was so wonderful to see one another again that we just wanted to hug and kiss. We were like a left shoe and a right shoe. Different, yes. But we were a pair that fit. All that macho talk went out the window as we cuddled together on the sofa while the pot roast sent tantalizing fragrances throughout the house. Moxie jumped in our laps and was especially attentive to Kurt, which made Kurt so proud. He'd never had a cat before and was relishing all this nuzzling only a cat can negotiate.

"I can't believe how addictive I've become to you, Eva. I missed you something terrible."

"I can't believe how slowly the month dragged on. When we're together it zips by."

When I poked at the roast, it was juicy and tender. Kurt poured glasses of White Zinfandel, and we toasted our relationship. "To our love," he said.

That night in bed, the things we'd discussed over the phone for four weeks returned with such a passion that pleasing one another was all that mattered. And that we did. It never ceases to amaze me how Kurt's touch that burns into my flesh can be so gentle. But that's one of the mysteries of love. Kurt says our intimacy is so intense that he loses himself in those moments, and it takes a while before his body and mind return to earth.

* * * * *

Before we realized it, Thanksgiving was here; and I decided to bake a turkey and invite Lexie and Stephen over, in addition to the neighbors that Kurt and I had become friends with. I was missing my California family during the holidays, although we talked on the phone a lot. That didn't make up for a personal visit, but it helped. Susan said she's baking a turkey using my stuffing recipe. I told her I'm also making a no-bake cheesecake, which takes ten minutes.

Kurt told his usual one-liners, and we all laughed like crazy. Willa is funny and outgoing and helped Lexie scrub the woodwork in my home before Kurt and I moved in. Her husband Harry is more reserved, but he enjoys Kurt's corny jokes.

Natalia, a pretty, unmarried woman, lives across the street with two dogs and one cat. She's always taking in strays and hooking them up with their owners or new owners.

Willa told us her white cat had been a bitty kitten when it stopped by her house one afternoon, and she took her in. "Now she's a fat twelve-year-old. What makes her special is that her tail is off-center at her behind."

I told my guests that my friend's husband had dementia that had gotten progressively worse, and she had to place him in a nursing home. Feeling sorry for leaving Moxie alone so often, she gave him to me. When she visited, she was surprised to see how quickly we bonded.

After our guests left, Kurt and I decided to make love on our den sofa. Hearing muffled noises sounding like giggles outside the French doors, we fled to our bedroom. Kurt asked, "Didn't you say we could look out the French doors but nobody could look in?"

"Obviously, someone made a *big* mistake," I replied curtly.

Thanksgiving was so enjoyable, we decided to have Christmas together. It snowed a few days before Christmas, and it was delightful to see and feel the snow again. It's been at least forty years since I've seen snow. Kurt and I tossed snowballs at one another, and Kurt made a small snowman that melted before Christmas day.

For a Christmas gift, Lexie and Stephen bought Kurt a memorial brick at the Smyrna Square. After our guests had gone, Stephen drove Lexie, Kurt, and me to the Square where Lexie led us to the Veteran's Memorial site where hundreds of bricks were displayed. She stopped at Kurt's memorial brick with Kurt's name and dates he served in the U.S. Military engraved on it. Wiping his eyes as he knelt beside the brick, I snapped a memorable moment. Kurt said this was one of the best gifts he's ever gotten. "And it will be here after I'm gone."

Stephen and Lexie drove us back home and thanked us for a lovely Christmas day.

After petting Moxie, I asked Kurt to sit beside me on the bed. Putting my hand on his knee, I asked, "Are we just playing house, or do we want to build a future together?"

Kurt looked confused. "I never thought about it. I'm just enjoying our relationship daily."

"Me, too, but I'm starting to feel like the lady wearing a scarlet letter on her chest."

"I love you, Eva, and I can't imagine a life without you."

"We've been together for a year and have been engaged for eight months. The bottom line is whether we want to spend the rest of our lives together or whether this is just a fling."

"I love you, Eva, and I'm committed to you, and that will never change; so, why don't we get married? I'll be very proud to have you for my wife."

Kurt dropped to his knee and asked, "Will you marry me, Eva, for better or worse?"

"Yes," I replied to a shower of the sweetest kisses in the world.

"What a precious moment," Kurt said. "And will you take my name?"

"I have to think about that since I'm published under Sandor."

"Whatever feels right," he said.

"Let's get married in the spring when the weather gets warmer," I said.

"You pick the date," Kurt said. "Where will this happen, and who do you want to perform the ceremony?"

"I'd be fine with the minister of The First Methodist Church performing the ceremony with a few friends in attendance."

"Would you be willing to do that, Eva? I'd love for Louie Cummings to officiate."

"Then it's a done deal." I would have liked for Father Goetz at the St. Thomas Catholic Church to perform the ceremony, but I knew Kurt would be amenable to having our marriage blessed by him later in the year.

"We'll talk to Pastor Louie about fitting us into his schedule." Kurt beamed.

* * * * *

Kurt was antsy to drive back to his Ohio home, and he wanted me to go with him. "We don't get much snow in

Ohio in the winters like when we were growing up," he said.

"I'll go if you promise not to stay longer than a month. Otherwise, I don't mind if you go alone. After all, it is your residence."

"A month this time of the year in Ohio is fine with me."

So, we packed and were gone within the week. Lexie and Stephen said they'd check on Aunt Wilma and our home while we are gone.

As Kurt drove, he voiced his enthusiasm about having a wedding reception in St. Clairsville with our classmates in attendance.

"I'd love that," I replied, "plus my cousin and her family, and Joe and Marla, and your neighbors, and Doug and Barb."

"I'm really getting into it," Kurt said.

"Let's each make a guest list, and then we'll consolidate the list. It would be great to have the reception at Mehlman's Cafeteria since their food and desserts are scrumptious."

"Aren't we having a wedding cake?" Kurt asked, disappointment in his voice.

"Of course. We'll have a two-tier white wedding cake with a bride and groom with white hair dancing on top."

"You know, I'm really getting excited about our wedding in Smyrna and a reception in St. Clairsville with our classmates there," Kurt said.

"Let's keep everything mum until we work out all the details. This is our moment."

Kurt agreed.

During our month in Ohio, Doug and Barb drove down from Maryland twice to see us. They stayed at their cabin and said they got some much-needed work done. Both times we had dinner with them when they arrived, and afterwards they came to Kurt's home to visit. Barb hardly acknowledged me while Doug and Kurt talked about the projects still to be done at the cabin. Both times we had breakfast with them at the Mall as they were heading back to Maryland. The conversation was strained, and since Barb was still maintaining a cold stance towards me, I lost interest in being her best friend. I got a handshake from Doug when they left. I wasn't happy with this relationship, but only Doug and Barb could make it better.

The phone rang, shaking me out of my doldrums, and I heard my friend Donna's sweet voice asking how I am. "First, let me know how you are. It's been a while since we've talked."

She said she's been in Bullhead City visiting our friends there and they send their love. I asked if they gambled at Laughlin, and Donna said she hit the five-hundred-dollar jackpot twice on the same machine. I congratulated her and told her about the way I'm being treated by Barb and Clara and she said since I don't see them very often to try to be pleasant for Kurt's sake and try to not let it get to me.

"I know you're right, but it's tough."

Donna said she couldn't understand their motives. "You've had two mothers-in-law with whom you've been very close, and you were close to Wes' mom and dad. I'd think that would be a good judge of your character. And every time you join a club, you're elected president. I think they're trying to make your life miserable so you break up with Kurt."

"I never thought about that. Grace thinks they're worried about their inheritance."

Donna said, "It's their loss because they're missing out on having a good friend."

"You always make me feel better, Donna." I then told her about Kurt's and my plans to get married in Smyrna and have a wedding reception in Ohio. I gave her dates we were considering for the reception in Ohio with the hope she could fly in for it.

"I'm very happy for the both of you, and you can count on me being there."

Chapter Forty

Louie Cummings of the First Methodist Church said he'd be happy to officiate at our wedding. Since he's leading a tour group to Israel, he gave us several dates in April, and Kurt and I selected April 2, 2011, for our wedding.

Since I was Lexie's maid of honor when she married Stephen, I asked her to be my maid of honor. Kurt asked Stephen to be his best man. Our neighbors will be our only guests.

Lexie's friend suggested a photographer, so I called him; and he said he was free on April 2 and quoted an affordable price to attend the ceremony and to snap pictures.

A few days later, Nancy called and asked if we'd like to take a nine-day Royal Caribbean Cruise with her and Brad and another couple.

I asked Kurt, and he said "yes" without hesitation. "Just find out where the ship departs from and where it's headed."

I was breathless when I told Nancy that we'd go, to just give us the details. She and I are both excited to go on a cruise together and knowing our husbands like one another makes it more appealing. Nancy said they'd met the other couple while taking dancing lessons. "You'll like them. They're both outgoing and a lot of fun."

After hanging up, I threw myself on Kurt's lap and kissed him a dozen times. "Thank you so much, darling."

"It will be our honeymoon," he said, grinning.

"A honeymoon comes after a marriage."

"So, ours will come before our marriage."

Nancy called the next day with all the details. The Royal Caribbean would leave Baltimore, Maryland and would cruise the high seas to the Bermudas and Bahamas and end up at Key West, Florida before returning to Baltimore. Nancy said the brochure touted the Caribbean beaches as the most beautiful in the world. "The food and entertainment on these ships is fantastic. I know because Brad and I took several cruises."

She gave me a number to call and said a Miss Hall has our names and will reserve a cabin next to the one she and Brad are sharing. "Make your reservation asap," she said.

I asked how they were getting to Baltimore, and she said she and Brad and the Ambroses would take a red-eye flight and would hail a cab to the Baltimore Harbor upon arrival.

I told her Kurt and I would drive to Kurt's Ohio home and spend the night and then spend the next night in Baltimore before boarding the ship the next morning. "I know I shouldn't be telling you this, but Kurt and I are getting married on April 2nd and this will be our honeymoon."

"I'm so excited for you," Nancy said. "I'll have to tell Brad, but he'll keep it secret."

"Okay, make sure. Before we go on the cruise, I want to buy my wedding dress." I told her Lexie would be my maid of honor and Stephen would be Kurt's best man."

"Are you going to be married in the Catholic Church?" she asked.

She sounded disappointed that I wouldn't be, but when I said we're going to have our marriage blessed in a Catholic Church, either in Smyrna or in Tiltonsville, where

I'd been baptized and confirmed, she thought that would be wonderful.

I spent the next few days shopping for my wedding dress and clothes to wear on the cruise. Nancy said there would be two formal dinners, and since I'd bought a black gown with sparkly gems woven into the top that I wore at a Ms. Senior California contest about six months ago, I'd pack that gown and a frilly black and white dress I wore when reading my humor essay in the talent contest. I'd supplement my beach ware by buying new capris, tops, and sandals.

Kurt asked me to accompany him to the Men's Wearhouse for a black suit and white brocade tie for our wedding. While there, he also bought a light grey suit and shirts that made the grey suit dazzle. Walking shorts, T-shirts, and tennies completed his cruise attire.

While Kurt bought his clothes at one store, I frequented several before finding my dusty-rose, short silk wedding dress. It has layers of semi-flat ruffles, running from the top of the dress to the bottom hem. Lexie wanted me to wear a long dress, but I couldn't find one I liked as well as the one I found on Macy's rack.

Greta, Lexie's friend who pet-sat Moxie on our trip to Warm Springs, was happy to take care of him during our nine-day cruise.

Before we had time to breathe deeply, it was time to head to Kurt's home in Ohio for the first stopover where we packed our bags, or I should say I packed my bag. Kurt was having difficulty packing his bag and ended up throwing his casual clothes in a heap in the bed of his truck. The weather report predicted a cold front, so Kurt drove his truck rather than my Nissan.

After six hours on the road, we pulled into the entrance of a swanky Baltimore hotel. I felt like one of the Beverly Hills' hillbillies in a red truck with flailing clothing in the truck bed. It didn't seem to bother Kurt as he checked us in, stacking the disarray of clothing on a hotel cart with our bags, that he pushed to our room. Along the way, we encountered guests laughing at us.

We placed the suitcases and clothes in our room, tended to our bladders, and walked a few blocks to a café where we had steaming clam chowder and shared a turkey sandwich.

Upon our return to the hotel, I unloaded Kurt's suitcase and put all of those clothes and his truck-bed clothes in a pile and rolled them neatly and repacked Kurt's suitcase.

"How did you get things to fit?" he asked, shaking his head.

"Patience," I replied. It just hit me that we're in Maryland where Doug and Barb live and I asked Kurt if he'd told them we're taking a cruise from Baltimore, and he said he had.

I asked if they wanted to get together while we are here, but Kurt said they don't live that close to Baltimore.

Getting up early, we checked out of the hotel and drove to the harbor where parking was marked off for Royal Caribbean passengers. Kurt parked the truck and found a wooden cart that he placed our two bags on and wheeled it to the ship's entrance. Kurt nor I had taken a cruise before and were amazed at the size of the ship and adroitness of the crew.

Once aboard, we found our cabin and looked out the porthole. The sea looked very calm, but I remember getting sick on a swing. Lexie said when she took a cruise, she wore a patch behind her ear, and her stomach was still upset. I planned to take seasickness pills and to let nature have its way with me because I was determined to enjoy my honeymoon.

Kurt loved looking at the ocean from the porthole. If I hadn't pulled him away, we'd still be in our cabin. Although the room was small, it contained everything we needed.

After settling in, we knocked lightly on Nancy and Brad's cabin door. Nancy opened it, and I remember thinking how beautiful she looked with her short red pixie cut and her lovely smile. She invited us in to greet Brad and said she'd introduce us to the Ambroses at breakfast.

Breakfast was a five-course production, and the banter around the table was great fun. Each couple introduced themselves and said whether it was their first cruise, where they were from, and said a little about themselves. Kurt said we're on our honeymoon, and everybody at the table congratulated us and wanted to know when we'd gotten married.

"Oh, we're not married yet," Kurt said.

All sorts of questions ensued, and Kurt answered by saying we decided to go on our honeymoon first, and that our wedding would take place on April 2nd.

"We want to find out if we're compatible," I said.

Kurt said that the small cabin we're sharing ought to reveal our temperaments.

"In other words, this is a trial run?" Roy Ambrose, half of the dancing couple, asked.

"Could be," I answered.

All table occupants had something funny to say about our honeymoon-first arrangement.

Dana, the other half of the dancing couple, sat next to me, and I told her about Moxie. She told me that she and Roy have two cats they leave alone with food, water, and an automatic kitty litter container. She said Nancy and Brad's son tends to their three cats.

After breakfast, I asked one of the cruise attendants where I could get some seasickness pills. Pulling out a bottle of pills from her pocket, she dumped some pills in my hand. "Start out by taking half a pill," she said. "Then take them as needed. If you want more, just look me up."

The six of us walked around the deck together, and then sat in lounge chairs. We'd cruise all day and night, and in the morning, we'd dock at King's Wharf, Bermuda, to tour the island.

That night, after a sumptuous dinner, we were entertained by a lady violinist. Kurt and I were mesmerized by what this slightly built, eighty-year-old woman did with her violin. At times it seemed to cry out, and at times it seemed to cackle with laughter.

Snacks were on every floor of the ship, loaded with goodies that tempted the most rigid dieter. I got addicted to the lemon/poppyseed cake. Kurt's sinful snack was almond croissants.

At bedtime, Kurt and I compared our bloated bellies and laughed. We then walked in place for ten minutes to eliminate the full feeling that seemed to overtake our sexual desires.

"How about a morning hour?" I asked.

"What do you mean an hour? I'll be lucky to go ten minutes."

"Okay. You can give me an hour before you start your ten minutes."

"Can you tell me how I can do that?"

"Figure it out. This is my honeymoon, too."

The next morning, we awoke to a very raw desire for one another. It was so intense that it must have lasted all of five minutes. We then showered and met our friends for breakfast.

"Any reason why you're late?" Roy asked. The rest of the occupants at our table teased us during the entire meal, referring to us as the honeymoon kids.

One of our new friends asked, "Well, is the wedding still on?"

Kurt smiled his foot-long grin, and I just nodded.

After breakfast, the Royal Caribbean docked at the King's Wharf, and passengers departed for the day to enjoy walking on the white sands, snorkeling, swimming, or sunbathing.

Another stop was at The Royal Naval Dockyard, which once served as an outpost for the British Royal Navy and has since become the busiest passenger ship port in the island. We three couples decided to part ways and to explore the tourist complex on our own. Kurt and I stopped to browse at the National Museum and bought T-shirts and souvenirs at The Clock Tower Shopping Mall. Since my legs were tired, we sat on a bench at an outdoor café drinking vanilla sodas and just enjoying being together and looking at phone camera pictures of our honeymoon.

The Grand Bahamas island was another delightful stop. A small boat took us to a secluded island where other ship passengers joined our group to enjoy food and beverage. Kurt regaled them with our reconnecting after sixty-two years and falling in love. Afterwards, Kurt and I walked the beach, hand in hand, before the small boat took us back to the ship.

That evening, the entertainment was a potty-mouthed comedian who told raunchy jokes that offended half of the crowd. Many couples left the room after his first joke, but our group of six remained a bit longer before we also departed. "Funny doesn't have to be filthy," Nancy said.

The ship also docked at Coco Cay, another island in the Bahamas, with pristine beaches. The most memorable docking, however, was at Nassau Bahamas on Providence island. Nassau is the capital and largest city. White beaches welcomed travelers from around the world with its rich culture and colonial architecture. Our walking tour took us to Parliament Square. As a paralegal, I was intrigued by the different cultures and legal processes. The Parliament buildings are pink that host a sixteen-member Senate and a thirty-eight-member House of Assembly. Vital decisions and debates concerning the future of the Bahamas take place here.

A honeymoon is a time for remembering why two people fell in love in the first place, and this dreamland honeymoon cruise proved to be all of that and more: simmering glances, sizzling kisses, loving touches, and passionate sex, all remind Kurt and me of our commitment to one another through sickness and in health because we love one another deeply and forever. We both believe that our union was destined from childhood. It just took us a while to figure it out.

One of our favorite entertainers was an Elton John impersonator who sang his heart out while pounding the keyboard. As coincidence would have it, we bumped into him in the lobby, and he was quite amendable to us having a picture taken together. So, Kurt snapped it. Best picture Kurt ever took. We were both smiling, and our heads were on the picture.

The Royal Caribbean cruised to Florida, where we toured Cape Canaveral and Key West before heading back to Baltimore. After goodbyes to the Randalls and Ambroses, we packed up the red truck and drove to St. Clairsville. After spending a day and night there, we drove back to Smyrna in my Nissan. I could hardly contain myself as I swept up my beautiful Moxie in my arms and listened to his passionate purring.

After a short nap with my favorite males, I got up and called Lexie. "No, I didn't get sick once. I took half of a seasickness pill every morning, given to me by a cruise attendant, and that did its magic on me. Other than gaining a few pounds, Kurt and I are fine."

Lexie told me that Aunt Wilma is happy eating her pureed food, "And she does very well without her teeth."

Lexie said she'd bought a long, grey dress; and we talked about the flower arrangements.

I told her I decided to hold the wedding dinner at 'The Old Vinings Inn' in Atlanta after reading a few reviews from regular customers.

"Our honeymoon was over the moon, and I know our wedding will be, as well."

Chapter Forty-One

Our wedding day had arrived. While Kurt dressed in his black suit, white shirt, and silk brocade white tie in the guest bedroom, I was busy making a headpiece out of small pearls and white roses that I fastened to a white headband. I applied my makeup and filled in my greying eyebrows with black eyeliner, drew a dusty pink lipstick across my lips, and combed my hair into an upsweep. I then placed the headband on. Wow! What a lovely bridal look that added.

Kurt walked into the room as I was finishing up. "You are a lovely bride," he said, stopping in his tracks and smiling engagingly.

"And you are a handsome groom," I replied.

Embracing, we professed our forever love.

"We better get moving," I said. "We need to stop by the florist to pick up the flowers."

* * * * *

When we arrived at the church, a car with markings on it reading "Paul's Photography" sat in the parking lot. A blond-haired gentleman with deep blue eyes and a winsome smile got out and introduced himself as Paul. We discussed the pictures we wanted him to snap.

Pastor Louie, waiting in the vestibule, greeted us warmly. "Are you ready for the big day?"

"We are," Kurt said, shaking his hand and introducing Paul.

Walking towards the altar, Louie explained the process. Before he was done, Lexie and Stephen joined us; and I pinned a red rose on Stephen's lapel and a white rose on Kurt's lapel.

In a matter of minutes, our neighbors arrived and sat in the first pew.

Lexie and I hugged; and she said what a beautiful bride I was in my pink dress and how much she liked my pink and white rose bouquet. I complimented her light grey gown and said it looked lovely on her. I then handed her the dark red and white rose bouquet that she aahed over.

I told Pastor Louie that Kurt and I had written our own vows; and he commenced the service. He said he's known us since we moved to Smyrna and that Kurt is a member of the First Methodist Church. He said he finds us to be a loving couple and that the marriage should work since we've known one another since we were children. Kurt and I repeated our special vows that we'd written, and after saying "I do's," the pastor pronounced us husband and wife. Kurt kissed me soundly; and the pastor presented us to our guests.

As we faced our neighbors, the photographer snapped Kurt and me with the pastor at the altar. He also took pictures of Lexie, Stephen, and our neighbors in various poses with us. Then he took some cutesy ones of me sitting on Kurt's lap and of us walking down the aisle and out of the church. Paul said he'd get proofs to us within a week.

* * * * *

Our wedding dinner was held at the 'Old Vinings Inn' in Atlanta, a historical site that housed a very popular, southern restaurant. Our party was seated in a private room; and when the chef found out the bride and groom were here, he came in and informed us of his specialties: Pecan-crusted Trout; Lump Crab Cakes; Shrimp and Grits; Southern-fried Chicken, and tasteful southern sides such as fried green tomatoes, creamed corn, and macaroni and cheese that a reviewer stated, "It's nothing like you've tasted before." The chef also suggested Baked Pork Chops with apricot glaze, and Pappardelle. My daughter, a vegetarian, chose the Pappardelle, and the rest of us chose other specialties that we shared.

The chef recommended a champagne that Kurt ordered. It was smooth, without the after-jolt, that our entire party enjoyed so much that we ordered a second bottle. The chef acted as our photographer, taking pictures of Kurt and me being toasted and roasted. The entire dining experience was elegant, gracious, and tasteful, adding to our perfect day.

Lexie and Stephen were married for thirty years and suggested tips for a happy life. Lexie's advice was to Kurt: "If you want a happy marriage, your wife is always right." Harry said to "Stuff your feelings if you should even think about disagreeing," and he should know as he and Willa have been married for fifty years. Since Kurt and I are still in the stage of thinking our mates are perfect, we ignored the tips. After a last toast, we bade adieu to our guests.

* * * * *

Kurt had made reservations at a Doubletree hotel nearby – destination unknown to our party. He'd requested the honeymoon suite, which had a jacuzzi tub in the living room. We thoroughly enjoyed the soak together, along with glasses of Grand Marnier. Although our minds were a little foggy, Kurt's navigator had no problem zeroing in on Ms. Vagina and entertaining her with his special of the day: a good old-fashioned f----ng. It wasn't long after, that Kurt started snoring. I conked out soon after Kurt had.

The next day, we walked across the street to IHOP for breakfast, and we talked about our wedding day.

"It was perfect," I ruminated.

"It looked like everyone was having a good time. I know I was," Kurt said. "And thanks for keeping your promise. It made my love for you even stronger."

"What promise are you talking about – our vows?"

"You know. The promise I was supposed to get on my birthday that I didn't get."

"You're dreaming. I didn't do that."

"Yes, you did."

"When did I supposedly do that?"

"After we got out of the Jacuzzi, I pointed out that Dickie had been soaking for an hour."

"I didn't do that."

"Yes, you did."

"Yes, I did.""

"You remember?"

"Yes. I remember thinking how much I love you and why don't I just put my mouth on it and fondle your balls to let you know just how much I love you."

"I'm glad it was a love act and not a drunken act."

"I was a little tipsy; however, it was a one-time love act for our wedding, okay?"

"Okay. But I was just thinking. Aren't we going to have our wedding blessed in the Catholic church?"

"Oh, no!" I shrieked. "Don't you understand that one time means one time?"

"Okay, I get it."

"Don't you mean, 'You got it?'"

"Yeah, whatever," Kurt said. "And I agree that our wedding day was perfect."

"Now we can plan our wedding reception in Ohio. We can set it two weeks away on a Saturday and send out invitations Monday. Lexie said any Saturday is good for her and Stephen."

"Let's put our guest lists together and do it. I'm excited to get all of our friends and classmates together," Kurt said.

"I can't believe how many still live in the Ohio Valley," I said.

Before sending the invitations, I called Mehlman's Cafeteria in St. Clairsville to see whether they could accommodate a guest list of forty. The manager, Janine, said she'd reserve a separate room next to the cafeteria and set up tables as we desired, suggesting we get there early to decorate. She said guests would go through the cafeteria line and select the items they want and tell the cashier they're attending the Miller reception. "We'll have servers help carry trays to the private room. And after the guests have gone," Janine said, "I'll tally up the bill."

"I want a head table for the bride-and-groom, maid of honor, best man, and three more settings for Doug, Barb, and Laura," I said. Janine suggested setting up ten tables that would seat four each, in addition to the guests seated at the head table. "We can always set up more tables."

Since I'd left my speaker phone on, Kurt heard the conversation and said, "I can't believe how easy that was. But you forgot to ask about the cake."

"We can buy the cake wherever we want, have it decorated, and then bring it to the reception, along with wedding decorations," I said.

"Although we'll be sending invitations, I'm going to call Doug with a heads up."

"Call Marla and Joe, also," I said. "And I'll call my cousin and family."

I was floating on a cloud when I called Lexie about our wedding reception. "I hope the date we selected is okay for you and Stephen."

"As long as it's on a Saturday, which it is."

I told her about the plans I'd made with Janine, and Lexie went on and on about how much she liked Mehlman's food. She said Aunt Sabrina held a wake there for Uncle Ed.

"If Stephen and I can help out, just let us know."

* * * * *

Kurt and I arrived at the reception room early and hung large letters spelling out Eva and Kurt, along with hearts and roses on a long ribbon that we tacked to the wall. We then covered the head table with sheets that looked like tablecloths. We placed two wedding albums of pictures of our honeymoon cruise on the table, along with two 8 x 10 pictures of Kurt and me in our wedding finery. We then set a 2-tiered white wedding cake decorated with fluffy white frosting, red roses, and green leaves, in the center of the head table with a bride and groom, with white hair, affixed to the top of the cake.

Covering the small tables with white paper, we set a swan ornament filled with candies at each place setting, plus we put a swan ornament at each nameplate at the head table.

A card table sat by the entrance door with a guest wedding album on it which each guest would sign upon entering the room.

My husband and I awaited our guests in coordinated attire. I wore a black dress with ruffles down the front, a red silk scarf, and red shoes. Kurt wore a black shirt with white pinstripes, complimented by a red tie.

Lexie and Stephen arrived, both dressed in classy suits. Lexie took charge of signing guests in. The guests streamed in steadily; and when I saw Donna come in with her brother Bill and his wife Joan, I ran to the door to greet them. "You know I wouldn't miss your wedding reception," Donna said, hugging me. Kurt then greeted them and ushered them to their table.

Kurt and I returned to the head table and welcomed all of our guests. Then we asked two tables of guests to return to the cafeteria for their food; then two more tables of guests, and so on, until everyone had gotten their food and were seated. Although nameplates sat at the head table for Doug, Barb, and Laura, they chose to sit with their Aunt Deena. In fact, I mentioned to Kurt that neither his son nor Barb nor Laura had spoken to me. A perplexed look crossed Kurt's face.

* * * * *

After we'd finished eating, but before we cut the cake, I saw Laura standing by the wedding album and went over to talk to her. I said I was glad she came and told her about me. She said, "I heard," and walked back to her table.

I was stunned. What had she heard that made her disrespect me in this manner? I walked back to the head table and asked Lexie if Doug or Barb had greeted them.

"No, but as soon as Doug came in, I introduced myself and joked that I was the sister he'd been wanting, and he just gave me a weird look and kept walking. He didn't acknowledge me at all and never spoke to Stephen. Barb nor Laura spoke to us, either."

I told her what Laura had said to me, and I said that neither Kurt's son nor Barb had said one word to me, not even to say hello, and I was fed up with their rude behavior. "But it can wait until tomorrow. Today is Kurt's and my day."

I announced that we'd be cutting the cake and servers would be bringing in coffee.

"If anyone wants a soft drink," I said, "please return to the cafeteria for drinks of your choice before we cut the cake."

I asked Kurt if he spoke with Doug. "We bumped into one another, and he congratulated me, but that's it."

We cut the cake and some of our friends made toasts to us. Not Doug, however. I was glad to see that all of our guests that were invited had come and were having a good time. After eating and talking with the guests, Lexie and Stephen decided to head back to Smyna to let us have time with Kurt's family. "We'll drive until we're tired and then stop for the night," Stephen said. Lexie said they enjoyed talking with Donna and her family. Kurt and I both told them how we appreciate them diving in for our reception, and that there was a separate bedroom for them at Kurt's home; but they'd made up their minds. Soon after, Doug and Barb said they were leaving, and they told Kurt they'd call him in the morning. No goodbyes to me, and no wedding card from them. Kurt and I had said in our invitation: "No presents, please," but we didn't say "No cards."

Most of the guests left wedding congratulatory cards and some enclosed gift cards to restaurants. It was fun to read what they'd written.

Kurt and I walked Donna, her brother, and his wife to their car. Donna said she'd call us as she'll be spending a long weekend with Bill and Joan before flying back to California.

* * * * *

Kurt and I got back to his home before seven. "I wonder why Doug, Barb, and Laura didn't join us?" he asked.

"I'd like to know why they didn't sit at the head table with you and me and my family. Their name cards were sitting at the head table."

"Also, did you know that none of them spoke to Lexie nor Stephen, although Lexie made an attempt to engage Doug in conversation? I'd told you at past gatherings how they'd shun me, remember? I even had you ask Doug what's going on, and he said something about a girl thing. Do you think this is a girl thing? Not speaking to me or my family who drove over seven hundred miles to be with us and to meet your family? I think this is very rotten behavior."

Then I told Kurt what Laura said after I introduced myself and made a point of saying how glad I was that she came.

Kurt said, "What the hell did she hear? And what made her act like that? I think it's time I find out what's going on."

"Why don't you call them in the morning? We're all tired now."

"Yes, I'll do that, and I'll ask if they can come by to talk; okay?"

Chapter Forty-Two

In the morning, Doug and Barb appeared, but Laura was noticeably absent. They greeted us and sat on the floor in the living room while Kurt and I sat on the sofa. They appeared nervous, and I'm relatively certain that was because they knew a confrontation about their not speaking to me nor my family at the reception was about to take place.

Kurt spoke first and repeated to them what Laura had said to me when I introduced myself to her. "'I heard' is what Laura said to Eva, and then she walked back to her table, leaving Eva standing there."

Both Doug and Barb feigned surprise.

Kurt went on. "What did Laura hear, I'd like to know, and who said something negative to her?"

Barb jumped in. "I don't know what made Laura say that. We never said anything to her to cause that reaction."

"This is crazy. If nobody said anything to her, why would she say that and then ignore Eva?" Kurt probed.

Barb and Doug shook their heads as if a mystery had been unfolding in front of them.

I spoke up. "It doesn't make sense for Laura to have such a dislike of me with no input from you."

"Eva's right," Kurt said. "This couldn't have come out of nowhere."

"Do you think Laura might have taken a cue from you," I said, "when she saw that neither you nor Doug spoke to me nor my daughter nor her husband? Why did you come to our wedding celebration if you had no intention to speak to me or my family?"

"We didn't plan anything--that just happened."

"It looks like things were coordinated," Kurt said.

"What I'd like to know is why you and Doug didn't sit at the head table and take that opportunity to meet my daughter and her husband. They drove over seven hundred miles to celebrate with us and to meet you."

Barb struggled for a while before answering. "Laura was with us and didn't feel comfortable sitting at the head table."

"Then why didn't you and Doug sit at the head table with your father and let Laura sit with her aunt?" I asked.

Doug spoke up: "Your daughter said something very weird to me when I was signing the wedding album."

"She told me she joked with you," I said, "about her being the sister you never had. What's so weird about that? You're always joking around. And if that's what made you not want to sit at the head table or get to know her or her husband, I think that's just an excuse. And what really doesn't make sense is how you and Barb ignored me at my own wedding reception. Why did you come if you were not going to speak to me? No wonder Laura treated me the way she did. She saw you disrespecting me."

"Right after dad started seeing you, he started giving me lots of pictures of him and mom and our family," Doug said.

"Wait a minute. I had nothing to do with that."

"Eva's right. I just wanted you to enjoy them. There was no hidden message in my giving family pictures to you. And Eva had nothing to do with that."

"And while we're on the subject, I'd like to know why the family is refusing to accept Eva?" Kurt asked.

Before anyone could answer, I said, "I've been shunned every time we've gotten together for the past five months. If it's about your inheritance, Kurt and I signed a prenup agreement, at *my* suggestion."

"No, no, it isn't that," Barb countered. "It's just that we liked Pam so much."

"I'm certainly not trying to take Pam's place. She was a good friend of mine; but she's gone, and I would think you'd want your dad to be happy."

"We do," Doug said.

I could hardly hold back my tears as I spoke. "I can remember clearly the times we've gotten together in which I was ignored, like yesterday. Your dad and I didn't meet in a bar – we've known one another since we were children. I don't need his money. I worked since I was sixteen, and I own my own home."

"Eva is my wife, and if you won't accept her, you won't be seeing me," Kurt said, surprising everyone with his dark intonation.

Barb immediately responded. "Why don't we just forget about the past and start out like nothing happened?"

"But something did happen," I said, "and I can't ignore how badly I was treated on purpose for months. I hope when we get to know one another that we can build a relationship, but I can't sweep my hurt under the carpet and pretend it didn't happen, because it did happen. I'll always wonder whether you're just placating me because of your dad. I need time to assess who you really are, and if I can trust you."

It was evident that they were taken aback by my response, but what did they expect? Neither Barb nor Doug apologized to me for their ill-contrived and hurtful treatment of me for months, yet they expected me to forgive them? If they couldn't say or show they were sorry, I guess we'd never have a relationship.

I wondered whether I should mention the change in Clara's attitude after she and Ron had spent the night with Doug and Barb at their cabin, but I decided against it. That's something I'd have to discuss with Clara.

* * * * *

Several months after our reception, Ron visited Kurt and me in Ohio. One night, Ron and I stayed up late, just talking about what popped in our heads, and he confided parts of himself that people don't do unless it's to a friend, and I readily reciprocated.

When Kurt talks to Doug on the phone, he often hands me the phone, and I get a sense that Doug and I are bonding, slowly. However, as far as Barb is concerned, she doesn't make the trips from Maryland to Ohio with Doug like she used to do. Now, it may be once a year. Doug says she's learning a complicated accounting program at work, or that he dropped her off in Martins Ferry to visit her sister and nieces. As I see it, she's ignoring me, but not in my presence.

I'm glad that Kurt has bonded with my family. But the more I think about it, I set the proper groundwork for that to happen. I told them I love Kurt and that he has a big heart. I also told them how he makes me laugh and that I respect him.

I know it must be more difficult to tell one's sons why you want to marry after their mother died. Maybe Kurt thought he'd just let his family meet me first and get to know me and things would naturally fall into place. Kurt's best friends, Marla and Joe, said that although they liked Pam, after meeting me and knowing me, they said they like me an awfully lot. And the feeling is mutual. Pam's sister Deena gave us her blessings, and we've become close.

Then I remember what my best friend Grace told me about her marriage to Al. It was a second marriage for both of them; and they're crazy about one another, like Kurt and me. Grace said Al's daughters never accepted her, and that her daughters never accepted Al. Grace commented that she feels his daughters are worried that she'll get their inheritance. Grace said her daughters said they feel left out of family affairs since she's married Al.

I feel very sad that my relationship with Doug, Barb, and Laura is at a stalemate, but I'm not the one that can make it better. And I'm not sure they're interested in making it better.

Kurt and I need to focus on *us* in order to keep our relationship strong, but we also need to find purpose in our lives. I believe that time will heal what's really bothering Barb and Clara when they see how happy Kurt and I are together. I think of it as a family in progress.

I'd enjoyed being a hospice volunteer for Kaiser. I'd been a one-on-one volunteer, listening to patients' life stories and making my new friends feel special. They confided that they told me things they'd never told their family.

I'm giving some serious thought about doing that again. But then I wonder whether there isn't some kind of charitable work Kurt and I can do together that he would enjoy. We'll have to explore that together, I concluded.

I feel that Kurt and I are two sides of the same coin. We're good for one another, make one another laugh, love each other deeply, and can't keep our hands off one another. That combination is hard to beat at eighty-one and eighty-two … or at any age. And yes, we still enjoy a hot and steamy sexual romp in bed.

The End

About the Author

Ethel Ann Shaffer was born and raised in Tiltonsville, Ohio, along the banks of the Ohio River. Her family lived three doors from the public library, and Ethel Ann read voraciously. After her first marriage dissolved, she headed for Ventura, California with her two daughters.

After relocating, her writing career took off. She worked in various law firms to support her daughters, becoming a paralegal. She also wrote of her experiences in her abusive marriage. Woman's World paid her $500 an essay. The abusive memories depressed her so she started writing humorous articles for local and national magazines and newspapers.

In her fifties, Ethel Ann graduated magna cum laude from California State University Northridge with a bachelor's degree in English literature. She was elected president of the San Fernando Valley branch of the California Writers Club for two separate terms, ten years apart. She is also a pro-member of the Romance Writers of America. She is a member of LinkedIn and has 2,889 followers at this time.

In 2004, she published her first novel titled *Secret Torment* under the name Ethel Ann Pemberton. Her new release, *The Last of the Red Hot Lovers*, a memoir, is about meeting up with a childhood sweetheart and rekindling their love decade later leading to love and marriage.

Ethel Ann and Theodore, her husband of fourteen years, live in Valencia, California with their Siamese cat, Coco. Theodore is the other half of the duo depicted in the memoir.